VENICE   *A Portable Reader*

Venice
A Portable Reader

EDITED BY TOBY COLE

Lawrence Hill & Company
WESTPORT, CONNECTICUT

Editor's foreword, notes and editorial concept
Copyright © 1979 by Toby Cole

ISBN: 0-88208-097-0

Library of Congress Catalog Card Number: 78-19857

Acknowledgments: See page V

First edition May, 1979

1   2   3   4   5   6   7   8   9   10

Lawrence Hill & Company, Publishers, Inc.

Library of Congress C I P Data
Main entry under title:

Venice, a portable reader.

    Bibliography: p.
    Includes index.
    1. Venice--Literary collections. I. Cole,
Toby, 1916-
PN6071.V4V4   808.8'032   78-19857
ISBN 0-88208-097-0

Manufactured in the United States of America
by RAY FREIMAN & COMPANY
Stamford, Connecticut 06903

ACKNOWLEDGMENTS

For permission to publish the various selections in this book, acknowledgment is made to the following. For complete bibliography of sources see page 235.

"The Spoils of Battle" and "Venice Preserved" from *Venice Preserved*, reprinted by permission of Mary McCarthy © copyright Sedo A.A. Lausanne 1956, © copyright USA, The New Yorker Magazine, 1956.

"Islanders" from *Venice* by James Morris. Reprinted by permission of Faber & Faber Ltd., London © copyright James Morris, 1960, 1974.

"The Venetian Painters" from *The Italian Painters of the Renaissance* by Bernhard Berenson, published by Oxford University Press (1930), London. Reprinted by permission of the publisher.

"Effie in Venice" from *Young Mrs. Ruskin in Venice*, edited by Mary Nutjen reprinted by permission of the publishers, Vanguard Press, New York, and John Murray, London © copyright 1965 by Mary Lints.

"Remembrance of Things Past" from *Remembrance of Things Past* by Marcel Proust © copyright 1934, 1962. Reprinted by permission of the publisher, Random House, Inc., New York.

"Death in Venice" selection reprinted from *Death in Venice and Seven Stories* by Thomas Mann, translated by H.T. Lowe-Porter © 1930, 1958. Reprinted by permission of the publisher, Alfred A. Knopf, New York.

"Across the River and Into the Trees" excerpts from the novel of the same title © 1950 by Ernest Hemingway. Reprinted by permission of Charles Scribner's Sons.

"Maladies of Venice" reprinted by permission of Dora Jane Hamblin © 1977. This article first appeared in Smithsonian Magazine.

CONTENTS

Contents

Editor's Foreword

This *Reader* is an introduction to the literature about Venice, which may well be the most voluminous on any city in the world. From this well-spring is drawn the present portrait and guide to the city. It differs from conventional travel books in that its "guides" are eminent men and women of letters, historians, essayists, aestheticians and journalists of the past five centuries. Accordingly, the reader will be experiencing Venice in the noblest prose the city has inspired and will surely perceive this sublime monument to human art in new and delightfully surprising ways.

In bold outline, through selective passages, the *Reader* charts the spectacular history of the longest-lived Republic the world has known—more than a millenium—the development of a landscape of the art and architecture emblematic of the city's rising and declining fortunes, and a sampling of the creative response Venice has evoked in poetry and prose. A volume such as this would be incomplete without a reference to the city's current ecological plight. Thus, the *Reader* ends with a diagnosis of Venice's "maladies" and a prognosis for survival.

An observation is in order on the disproportionate number of foreign to native contributors. There is an apparent incongruity in the fact that, save for the Venetian-born Carlo Goldoni, who was to become the first great Italian playwright, Venice never had a Petrarch, Boccaccio or Dante—all Florentines—in a word, no poet laureate until an Englishman, Lord Byron, appeared on the scene in the early nineteenth century after the fall of the Republic to Napoleon.

Although Venice had her poets—prominent among them two women, Veronica Franco and Cassandra Fedele, and in the recent past Diego Valeri—the city's native literature was history, such as Samuele Romanin's capacious *Storia documentata di Venezia* and Pompeo Molmenti's *La storia di Venezia*. Marino Sanuto's diary of Venetian daily life which spanned fifty-one years, 1482–1533, fills over fifty volumes and has been called the "greatest storehouse of minute information existing in the world." Venice was once also a hub of printing and publishing in many languages, Armenian and Hebrew among them; the home of the famed *Stamparia Aldine* now marked by a plaque on the jarring modern facade of a bank which reads: "Aldo, Pio, Paulo and Aldo II, Manuzio, Princes in the Art of Typography in the sixteenth century diffused with classic

books a new light of culture and wisdom" and invented a typeface—
Italic—said to have been based on Petrarch's handwriting. It is also said
that the first periodical—*La Gazeta*—was issued in Venice, named for
the coin with which one purchased it.

In sum, it would appear that while the Venetians "toiled for their city,
determined that she should be great, that she should be beautiful beyond
all other races, that her power and splendor should outdo every rival"
they left it to the foreigner to zealously sample and rhapsodically record
the infinite pleasures of their creation.

The primary source for this book was the *Fondazione Tursi,* a special
collection of books by foreign travellers to Italy, in the Marciana Library,
Venice. I most humbly inscribe this *Reader* to Angiolo Tursi (1885–
1977) bibliophile and creater of the collection. Access to materials was
facilitated by Maria Teresa Muraro, Luigi Ferrari and Stefania Rossi, and
continuous assistance was cheerfully given by librarians Anna Maria
Galante and Anna Maria Zanotto. A debt is also due to that great national
resource, the New York Public Library and its staff. May New Yorkers
refuse to allow any more chipping away at its services in the name of
"economy"! Gino Carraro was an invaluable guide to literary sites;
Philip Rylands of the Venice in Peril Fund, Jane Rylands, Mary Lutyens
and Meg Bogin made useful comments; Natale Rusconi, Nicola Passante
and Maurizio Scoccimarro extended Venetian courtesies; Minna and
Milton Abernethy and Manina Jouffroy helped in many ways and my
publisher Lawrence Hill and his staff collaborated in editorial matters.
My most agreeable duty is to say *grazie infinite* to the Venetian people and
in particular to my neighbors on the Giudecca who so graciously admit
me into the life of their city which is, and which, with determination, will
remain "the joy of the whole earth."

Toby Cole

VENICE *A Portrait*

AN INTRODUCTION

BY HENRY JAMES

VENICE HAS BEEN PAINTED and described many thousands of times, and of all the cities of the world it is the easiest to visit without going there. Open the first book and you will find a rhapsody about it; step into the first picture-dealer's and you will find three or four high-colored "views" of it. There is nothing more to be said about it. Everyone has been there, and everyone has brought back a collection of photographs. There is as little mystery about the Grand Canal as about our local thoroughfare; and the name of St. Mark is as familiar as the postman's ring. It is not forbidden, however, to speak of familiar things, and I believe that, for the true Venice-lover, Venice is always in order. There is nothing new to be said about it certainly, but the old is better than any novelty. It would be a sad day, indeed, when there should be something new to say. I write these lines with the full consciousness of having no information whatever to offer. I do not pretend to enlighten the reader; I pretend only to give a fillip to his memory; and I hold any writer sufficiently justified who is himself in love with his topic.

* * * *

One may doubtless be very happy in Venice without reading at all—without criticizing or analyzing or thinking a strenuous thought. It is a city in which, I suspect, there is very little strenuous thinking, and yet it is a city in which there must be almost as much happiness as misery. The misery of Venice stands there for all the world to see; it is part of the spectacle—a thorough-going devotee of local color might consistently say it is part of the pleasure. The Venetian people have little to call their own—little more than the bare privilege of leading their lives in the most beautiful of towns. Their habitations are decayed; their taxes heavy; their pockets light; their opportunities few. One receives an impression, however, that life presents itself to them with attractions not accounted for in this meager train of advantages, and that they are on better terms with it than many people who have made a better bargain. . . . The way to enjoy

Venice is to follow the example of these people and make the most of simple pleasures. Almost all the pleasures of the place are simple; this may be maintained even under the imputation of ingenious paradox. There is no simpler pleasure than looking at a fine Titian—unless it be looking at a fine Tintoretto, or strolling into St. Mark's—it is abominable, the way one falls into the habit—and resting one's light-wearied eyes upon the windowless gloom; or than floating in a gondola, or hanging over a balcony, or taking one's coffee at Florian's. It is of these superficial pastimes that a Venetian day is composed, and the pleasure of the matter is in the emotions to which they minister. These, fortunately, are of the finest; otherwise, Venice would be insufferably dull. Reading Ruskin is good; reading the old records is, perhaps, better; but the best thing of all is simply staying on. The only way to care for Venice as she deserves it, is to give her a chance to touch you often—to linger and remain and return.

* * * *

The danger is that you will not linger enough—a danger of which the author of these lines had known something. It is possible to dislike Venice, and to entertain the sentiment in a responsible and intelligent manner. There are travellers who think the place odious, and those who are not of this opinion often find themselves wishing that the others were only more numerous. The sentimental tourist's only quarrel with his Venice is that he has too many competitors there. He likes to be alone; to be original; to have (to himself, at least) the air of making discoveries. The Venice of today is a vast museum where the little wicket that admits you is perpetually turning and creaking, and you march through the institution with a herd of fellow-gazers. There is nothing left to discover or describe, and originality of attitude is completely impossible. This is often very annoying; you can only turn your back on your impertinent playfellow and curse his want of delicacy. But this is not the fault of Venice; it is the fault of the rest of the world. The fault of Venice is that, though it is easy to admire it, it is not so easy to live in it. After you have been there a week, and the bloom of novelty has rubbed off, you wonder whether you can accommodate yourself to the peculiar conditions. Your old habits become impracticable, and you find yourself obliged to form new ones of an undesirable and unprofitable character. You . . . have seen all the principal pictures and heard the names of the palaces announced a dozen times by your gondolier, who brings them out almost as impressively as if he were an English butler bawling titles into a drawing-room.

Introduction

You have walked several hundred times round the Piazza, and bought several bushels of photographs. You have visited the antiquity-mongers whose horrible signboards dishonor some of the grandest vistas in the Grand Canal; you have tried the opera and found it very bad; you have bathed at the Lido and found the water flat. You have begun to have a shipboard feeling—to regard the Piazza as an enormous saloon and the Riva degli Schiavoni as a promenade deck. . . .

This is the state of mind of those shallow inquirers who find Venice all very well for a week; and if in such a state of mind you take your departure, you act with fatal rashness. The loss is your own, moreover; it is not—with all deference to your personal attractions—that of your companions who remain behind; for though there are some disagreeable things in Venice, there is nothing so disagreeable as the visitors. The conditions are peculiar, but your intolerance of them evaporates before it has had time to become a prejudice. When you have called for the bill to go, pay it and remain, and you will find on the morrow that you are deeply attached to Venice. It is by living there from day to day that you feel the fullness of its charm; that you invite its exquisite influence to sink into your spirit. The place is as changeable as a nervous woman, and you know it only when you know all the aspects of its beauty. It has high spirits or low, it is pale or red, gray or pink, cold or warm, fresh or wan, according to the weather or the hour. It is always interesting and almost always sad; but it has a thousand occasional graces and is always liable to happy accidents. You become extraordinarily fond of these things; you count upon them; they make part of your life. Tenderly fond you become; there is something indefinable in those depths of personal acquaintance that gradually establish themselves. The place seems to personify itself, to become human and sentient, and conscious of your affection. You desire to embrace it, to caress it, to possess it; and finally, a soft sense of possession grows up, and your visit becomes a perpetual love affair.

PART I

THE GRAND DESIGN

On the Extinction of the Venetian Republic

Once did She hold the gorgeous east in fee;
And was the safeguard of the west: the worth
Of Venice did not fall below her birth,
Venice, the eldest Child of Liberty.
She was a maiden City, bright and free;
No guile seduced, no force could violate;
And, when she took unto herself a Mate,
She must espouse the everlasting Sea.
And what if she had seen those glories fade,
Those titles vanish, and that strength decay;
Yet shall some tribute of regret be paid
When her long life hath reached its final day:
Men are we, and must grieve, when even the Shade
Of that which once was great, is passed away.

WILLIAM WORDSWORTH

John Ruskin

John Ruskin first visited Venice in 1835, at age sixteen. The future art critic and aesthetician began his studies of art and twelfth-century Italian architecture in Paris. In 1848, now the author of the first volume of Modern Painters *(five volumes would be published by 1860), the twenty-nine-year-old Englishman arrived in Venice with his youthful Scottish bride, Euphemia Gray. Ruskin, ever mindful of the enduring nature of works of art and the comparative evanescence of architecture, focussed his studies on the city he believed afforded "the richest example of architecture raised by a mercantile community, for civil uses and domestic magnificence." Learning to his "consternation, that Venetian antiquaries were not agreed within a century as to the date of the building of the facades of the Ducal Palace, and that nothing was known of any other civil edifice of the early city . . . it became necessary . . . to examine not only every one of the older palaces, stone by stone, but every fragment throughout the city which afforded any clue to the formation of its style." In this laborious task Ruskin "endeavored to trace the lines of this image before it be for ever lost and to record . . . the warning . . . which seemed to be uttered by every one of the fast-gaining waves, that beat, like passing bells, against the Stones of Venice." Thus, in incomparable prose and highly detailed illustrations, Ruskin composed* The Stones of Venice *(1849–1853), a massive work, considered one of the noblest monographs on a city and its architecture ever written. During a prolonged residence in Venice in 1877, nearing sixty and a descent into episodes of insanity, Ruskin wrote* St. Mark's Rest, *a history of Venice, and a* Guide to the Principal Pictures of the Academy of Venice.

THE BIRTH OF VENICE, 421 A.D.

I find the chroniclers agree in fixing the year 421, if any: the following sentence from de Monaci may perhaps interest the reader.

3

"God, who punishes the sins of men by war sorrows, and whose ways are past finding out, willing both to save innocent blood, and that a great power, beneficial to the whole world, should arise in a spot strange beyond belief, moved the chief men of the cities of the Venetian province . . . both in memory of past and in dread of future distress, to establish states upon the nearer islands of the inner gulphs of the Adriatic, to which, in the last necessity, they might retreat for refuge. And . . . by the command of their king and the desire of the citizens, laid the foundations of the new commonwealth, under good auspices, on the island of the Rialto, the highest and nearest to the mouth of the deep river now called the Brenta, in the year of our Lord, as many writers assure us, four hundred and twenty one, on the 25th of March."

Finally the conjecture as to the origin of her name, recorded by Sansovino, will be accepted willingly by all who love Venice: *"Fu interpretato da alcuni, che questa voce Venetia, voglia dire VENI ETIAM, cioè, vieni ancora, e ancora, perciò che quante volti verrai, sempre vedrai nuove cose, e nuove bellezze."*

* * * *

When the eye falls casually on a map of Europe, there is no feature by which it is more likely to be arrested than the strange sweeping loop formed by the junction of the Alps and Apennines, and enclosing the great basin of Lombardy. This return of the mountain chain upon itself causes a vast difference in the character of the distribution of its debris on its opposite sides. The rock fragments and sediments which the torrents on the north side of the Alps bear into the plains are distributed over a vast extent of country, and, though here and there lodged in beds of enormous thickness, soon permit the firm substrata to appear from underneath them; but all the torrents which descend from the southern side of the High Alps, and from the northern slope of the Apennines, meet concentrically in the recess or mountain bay which the two ridges enclose; every fragment which thunder breaks out of their battlements, and every grain of dust which the summer rain washes from their pastures, is at last laid at rest in the blue sweep of the Lombardic plain; and that plain must have risen within its rocky barriers as a cup fills with wine, but for two contrary influences which continually depress, or disperse from its surface, the accumulation of the ruins of ages.

I will not tax the reader's faith in modern science by insisting on the singular depression of the surface of Lombardy, which appears for many centuries to have taken place steadily and continually; the main fact with which we have to do is the gradual transport, by the Po and its great collateral rivers, of vast masses of the finer sediment to the sea. The character of the Lombardic plains is most strikingly expressed by the ancient walls of its cities, composed for the most part of large rounded Alpine pebbles alternating with narrow courses of brick; and was curiously illustrated in 1848, by the ramparts of these same pebbles thrown up four or five feet high round every field, to check the Austrian cavalry in the battle under the walls of Verona. The finer dust among which these pebbles are dispersed is taken up by the rivers, fed into continual strength by the Alpine snow, so that, however pure their waters may be when they issue from the lakes at the foot of the great chain, they become of the color and opacity of clay before they reach the Adriatic; the sediment which they bear is at once thrown down as they enter the sea, forming a vast belt of low land along the eastern coast of Italy. The powerful stream of the Po of course builds forward the fastest; on each side of it, north and south, there is a tract of marsh, fed by more feeble streams, and less liable to rapid change than the delta of the central river. In one of these tracts is built Ravenna, and in the other *Venice*.

What circumstances directed the peculiar arrangement of this great belt of sediment in the earliest times it is not here the place to inquire. It is enough for us to know that from the mouths of the Adige to those of the Piave there stretches, at a variable distance of from three to five miles from the actual shore, a bank of sand, divided into long islands by narrow channels of sea. The space between this bank and the true shore consists of the sedimentary deposits from these and other rivers, a great plain of calcareous mud, covered, in the neighborhood of Venice, by the sea at high water, to the depth in most places of a foot or a foot and a half, and nearly everywhere exposed at low tide, but divided by an intricate network of narrow and winding channels, from which the sea never retires. In some places, according to the run of the currents, the land has risen into marshy islets, consolidated, some by art, and some by time, into ground firm enough to be built upon, or fruitful enough to be cultivated: in others on the contrary, it has not reached the sea level; so that, at the average low water, shallow lakelets glitter among its irregularly exposed fields of seaweed. In the midst of the largest of these, increased in importance by the confluence of several large river channels towards one of the openings in the sea bank, the city of Venice itself is built, on a crowded cluster of islands; the various plots of higher ground which appear to the north and south of this central cluster have at different periods been also thickly inhabited, and now bear, according to their size, the remains of cities, villages, or isolated convents and churches, scattered among spaces of open ground, partly waste and encumbered by ruins, partly under cultivation for the supply of the metropolis.

The average rise and fall of the tide is about three feet (varying considerably with the seasons); but this fall, on so flat a shore, is enough to cause continual movement in the waters, and in the main canals to produce a reflux which frequently runs like a mill stream. At high water no land is visible for many miles to the north or south of Venice, except in the form of small islands crowned with towers or gleaming with villages: there is a channel, some three miles wide, between the city and the mainland, and some mile and a half wide between it and the sandy breakwater called the Lido, which divides the lagoon from the Adriatic, but which is so low as hardly to disturb the impression of the city's having been built in the midst of the ocean, although the secret of its true position is partly, yet not painfully, betrayed by the clusters of piles set to mark the deep-water channels, which undulate far away in spotty chains like the studded backs of huge sea snakes, and by the quick glittering of the crisped and crowded waves that flicker and dance before the strong winds upon the uplifted level of the shallow sea. But the scene is widely different at low tide. A fall of eighteen or twenty inches is enough to show ground over the greater part of the lagoon; and at the complete ebb the city is seen standing in the midst of a dark plain of seaweed, of gloomy green, except only where the larger branches of the Brenta and its associated streams converge towards the port of the Lido. Through this salt and somber plain the gondola and the fishing boat advance by tortuous channels, seldom more than four or five feet deep, and often so choked with slime that the heavier keels furrow the bottom till their crossing tracts are seen through the clear sea water like the ruts upon a wintry road, and the oar leaves blue gashes upon the ground at every stroke, or is entangled among the thick weed that fringes the banks with the weight of its sullen waves, leaning to and fro upon the uncertain sway of the exhausted tide.

The scene is often profoundly oppressive, even at this day, when every plot of higher ground bears some fragment of fair building: but, in order to know what it was once, let the traveller follow in his boat at evening the windings of some unfrequented channel far into the midst of the melancholy plain; let him remove, in his imagination, the brightness of the great city that still extends itself in the distance, and the walls and towers from the islands that are near; and so wait, until the bright investitute, and sweet warmth of the sunset are withdrawn from the waters, and the black desert of their shore lies in its nakedness beneath the night, pathless,

6

comfortless, infirm, lost in dark languor and fearful silence, except where the salt runlets plash into the tideless pools, or the sea birds flit from their margins with a questioning cry; and he will be enabled to enter in some sort into the horror of heart with which this solitude was anciently chosen by man for his habitation.

They little thought, who first drove the stakes into the sand, and strewed the ocean reeds for their rest, that their children were to be the princes of that ocean, and their palaces its pride; and yet, in the great natural laws that rule that sorrowful wilderness, let it be remembered what strange preparation had been made for the things which no human imagination could have foretold, and how the whole existence and fortune of the Venetian nation were anticipated or compelled, by the setting of those bars and doors to the rivers and the sea. Had deeper currents divided their islands, hostile navies would again and again have reduced the rising city into servitude; had stronger surges beaten their shores all the richness and refinement of the Venetian architecture must have been exchanged for the walls and bulwarks of an ordinary seaport. Had there been no tide, as in other parts of the Mediterranean, the narrow canals of the city would have become noisome, and the marsh in which it was built pestiferous. Had the tide been only a foot or eighteen inches higher in its rise the water-access to the doors of the palaces would have been impossible: even as it is, there is sometimes a little difficulty, at the ebb, in landing without setting foot upon the lower and slippery steps; and the highest tides sometimes enter the courtyards, and overflow the entrance halls. Eighteen inches more of difference between the level of the flood and ebb would have rendered the doorsteps of every palace, at low water, a treacherous mass of weeds and limpets, and the entire system of water-carriage for the higher classes, in their easy and daily intercourse, must have been done away with. The streets of the city would have been widened, its network of canals filled up, and all the peculiar character of the place and the people destroyed.

The reader may perhaps have felt some pain in the contrast between this faithful view of the site of the Venetian Throne and the romantic conception of it which we ordinarily form. . . . If, two thousand years ago, we had been permitted to watch the slow settling of the slime of those turbid rivers into the polluted sea, and the gaining upon its deep and fresh waters of the lifeless, impassable, unvoyageable plain, how little could we have understood the purpose with which those islands were shaped out of the void, and the torpid waters enclosed with their desolate walls of sand! . . . How little imagined that in the laws which were stretching forth the gloomy margins of those fruitless banks, and feeling the bitter grass among their shallows, there was indeed a preparation, and *the only preparation possible,* for the founding of a city which was to be set like a golden clasp on the girdle of the earth, to write her history on the white scrolls of the sea-surges, and to word it in their thunder, and to gather and give forth, in worldwide pulsation, the glory of the West and of the East, from the burning heart of her fortitude and splendor!

Niccolo Machiavelli

◄ 1469–1527 ►

Niccolo Machiavelli, statesman, political philosopher and historian, was born in Florence and is buried in the Church of Santa Croce beside Michelangelo. During his service to the Florentine Republic he carried out twenty-three diplomatic missions abroad and is known to have visited Venice late in life. Among his best known works are The Prince *and* The History of Florence *(1532), from which these observations on the Venetian Republic are drawn.*

THE CITY REPUBLIC

Venice, being a republic, which, both on account of its power and internal regulations, deserves to be celebrated above any principality of Italy. . . . I speak of their city from a remote period. . . . When Attila, king of the Huns, besieged Aquileia, the inhabitants, after defending themselves a long time, began to despair of effecting their safety, and fled for refuge to several uninhabited rocks, situate at the point of the Adriatic Sea, now called the Gulf of Venice, carrying with them whatever moveable property they possessed. The people of Padua, finding themselves in equal danger, and knowing that, having become master of Aquileia, Attila would next attack themselves, also removed with their most valuable property to a place on the same sea, called Rialto, to which they brought their women, children, and aged persons, leaving the youth in Padua to assist in her defense. Besides these, the people of Monselice, with the inhabitants of the surrounding hills, driven by similar fears, fled to the same rocks. But after Attila had taken Aquileia, and destroyed Padua, Monselice, Vicenza, and Verona, the people of Padua, and others who were powerful continued to inhabit the marshes about Rialto and in like manner all the people of the province anciently called Venetia, driven by the same events, became collected in these marshes. Thus, under the pressure of necessity, they left an agreeable and fertile country to occupy one sterile and unwholesome. However, in consequence of a great number of people being drawn together into a comparatively small space, in a short time they made those places not only habitable, but delightful; and having established among themselves laws and useful regulations, enjoyed themselves in security amid the devastations of Italy, and soon increased both in reputation and strength. For, besides the inhabitants already mentioned, many fled to these places from the cities of Lombardy, principally to escape from the cruelties of Clefis, king of the Lombards, which greatly tended to increase the numbers of the new city; and in the conventions which were made betwixt Pepin, king of France, and the emperor of Greece when the former, at the entreaty of the pope, came to drive the Lombards out of Italy, the duke of Benevenuto and the Venetians did not render obedience to either the one or the other, but alone enjoyed their liberty. As necessity had led them to dwell on sterile rocks, they were compelled to seek the means of subsistence elsewhere; and voyaging with their ships to every port of the ocean, their city became a depository for the various products of the world, and was itself filled with men of every nation.

For many years the Venetians sought no other dominion than that which tended to facilitate their commercial enterprises, and thus acquired many ports in Greece and Syria; and as the French had made frequent use of their ships in voyages to Asia, the island of Candia was assigned to them, in recompense for these services. Whilst they lived in this manner, their name spread terror over the seas, and was held in veneration throughout Italy. This was so completely the case, that they were generally chosen to arbitrate in controversies arising betwixt the states, as occurred in the difference betwixt the Colleagues, on account of the cities they had divided amongst themselves; which being referred to the Venetians, they awarded Brescia and Bergamo to the Visconti. But when, in the course of time, urged by their eagerness for dominion, they had made themselves masters of Padua, Vicenza, Treviso, and afterwards of Verona, Bergamo, and Brescia, with many cities in Romagna, and the kingdom of Naples, other nations were impressed with such an opinion of their power, that they were a terror, not only to the princes of Italy, but to the Ultramontane kings. These states entered into an alliance against them, and in one day wrested from them the provinces they had obtained with so much labor and expense; and although they have in latter times reacquired some portions, still, possessing neither power nor reputation, like all the other Italian powers, they live at the mercy of others. . . .

Amongst the great and wonderful institutions of the republics and principalities of antiquity that have now gone into disuse, was that by means of which towns and cities were from time to time established; and there is nothing more worthy the attention of a great prince, or of a well-regulated republic, or that confers so many advantages upon a province, as the settlement of new places, where men are drawn together for mutual accommodation and defense. This may easily be done, by sending people to reside in recently acquired or uninhabited countries. Besides causing the establishment of new cities, these removals render a conquered country more secure, and keep the inhabitants of a province properly distributed. Thus deriving the greatest attainable comfort, the inhabitants increase rapidly, are more prompt to attach others, and defend themselves with greater assurance. This custom, by the unwise practice of princes and republics, having gone into desuetude, the ruin and weakness of territories has followed; for this ordination is that by which alone empires are made secure, and countries become populated. Safety is the result of it; because the colony which a prince establishes in a newly acquired country is like a fortress and a guard, to keep the inhabitants in fidelity and obedience. Neither can a province be wholly occupied and preserve a proper distribution of its inhabitants without this regulation; for all districts are not equally healthy, and hence some will abound to overflowing, whilst others are void. . . . With cultivation the earth becomes fruitful, and the air is purified with fires—remedies which Nature cannot provide. The city of Venice proves the correctness of these remarks. Being placed in a marshy and unwholesome situation, it became healthy only by the number of industrious individuals who were drawn together.

Edward Gibbon

-◄ 1737–1794 ►-

Edward Gibbon had little formal education, yet became a great histo-rian. Forced to leave Oxford University because he converted to Catholicism, he was sent to Lausanne, Switzerland, where he recon-verted. There he read widely, his study, as he described it, being "chiefly preparations for my classic tour—Latin poets, historians—topography and antiquities of Rome. . . ." And, he added, "perhaps I might boast that few travellers more completely armed and instructed have ever followed the footsteps of Hannibal."

This knowledge and particular religious background were soon put to good use, for it was on a visit to Rome in 1764 that Gibbon conceived the idea of his great work, The History of the Decline and Fall of the Roman Empire *(6 volumes, 1776–88). His first reaction to Venice, in 1765, was alternately "astonishment" and "disgust," but later he was moved to speak of "the beauties of Florence, the wonders of Rome, the curiosities of Naples and the singular aspect of Venice."*

In the excerpt from Decline and Fall *included here, Gibbon describes the Venetian conquest and sack of Constantinople and her emergence as one of the wealthiest and most powerful city states of the middle ages.*

SACK OF CONSTANTINOPLE, 1204 A.D.

In the invasion of Italy by Attila, I have mentioned the flight of the Venetians from the fallen cities of the continent, and their obscure shelter in the chain of islands that line the extremity of the Adriatic Gulf. In the midst of the waters, free, indigent, laborious, and inaccessible, they gradually coalesced into a republic: the first foundations of Venice were laid in the island of Rialto; and the annual election of the twelve tribunes was superseded by the permanent office of a duke or doge. The inhabit-ants of Venice owned the authority of the Greek emperors: but the bands

13

of dependence, which was never absolute or rigid, were imperceptibly relaxed by the ambition of Venice, and the weakness of Constantinople. The sea was their patrimony: the western parts of the Mediterranean, from Tuscany to Gibraltar, were indeed abandoned to their rivals of Pisa and Genoa; but the Venetians acquired an early and lucrative share of the commerce of Greece and Egypt. Their riches increased with the increasing demand of Europe; their manufacturers of silk and glass, perhaps the institution of their bank, are of high antiquity; and they enjoyed the fruits of their industry in the magnificence of public and private life. To assert her flag, to avenge her injuries, to protect the freedom of navigation, the republic could launch and man a fleet of 100 galleys; and the Greeks, the Saracens, and the Normans were encountered by her naval arms.

The primitive government of Venice was a loose mixture of democracy and monarchy: the doge was elected by the votes of the general assembly; as long as he was popular and successful, he reigned with the pomp and authority of a prince; but in the frequent revolutions of the state he was deposed, or banished, or slain, by the justice or injustice of the multitude. The 12th century produced the first rudiments of the wise and jealous aristocracy, which reduced the doge to a pageant, and the people to a cipher.

When the six ambassadors of the French pilgrims arrived at Venice (1201 A.D.), they were hospitably entertained in the palace of St. Mark by the reigning duke: his name was Enrico Dandolo; and he shone in the last period of human life as one of the most illustrious characters of the times. Under the weight of years, and after the loss of his eyes, Dandolo retained a sound understanding and a manly courage: the spirit of a hero, ambitious to signalize his reign by some memorable exploits; and the wisdom of a patriot, anxious to build his fame on the glory and advantage of his country. The proposal of the French was first debated by the six *sages* who had been recently appointed to control the administration of the doge: it was next disclosed to the 40 members of the council of state; and finally communicated to the legislative assembly of 450 representatives, who were annually chosen in the six quarters of the city. Dandolo supported warmly the application of the crusaders: his arguments of public interest were approved; and he was authorized to inform the ambassadors of the following conditions of the treaty. It was proposed that the crusaders should assemble at Venice on the feast of St. Giovanni of the ensuing year; that a sufficient number of ships should be prepared for their embarkation; that during a term of nine months they should be supplied with provisions, and transported to whatsoever coast the service of God and Christendom should require; and that the republic should join the armament with a squadron of 50 galleys. It was required that the pilgrims should pay, before their departure, a sum of 85,000 marks of silver; and that all conquests, by sea and land, should be equally divided between the confederates. The terms were hard; but the emergency was pressing, and the French barons were not less profuse of money than of blood.

The French barons elected as their general Boniface marquis of Montferrat, descended of a race of heroes, and himself of conspicuous fame in the wars and negotiations of the times. Upon their arrival at Venice they found that their allies had fulfilled, and even surpassed, their engagements; and the fleet of transports, ships, and galleys, was ready to hoist sail as soon as the republic had received the price of the freight and armament (1202 A.D.). But that price far exceeded the wealth of the crusaders who were assembled at Venice; and after all their efforts, 34,000 marks were still wanting to complete the stipulated sum. The obstacle was removed by the policy and patriotism of the doge, who proposed to the barons that, if they would join their arms in reducing some revolted cities of Dalmatia, he would expose his person in the holy war, and obtain from the republic a long indulgence, till some wealthy conquest should afford the means of satisfying the debt. After much scruple and hesitation, they chose rather to accept the offer than to relinquish the enterprise; and the first hostilities of the fleet and army were directed against Zara, a strong city of the Slavonian coast, which had renounced its allegiance to Venice, and implored the protection of the king of Hungary. The crusaders easily made themselves masters of Zara: and as the season was far advanced, they resolved to pass the winter in a secure harbor and plentiful country.

The assembly of such formidable powers by sea and land had revived the hopes of young Alexius, and both at Venice and Zara he solicited the arms of the crusaders for his own restoration and his father's deliverance. He promised, in his own and his father's name, that, as soon as they should be seated on the throne of Constantinople, they would terminate the long schism of the Greeks, and submit themselves and their people to the lawful supremacy of the Roman church. He engaged to recompense the labors and merits of the crusaders by the immediate payment of 200,000 marks of silver; to accompany them in person to Egypt; or, if it should be judged more advantageous, to maintain, during a year, 10,000 men, and, during his life, 500 knights, for the service of the Holy Land. These tempting conditions were accepted; but many pilgrims, distinguished for their valor and piety, refused their consent; they alleged the sanctity of their vow, and withdrew from the camp.

Notwithstanding this defection, the departure of the fleet and army was vigorously pressed by the Venetians, whose zeal for the service of the royal youth concealed a just resentment to his nation and family. They were mortified by the recent preference which had been given to Pisa, the rival of their trade; and they had a long arrear of debt and injury to liquidate with the Byzantine court. No resistance was offered by the Byzantine monarch to the passage of the fleet through the Greek seas; and after a prosperous voyage, the crusaders reposed for nine days in Scutari, the Asiatic suburb of Constantinople (1203 A.D.). On the tenth day they traversed the Bosporus without encountering an enemy or an obstacle; and the 70,000 Greeks, who had been drawn up on the opposite shore, fled on their approach. In the first consternation of the flying enemy, the Latins resolved, by a double attack, to open the entrance of the harbor. The tower of Galata, in the suburb of Pera, was attacked and stormed by the French, while the Venetians assumed the more difficult task of forcing the boom or chain that was stretched from that tower to the Byzantine shore. After some fruitless attempts their intrepid perseverance prevailed; 20 ships of war, the relics of the Grecian navy, were either sunk or taken; the enormous and massy links of iron were cast asunder by the shears or broken by the weight of the galleys; and the Venetian fleet, safe and triumphant, rode at anchor in the port of Constantinople. By these daring achievements a remnant of 20,000 Latins solicited the license of besieging a capital which contained above 400,000 inhabitants, able, though not willing, to bear arms in the defense of their country. Such an account would indeed suppose a population of near 2,000,000: but whatever abatement may be required in the numbers of the Greeks, the *belief* of those numbers will equally exalt the fearless spirit of their assailants.

It was arranged that the French should attack the city by land and the Venetians by sea. After ten days incessant labor the Latins effected a breach, and attempted to scale the walls; but they were driven back by the numbers that defended the vantage-ground. The naval attack was more successful; the soldiers, who leaped from the galleys on shore, immediately planted and ascended their scaling-ladders, while the large ships, advancing more slowly into the intervals, and lowering a drawbridge, opened a way through air from their masts to the rampart. In the midst of the conflict the doge, a venerable and conspicuous form, stood aloft in complete armor on the prow of his galley. The great standard of St. Mark was displayed before him; his vessel was the first that struck; and Dandolo was the first warrior on the shore. On a sudden, by an invisible hand (for the standard-bearer was probably slain), the banner of the republic was fixed on the rampart: 25 towers were rapidly occupied; and, by the cruel expedient of fire, the Greeks were driven from the adjacent quarter. The doge had despatched the intelligence of his success, when he was checked by the danger of his confederates. Nobly declaring that he would rather die with the pilgrims than gain a victory by their destruction, Dandolo relinquished his advantage, recalled his troops, and hastened to the scene of action. He found the French encompassed by 60 squadrons of the Greek cavalry. Shame and despair had provoked Alexius to the last effort of a general sally: but he was awed by the firm order and manly aspect of the Latins; and, after skirmishing at a distance, withdrew his troops in the close of the evening. The silence or tumult of the night exasperated his fears, and the timid usurper, collecting a treasure of 10,000 pounds of gold, basely deserted his wife, his people, and his fortune; threw himself into a bark; stole through the Bosporus; and landed in a shameful safety in an obscure harbor of Thrace. As soon as they were apprized of his flight, the Greek nobles sought pardon and peace in the dungeon where the blind Isaac expected each hour the visit of the executioner. At the dawn of day hostilities were suspended, and the Latin chiefs were surprised by a message from the lawful and reigning emperor, who was impatient to embrace his son and to reward his generous deliverers (July 18).

The barons mounted on horseback and introduced the heir of Constantinople to the city and palace: his youth and marvelous adventures engaged every heart in his favor, and Alexius was solemnly crowned with his father in the dome of St. Sophia. The mixture of two discordant nations in the same capital might have been pregnant with mischief and danger; and the suburb of Galata, or Pera, was assigned for the quarters of the French and Venetians. It was agreed between the young Alexius and his allies that the reunion of the two churches must be the result of patience and time; but avarice was less tractable than zeal; and a large sum was instantly disbursed to appease the wants and silence the importunity of the crusaders. Alexius was alarmed by the approaching hour of their departure: their absence would have left him, naked and alone, to the caprice and prejudice of a prefidious nation; and he wished to bribe their stay, the delay of a year, by undertaking to defray their expense, and to satisfy, in their name, the freight of the Venetian vessels. The offer was agitated in the council of the barons; and, after a repetition of their debates and scruples, a majority of votes again acquiesced in the advice of the doge and the prayer of the young emperor. At the price of 1600 pounds of gold, he prevailed on the marquis of Montferrat to lead him with an army round the provinces of Europe; to establish his authority, and pursue his uncle, while Constantinople was awed by the presence of Baldwin and his confederates of France and Flanders.

By the recent invasion the Greeks were awakened from a dream of nine centuries; from the vain presumption that the capital of the Roman empire was impregnable to foreign arms. The strangers of the west had violated the city, and bestowed the sceptre, of Constantine: their Imperial clients soon became as unpopular as themselves: the well-known vices of Isaac were rendered still more contemptible by his infirmities, and the young Alexius was hated as an apostate who had renounced the manners and religion of his country. His secret covenant with the Latins was divulged or suspected; the people, and especially the clergy, were devoutly attached to their faith and superstition; and every convent, and every shop, resounded with the danger of the church and the tyranny of the pope. During the absence of marquis Boniface and his Imperial pupil, Constantinople was visited with a calamity which might be justly imputed to the zeal and indiscretion of the Flemish pilgrims. In one of their visits to the city they were scandalized by the aspect of a mosque or synagogue. They set fire to the building of the infidels; but during eight days and nights the conflagration spread above a league in front, from the harbor to the Propontis, over the thickest and most populous regions of the city. By this outrage the name of the Latins became still more unpopular; and the colony of that nation, above 15,000 persons, consulted their safety in a hasty retreat from the city to the protection of their standard in the suburb of Pera. The young emperor returned in triumph: his own inclination, and his father's advice, attached him to his benefactors; but Alexius hesitated between gratitude and patriotism, between the fear of his subjects and of his allies. By his feeble and fluctuating conduct he lost the esteem and confidence of both. The Latins chiefs repeated their demands, resented his delays, suspected his intentions, and exacted a decisive answer of peace or war. Among the Greeks all authority and wisdom were overborne by the impetuous multitude, who mistook their rage for valor, their numbers for strength, and their fanaticism for the support and inspiration of Heaven. The author of the tumult was a prince of the house of Ducas; and his common appellation of Alexius must be discriminated by the epithet of Mourzoufle, which in the vulgar idiom expressed the close junction of his black and shaggy eyebrows. He insinuated himself into the favor and confidence of Alexius, and by a stratagem seized the young emperor, and after a few days' confinement put him to death. The emperor Isaac Angelus soon followed his son to the grave; and Mourzoufle, perhaps, might spare the superfluous crime of hastening the extinction of impotence and blindness (1204 A.D.).

The death of the emperors, and the usurpation of Mourzoufle, had changed the nature of the quarrel. The French and Venetians forgot their

18

complaints against Alexius, and swore revenge against the perfidious nation who had crowned his assassin. The second seige of Constantinople was far more laborious than the first. Near three months, without excepting the holy season of Lent, were consumed in skirmishes and preparations, before the Latins were ready for or resolved for a general assault. The land fortifications had been found impregnable; and it was therefore determined to attack the city from the harbor. The first assault was repelled; but the second was crowned with success. Four towers were scaled; three gates were burst open; the Latins entered the city under the banners of their leaders; and either design or accident kindled a third conflagration, which consumed in a few hours the measure of three of the largest cities in France. In the close of the evening the barons checked their troops and fortified their stations: but in the morning a suppliant procession, with crosses and images, announced the submission of the Greeks and deprecated the wrath of the conquerors: the usurper escaped through the golden gate; and the empire, which still bore the name of Constantine and the title of Roman, was subverted by the arms of the Latin pilgrims. Constantinople had been taken by storm; and no restraints except those of religion and humanity were imposed on the conquerors by the laws of war. Their cruelty and lust were moderated by the authority of the chiefs and feelings of the soldiers; but a free scope was allowed to their avarice, which was glutted, even in the holy week, by the pillage of the city. The magnitude of the prize surpassed the largest scale of experience or expectation. After the whole had been equally divided between the French and Venetians, 50,000 marks were deducted to satisfy the debts of the former and the demands of the latter. The residue of the French amounted to 400,000 marks of silver, about 800,000 pounds sterling; nor can I better appreciate the value of that sum in the public and private transactions of the age than by defining it as seven times the annual revenue of the kingdom of England.

After the death of the lawful princes, the French and Venetians, confident of justice and victory, agreed to divide and regulate their future possessions. It was stipulated by treaty that twelve electors, six of either nation, should be nominated; and that a majority should choose the emperor of the east. To him, with all the titles and prerogatives of the Byzantine throne, they assigned a fourth part of the Greek monarchy. It was defined that the three remaining portions should be equally shared between the republic of Venice and the barons of France; that each feudatory, with an honorable exception for the doge, should acknowledge and perform the duties of homage and military service to the supreme head of the empire; and that the nation which gave an emperor should resign to their brethren the choice of a patriarch. After the conquest of Constantinople by the Latins, the treaty was confirmed and executed; and the first and most important step was the creation of an emperor. A just impulse of respect and gratitude prompted the twelve electors to crown the virtues of the doge: but the patriot Dandolo was devoid of all personal ambition, and his nomination was overruled by the Venetians themselves. The exclusion of the doge left room for the more equal merits of Boniface and Baldwin. The marquis of Montferrat was recommended by his mature age and fair reputation, by the choice of the adventurers, and the wishes of the Greeks. But the count of Flanders was the chief of a wealthy and warlike people: he was valiant, pious, and chaste; in the prime of life, since he was only 32 years of age; a descendant of Charlemagne, and a cousin of the king of France. The electors decided in favor of Baldwin. Boniface was the first to kiss the hand of his rival, and to raise him on the buckler; and Baldwin was transported to the cathedral, and solemnly invested with the purple buskins. At the end of three weeks he was crowned by the legate, in the vacancy of a patriarch; but the Venetian clergy soon filled the chapter of St. Sophia, and seated Tommaso Morosini on the ecclesiastical throne.

In the division of the Greek provinces the share of the Venetians was more ample than that of the Latin emperor. No more than one-fourth was appropriated to his domain; a clear moiety of the remainder was reserved for Venice; and the other moiety was distributed among the adventurers of France and Lombardy. The venerable Dandolo was proclaimed despot of Romania, but ended at Constantinople his long and glorious life. The Venetians formed a chain of factories, and cities, and islands, along the maritime coast, from the neighborhood of Ragusa to the Hellespont and the Bosporus. The marquis Boniface became king of Thessalonica or Macedonia. The lots of the Latin pilgrims were regulated by chance, or choice, or subsequent exchange; and they abused, with intemperate joy, their triumph over the lives and fortunes of a great people.

Mary McCarthy

Mary McCarthy visited Venice in 1946. One of the American novelist's short stories, "The Guide," was suggested by that visit. At the end of August, 1955, she returned for three months expressly to write a series of articles about the city for the New Yorker magazine. In 1956 Venice Observed, *with colored photo illustrations by André Chastel, was published simultaneously in London and Paris. The book, which Jan Morris has called a "magnificent essay" and "perhaps the best" of the recent books on Venice, apparently caused a small tempest among some citizens of the city who objected to the author's "observations" on the Venetian character. In an interview she stated that she felt the book was misunderstood. She had not criticized Venice, she said, but rather had called it "the world's loveliest city." Without doubt Venice was already gray, with several boils on her face, many lines around the eyes, but still a charming, delightful creature. Mary McCarthy's* The Group, The Stones of Florence *and* Vietnam *have been published in Italy.*

THE SPOILS OF THE SACK

The fall of Constantinople marked the end of Venetian involvement in the holy work of the Crusades. Having got what they wanted—their "quarter and a half-quarter," plus Crete—St. Mark's merchants withdrew to the sidelines. In 1268, they signed a contract with St. Louis for transport only on the eighth crusade. During the same century, the Emperor Baldwin II pawned his Crown of Thorns to the Venetian Morosini family for a loan of seven thousand ducats; in fact, he pawned it twice. Later, he pawned his son Philip to a Cappello of Venice. The boy was redeemed by St. Louis. Toward the end of the century, Venice lay under the pope's interdict and was also punished (it was thought) by heaven with earthquakes and floods for having made an anti-crusade treaty with one of the Palaeologues. Not long after, unregenerate, the Venetians signed a treaty with the Turks and began trading in "goods forbidden to Christians"—i.e., slaves, arms, and wood for shipbuilding. . . . During this period, the only serious fighting the Venetians did in the Holy Land was with the Genoese, their rival traders. Trophies of their victory at Acre stand on the Piazzetta side of St. Mark's: the Pietra del Bando, a short reddish column from which the Laws of the Republic were proclaimed, and the two strangely decorated pillars, Syrian art of the fifth or sixth century, carried off from the church of San Saba.

But it was the great Sack of Constantinople, in 1204, under the blind doge, that had netted the richest booty: the four little porphyry Moors (thought to be really four Roman Emperors who ruled jointly); the Horses (which had stood on high pedestals in the Hippodrome, a fact which saved their lives when the Crusaders set the town on fire); St. Mark's wonder-working ikon, the Madonna Nicopeia, said to have been painted by St. Luke; the top section (probably) of the Pala d'Oro, St. Mark's great altarpiece in gold and jewels and enamels, which tourists today, having paid a fee, stand in line bug-eyed to examine. This top section was rifled, it is thought, from the Church of the Pantocrator. From Constantinople, certainly, came one of the bottom panels in which the Virgin is shown between the Empress Irene and the Emperor John Comnenus II, who has turned into the Doge Ordelaffo Falier. Such agile transformations were easy for the resourceful Venetians—the chimera into the winged lion, the emperor into the saint. The Emperor Justinian the Noseless, on St. Mark's façade, a Syrian portrait of the eighth century, is called by the Venetians Count Carmagnola, after the general they decapitated nearby, on the Piazzetta. In the same way, by a characteristic turnabout the four little stolen Emperors have been converted by popular tradition into four Saracens who were turned to stone while trying to rob St. Mark's treasury, outside which they stand embracing.

From the outside, as is often observed, St. Mark's looks like an Oriental pavilion—half pleasure house, half war tent, belonging to some great satrap. Inside, glittering with jewels and gold, faced with precious Eastern marbles, jasper and alabaster, porphyry and verd-antique, sustained by Byzantine columns in the same materials, of varying sizes and epochs, scarcely a pair alike, this dark cruciform cave has the look of a robber's den. In the chapel of the Crucifix, with a pyramidal marble roof topped by a huge piece of Oriental agate and supported by six Byzantine columns in black and white African marble, stands a painted crucifix, of special holiness, taken from Constantinople. In the atrium, flanking St.

Clement's door, are two pairs of black and white marble columns, with wonderful lion's and eagle's heads in yellowish ivory; tradition says they came from the Temple of Solomon in Jerusalem. From Tyre came the huge block of Mount Tabor granite on the altar in the Baptistery—said to be the stone on which Christ was wont to pray. In the Zen chapel, the wall is lined with onion marbles and verd-antique, reputedly the gravestones of the Byzantine Emperors.

In the chapel of St. Isidore sleeps the saint stolen from Chios; he was hidden for two centuries for fear of confiscation. St. Theodore, stolen from Byzantium, was moved to San Salvatore. St. Mark himself was lost for a considerable period, after a fire in 976, which destroyed most of the early church; he revealed his presence by thrusting forth his arm. He was not the original saint of Venice, but, so to speak, a usurper, displacing St. Theodore. Thus, he himself, the patron, was a kind of thieving cuckoo bird, and his church, which was only the doge's private chapel, imitated him by usurping the functions of San Pietro in Castello, the seat of the Patriarch and the real Cathedral (until very recent times) of Venice. In the same style, the early doges had themselves buried, in St. Mark's porch, in sarcophagi that did not belong to them, displacing the bones of old pagans and paleo-Christians.

Venice, unlike Rome or Ravenna or nearby Verona, had nothing of its own to start with. Venice, as a city, was a foundling, floating upon the waters like Moses in his basket among the bulrushes. It was therefore obliged to be inventive, to steal and improvise. Cleverness and adaptativity were imposed by the original situation, and the get-up-and-go of the early Venetian business men was typical of a self-made society. St. Mark's Church is a (literally) shining example of this spirit of initiative, this gift for improvisation, for turning everything to account. It is made of bricks, like most Venetian churches, since brick was the easiest material to come by. Its external beauty comes from the thin marble veneers with which the brick surface is coated, just as though it were a piece of furniture. These marbles for the most part, like the columns and facing inside, were the spoils of war, and they were put on almost haphazardly, green against grey, against red or rose or white with red veining, without any general principle of design beyond the immediate pleasure of the eye. On the Piazzetta side, this gives the effect of gay abstract painting. Parvenu art, more like painting than architecture (as Herbert Spencer might say), and yet it "worked." The marble veneers of St. Mark's sides, especially when washed by the rain so that they look like oiled silk, are among the most beautiful things in Venice. And it is their very thinness, the sense they give of being a mere lustrous coating, a film, that makes them beautiful. A palace of solid marble, rain washed, simply looks bedraggled.

St. Mark's as a whole, unless seen from a distance or at twilight, is not beautiful. The modern mosaics (seventeenth century) are generally admitted to be extremely ugly, and I myself do not care for some of the Gothic statuary of the pinnacles. The horses, the colored marble veneers, the Byzantine Madonna of the front, the old mosaic on the left, the marble columns of the portal, the gold encrustations of the top, the five grey domes with their strange ornaments, like children's jacks—these are the details that captivate. As for the rest, it is better not to look too closely, or the whole will begin to seem tawdry, a hodge-podge, as so many critics have said. The whole is not beautiful, and yet again it is. It depends on the light and the time of day or on whether you narrow your eyes, to make it look flat, a painted surface. And it can take you unawares, looking beautiful or horribly ugly, at a time you least expect. Venice, Henry James said, is as changeable as a nervous person, and this is particularly true of St. Mark's façade.

But why should it be beautiful at all? why should Venice, aside from its situation, be a place of enchantment? One appears to be confronted with a paradox. A commercial people who lived solely for gain—how could they create a city of fantasy, lovely as a dream or a fairy tale? This is the central puzzle of Venice, the stumbling block that one keeps coming up against if one tries to *think* about her history, to put facts of her history together with the visual fact that is there before one's eyes. It cannot be that Venice is a happy accident or a trick of light. I have thought about this a long time, but now it occurs to me that, as with most puzzles, the clue to the answer lies in the way the question is framed. "Lovely as a dream or a fairy tale . . ." There is no contradiction, once you stop to think what images of beauty arise from fairy tales. They are images of money. Gold, caskets of gold, caskets of silver, the miller's daughter spinning gold all night long, thanks to Rumpelstiltskin, the cave of Ali Baba stored with stolen gold and silver, the underground garden in which Aladdin found jewels growing on trees, so that he could gather them in his hands, rubies and diamonds and emeralds, the Queen's lovely daughter whose hair is black as ebony and lips are red as rubies, treasure buried in the forest, treasure guarded by dogs with eyes as big as carbuncles, treasure guarded by a Beast—this is the spirit of the enchantment under which Venice lies, pearly and roseate, like the Sleeping Beauty, changeless throughout the centuries, arrested, while the concrete forest of the modern world grows up around her.

A wholly materialist city is nothing but a dream incarnate. Venice is the world's unconscious: a miser's glittering hoard, guarded by a beast whose eyes are made of white agate, and by a saint who is really a prince who has just slain a dragon.

A list of goods in which the early Venetian merchants trafficked arouses a sense of pure wonder: wine and grain from Apulia, gems and drugs from Asia, metal-work, silk, and cloth of gold from Byzantium and Greece. These are the gifts of the Magi, in the words of the English hymn "Pearls from the ocean and gems from the mountain; myrrh from the forest and gold from the mine." During the Middle Ages, as a part of his rightful revenue, the doge had his share in the apples of Lombardy and the crayfish and cherries of Treviso—the Venetian mind, interested only in the immediate and the solid, leaves behind it for our minds, clear, dawn-fresh images out of fairy tales.

William Dean Howells

◄ 1837–1920 ►

William Dean Howells was appointed by Abraham Lincoln to be American Consul in Venice, 1861–1865. There "the almost uninterrupted leisure for study and literary work" gave the future novelist, dramatist, critic and editor "a wider outlook on the world." Twenty-two of his thirty-eight volumes of fiction contain characters who have been or go to Italy. Venetian Life (1866), *which Henry James called "a delightful volume of impressions," was the first of Howells' many travel books, and provides a unique account of the city's popular life during the reoccupation of it by Austrian forces after the briefly reconstituted republic under Daniele Manin of 1848–49. In the first chapter Howells speaks of an evening in a little theatre in Padua in which he's been given a stage-box from which he could watch the play and the by-play, and continues: "It has sometimes seemed to me as if fortune had given me a stage-box at another and grander spectacle, and I had been suffered to see this VENICE, which is to other cities like the present improbability of the theatre to everyday, commonplace life, to much the same effect as that melodrama in Padua. I could not, indeed, dwell three years in the place without learning to know it differently from those writers who have described it in romances, poems, and hurried books of travel, nor help seeing from my point of observation the sham and cheapness with which Venice is usually brought out, if I may so speak, in literature. At the same time, it has never lost for me its claim upon constant surprise and regard, nor the fascination of its excellent beauty, its peerless picturesqueness, its sole and wondrous grandeur."*

AUSTRIA IN VENICE, 1815–1866

If there be more than one opinion among men elsewhere concerning the means by which Austria acquired Venetia and the tenure by which she holds the province, there would certainly seem to be no division on the question in Venice. To the stranger first inquiring into public feeling, there is something almost sublime in the unanimity with which the Venetians appear to believe that these means were iniquitous, and that this tenure is abominable. . . .

Consigned to the Austrians by Napoleon I, confirmed in the subjection into which she fell a second time after Napoleon's ruin, by the treaties of the Holy Alliance, defeated in several attempts to throw off her yoke, and loaded with heavier servitude after the fall of the short-lived Republic of 1849—Venice has always hated her masters with an exasperation deepened by each remove from the hope of independence, and she now detests them with a rancor which no concession short of some relinquishment of dominion would appease.

Instead, therefore, of finding that public gaiety and private hospitality in Venice for which the city was once famous, the stranger finds himself planted between two hostile camps, with merely the choice of sides open to him. Neutrality is solitude and friendship with neither party; society is exclusive association with the Austrians or with the Italians. The latter do not spare one of their own number if he consorts with their masters, and though a foreigner might expect greater allowance, it is seldom shown to him. To be seen in the company of officers is enmity to Venetian freedom, and in the case of Italians it is treason to country and to race. Of course, in a city where there is a large garrison and a great many officers who have nothing else to do, there is inevitably some international love-making, although the Austrians are rigidly excluded from association with the citizens. But the Italian who marries an Austrian severs the dearest ties and remains an exile in the heart of her country. Her friends mercilessly cast her off, as they cast off everybody who associates with the dominant race. In rare cases I have known Italians to receive foreigners who had Austrian friends, but this with the explicit understanding that there was to be no sign of recognition if they met them in the company of these detested acquaintances.

There are all degrees of intensity in Venetian hatred, and after hearing certain persons pour out the gall of bitterness upon the Austrians, you may chance to hear these persons spoken of as tepid in their patriotism by yet more fiery haters. Yet it must not be supposed that the Italians hate the Austrians as individuals. On the contrary, they have rather a liking for them—rather a contemptuous liking, for they think them somewhat slow and dull-witted—and individually the Austrians are amiable people, and try not to give offense. The government is also very strict in its control of the military. I have never seen the slightest affront offered by a soldier to a citizen; and there is evidently no personal ill-will engendered. The Austrians are simply hated as the means by which an alien and despotic government is imposed upon a people believing themselves born for freedom and independence. . . .

* * * *

The Venetians are now, therefore, a nation in mourning, and have, as I said, disused all their former pleasures and merry-makings. Every class, except a small part of the resident *titled* nobility (a great part of the nobility is in either forced or voluntary exile), seems to be comprehended by this feeling of despondency and suspense. The poor of the city formerly found their respite and diversion in the numerous holidays which fell in different parts of the year, and which, though religious in their general character, were still inseparably bound up in their origin with ideas of patriotism and national glory. Such of these holidays as related to the victories and pride of the Republic naturally ended with her fall. Many others, however, survived this event in all their splendor, but there is not one celebrated now as in other days. It is true that the churches still parade their pomps in the Piazza on the day of Corpus Christi; it is true that the bridges of boats are still built across the Grand Canal to the church of Santa Maria della Salute and across the Canal of the Giudecca to the temple of the Redentore on the respective festivals of these churches; but the concourse is always meager, and the mirth is forced and ghastly. The *Italianissimi** have so far imbued the people with their own ideas and feelings, that the recurrence of the famous holidays now merely awakens them to lamentations over the past and vague longings for the future.

As for the carnival, which once lasted six months of the year, charming hither all the idlers of the world by its peculiar splendor and variety of pleasure, it does not, as I said, any longer exist. It is dead, and its shabby, wretched ghost is a party of beggars, hideously dressed out with masks and horns and women's habits, who go from shop to shop droning forth a stupid song, and levying tribute upon the shopkeepers. The crowd through which these melancholy jesters pass, regards them with a pensive scorn, and goes about its business untempted by the delights of carnival.

All other social amusements have shared in greater or less degree the fate of the carnival. At some houses *conversazioni* are still held, and it is impossible that balls and parties should not now and then be given. But

---

*   *Italianissim* are those who favor union with Italy at any cost. *Austriacanti* (see p. 30) are people of Austrian politics, though not of Austrian birth.

the greater number of the nobles and the richer of the professional classes lead for the most part a life of listless seclusion, and attempts to lighten the general gloom and heaviness in any way are not looked upon with favor. By no sort of chance are Austrians, or *Austriacanti,* ever invited to participate in the pleasures of Venetian society.

As the social life of Italy, and especially of Venice, was in great part to be once enjoyed at the theaters, at the cafe and at the other places of public resort, so is its absence now to be chiefly noted in those places. No lady of perfect standing among her people goes to the opera, and the men never go in the boxes, but if they frequent the theater at all, they take places in the pit, in order that the house may wear as empty and dispirited a look as possible. Occasionally a bomb is exploded in the theater, as a note of reminder, and as means of keeping away such of the nobles as are not enemies of the government. As it is less easy for the Austrians to participate in the diversion of comedy, it is a less offense to attend the comedy, though even this is not good *Italianissimism.* In regard to the cafe, there is a perfectly understood system by which the Austrians go to one, and the Italians to another; and Florian's, in the Piazza, seems to be the only common ground in the city on which the hostile forces consent to meet. This is because it is thronged with foreigners of all nations, and to go there is not thought a demonstration of any kind. But the other cafes in the Piazza do not enjoy Florian's cosmopolitan immunity, and nothing would create more wonder in Venice than to see an Austrian officer at the Specchi, unless, indeed, it were the presence of a good Italian at the Quadri.

It is in the Piazza that the tacit demonstration of hatred and discontent chiefly takes place. Here, thrice a week, in winter and summer, the military band plays that exquisite music for which the Austrians are famous. The selections are usually from Italian operas, and the attraction is the hardest of all others for the music-loving Italian to resist. But he does resist it. There are some noble ladies who have not entered the Piazza while the band was playing there, since the fall of the Republic of 1849; and none of good standing for patriotism has attended the concerts since the treaty of Villafranca in '59. Until very lately, the promenaders in the Piazza were exclusively foreigners, or else the families of such government officials as were obliged to show themselves there. Last summer, however, before the Franco-Italian convention for the evacuation of Rome revived the drooping hopes of the Venetians, they had begun visibly to falter in their long endurance. But this was, after all, only a slight and transient weakness. As a general thing, now, they pass from the Piazza when the music begins, and walk upon the long quay at the seaside of the Ducal Palace; or if they remain in the Piazza they pace up and down under the arcades on either side; for Venetian patriotism makes a delicate distinction between listening to the Austrian band in the Piazza and hearing it under the Procuratie, forbidding the first and permitting the last. As soon as the music ceases the Austrians disappear, and the Italians return to the Piazza.

But since the catalog of demonstrations cannot be made full, it need not be made any longer. The political feeling in Venice affects her prosperity in a far greater degree than may appear to those who do not understand how large an income the city formerly derived from making merry. The poor have to lament not merely the loss of their holidays, but also of the fat employments and bountiful largess which these occasions threw into their hands. With the exile or the seclusion of the richer families, and the reluctance of foreigners to make a residence of the gloomy and dejected city, the trade of the shopkeepers has fallen off; the larger commerce of the place has also languished and dwindled year by year; while the cost of living has constantly increased, and heavier burdens of taxation have been laid upon the improverished and despondent people. And in all this, Venice is but a type of the whole province of Venetia.

The alien life to be found in the city is scarcely worth noting. The Austrians have a casino, and they give balls and parties, and now and then make some public manifestation of gaiety. But they detest Venice as a place of residence, being naturally averse to living in the midst of a people who shun them like a pestilence. Other foreigners, as I said, are obliged to take sides for or against the Venetians, and it is amusing enough to find the few English residents divided into *Austriacanti* and *Italianissimi*. . . .

* * * *

For the present, it is certain that the discontent of the people has its peculiar effect upon the city as the stranger sees its life, casting a glamor over it all, making it more and more ghostly and sad, and giving it a pathetic charm which I would fain transfer to my pages; but failing that, would pray the reader to remember as a fact to which I must be faithful in all my descriptions of Venice.

James Morris

James Morris's articles on Venice for the Manchester Guardian *led to a commission from a British and an American publisher for a book on the city. From a sojourn in the city during the major part of* 1959 *evolved* The World of Venice, *an all-inclusive account of the day-to-day life of the Venetian, as well as his history and traditions. Morris, now a special correspondent of the London* Times, *has said "I like to think, in moments of pretentious fancy, that my connection with Venice began with my maternal ancestor Philippe de Commynes, who wrote his report on the city in* 1495. . . ."

ISLANDERS

The estuaries of three virile rivers first formed the Venetian lagoon, rushing down from the Alps with their sediments of sand, shale and mud, and falling into the northwestern corner of the Adriatic. For many centuries, sheltered from the open sea by a bulwark of sandy reefs, it remained obscure and anonymous, on the edge of the Pax Romana. Scattered communities of fishermen and salt-gatherers lived among its marshes. Traders sometimes wandered through it. A few of the Roman sporting rich built villas, picnicked, idled or hunted duck on its islands. Some historians say the people of Padua maintained a port upon its outer reefs; others believe it was much less watery then, and that half of it was under the plough. Around its perimeter, on the mainland of Roman Veneto, celebrated cities flourished—Aquileia, Concordia, Padua, Altinum, all rich in the imperial civilization: but the lagoon itself stood aside from history, and remained shrouded in myth and malaria.

Then in the fifth and sixth centuries there fell out of the north, in successive waves, the Goths, Huns, Avars, Herulians and Lombards who were the scavengers of empire. The hinterland was lost in fire and

33

vengeance. Driven by barbarism, brutality and even the threat of Christian heresy, the peoples of the Veneto cities abandoned their comforts and fled into their obvious refuge—the lagoon. Sometimes, when a phase of barbaric invasion had passed, they went home again: but gradually, over the years, their exodus became an emigration. They became Venetians in fits and starts. Some were ordered into the lagoon by direct divine command, and were led by their formidable bishops, clutching vestments and chalices. Some saw guiding omens, of birds, stars or saints. Some took the tools of their trades with them, even the stones of their churches. Some were destitute—"but they would receive no man of servile condition," so the traditions assure us, "or a murderer, or of wicked life."

Many of these people went to the northern islands of the lagoon, fringed in reeds and soggy grass (where St. Peter himself, for example, assigned one fertile estate to the citizens of Altinum). Others went to the outer perimeter, as far as possible from the fires of Attila. Gradually, in a movement sanctified by innumerable miracles and saintly interventions, the original humble islanders were overwhelmed, rights of property were established, the first council chambers were built, the first austere churches. Venice was founded in misfortune, by refugees driven from their old ways and forced to learn new ones. Scattered colonies of city people, nurtured in all the ease of Rome, now struggled among the dank miasmas of the fenlands (their "malarious exhalations," as Baedeker was to call them, fussily adjusting his mosquito-net 1,400 years later). They learnt to build and sail small boats, to master the treacherous tides and shallows of the lagoon, to live on fish and rain-water. They built houses of wattles and osiers, thatched and mounted on piles.

Guided by priests and patricians of the old order, they devised new institutions based upon Roman precedents: there were, governing tribunes in each settlement, slowly uniting, with bickering and bloodshed, into a single administration under the presidency of a non-hereditary doge, elected for life—"rich and poor under equal laws," said the first of Venice's innumerable sycophants, "and envy, that curse of all the world, hath no place there." The lagoon people were pioneers, like settlers in the early West, or colonials on the Veldt. Crèvecoeur once wrote of "this new man, the American": But Goethe used precisely the same phrase to describe the first of the Venetians, whose old world had died around them.

Their beginnings are distinctly blurred, and were certainly not so uniformly edifying as their early apologist would have us believe. It took many years for the lagoon to spring into life and vigor; and several centuries for these new men to stop quarrelling with each other, develop into nationhood, and build the great city of Venice proper, until they could say of themselves (as they said haughtily to the Byzantine kings): "This Venice, which we have raised in the lagoons, is our mighty habitation, and no power of Emperor or Prince can touch us!" The early chronology of Venice is hazy and debatable, and nobody really knows what happened when, if at all.

Legend, though, is always precise, and if we are to believe the old chronicles, the foundation of Venice occurred on 25th March 421, at midday exactly. It was, according to my perpetual calendar, a Friday.

* * * *

So the Venetians became islanders, and islanders they remain, still a people apart, still tinged with the sadness of refugees. The squelchy islands of their lagoon, welded over the centuries into a glittering Republic, became the greatest of trading States, mistress of the eastern commerce and the supreme naval power of the day. For more than a thousand years Venice was something unique among the nations, half eastern, half western, half land, half sea, poised between Rome and Byzantium, between Christianity and Islam, one foot in Europe, the other paddling in the pearls of Asia. She called herself the Serenissima, she decked herself in cloth of gold, and she even had her own calendar, in which the years began on March 1st, and the days began in the evening. This lonely hauteur, exerted from the fastnesses of the lagoon, gave to the old Venetians a queer sense of isolation. As their Republic grew in grandeur and prosperity, and their political arteries hardened, and a flow of dazzling booty enriched their palaces and churches, so Venice became entrammelled in mystery and wonder. She stood, in the imagination of the world, somewhere between a freak and a fairy tale.

She remained, first of all uncompromisingly a city of the waters. In the early days the Venetians made rough roads in their islands, and rode about on mules and horses: but presently they evolved the system of canals, based on existing water-channels and rivulets, that is to this day one of the piquant wonders of the world. Their capital, the city of Venice proper, was built upon an archipelago in the heart of the lagoon. Their esplanade was the Grand Canal, the central highway of this city, which swung in a regal curve through a parade of palaces. Their Cheapside or Wall Street was the Rialto, first an island, then a district, then the most famous bridge in Europe. Their doges rode in fantastic golden barges, and outside each patrician's house the gondolas lay gracefully at their mooring. Venice evolved an amphibious society peculiar to herself, and the ornate front doors of her mansions opened directly upon the water.

Against this extraordinary physical background, the Venetians erected a no less remarkable kind of State. At first a kind of patriarchal democracy, it became an aristocratic oligarchy of the tightest kind, in which (after 1297) power was strictly reserved to a group of patrician families. Executive authority passed first to this aristocracy; then to the inner Council of Ten; and later, more and more, to the still more reclusive and reticent Council of Three, which was elected in rotation, a month at a time. To maintain this supremacy, and to prevent both popular rising and personal dictatorships, the structure of the State was buttressed with tyranny, ruthless, impersonal, bland and carefully mysterious. Sometimes the stranger, passing by the Doge's Palace, would find a pair of anonymous conspirators hanging mangled from a gibbet, or hear a whisper of appalling torture in the dungeons of the Ten. Once the Venetians awoke to discover three convicted traitors buried alive, head downwards, among the flagstones of the Piazzetta, their feet protruding between the pillars. Time and again they learnt that some celebrated national leader, admiral or *condottiere*, had grown too big for his buskins, and had been strangled or thrown into gaol. Venice was a sort of police State, except that instead of worshipping power, she was terrified of it, and refused it to any single one of her citizens: and by these means, at once fair and ferocious, she outlived all her rivals, and preserved her republican independence until the very end of the eighteenth century.

All this was wonderful, but no less marvellous was the wealth and strength of Venice—which was, so the Venetians assiduously let it be known, divinely granted. First St. Theodore, then St. Mark the Evangelist surpervised the destinies of the Republic, and all kinds of sacred relics and allusions gave power to the Venetian elbow. *"Pax tibi, Marce, Evangelista Meus."* So said a heavenly messenger to St. Mark, when the Evangelist was once stranded on an apocryphal sand-bank in this very lagoon: and the words became the national slogan of the Venetian Republic, a divine writ of recommendation.

She was the greatest sea-power of her day, unrivalled in tonnage, fire-power and efficiency. Her great Arsenal was the supreme shipyard of the world, its secrets as jealously guarded as any nuclear armory; its walls were two miles round, its payroll numbered 16,000, and in the sixteenth-century wars against the Turks a new galley left its yards every morning for 100 days. The Venetian Navy, manned by free men until the slavers' seventeenth-century heyday, was a most formidable instrument of war, and long after the rise of Genoa and Spain as naval powers, Venetian gunnery remained incomparable.

Venice stood at the mouth of the great Po valley, facing eastwards, protected in the north by the Alps. She was a natural funnel of intercourse between east and west, and her greatness was built upon her geography. She was hazily subject first to Ravenna and then to Byzantium, but she established herself as independent both of east and of west. She became mistress of the Adriatic, of the eastern Mediterranean, and finally of the trade routes to the Orient—Persia, India and the rich mysteries of China. She lived by the eastern commerce. She had her own caravanserai in the cities of the Levant: and "all the gold in Christendom," as one mediaeval chronicler querulously observed, "passes through the hands of the Venetians."

In Venice the Orient began. Marco Polo was a Venetian, and Venetian merchants, searching for new and profitable lines of commerce, travelled widely throughout central Asia. Decked in Oriental fineries, Venice became the most flamboyant of all cities—"the most triumphant Citie I ever set eyes on," wrote de Commynes in 1495. She was a place of silks, emeralds, marbles, brocades, velvets, cloth of gold, porphyry, ivory, spices, scents, apes, ebony, indigo, slaves, great galleons, mosaics, shining domes, rubies, and all the gorgeous commodities of Arabia, China and the Indies. She was a treasure-box. Venice was ruined, in the long run, by the Muslim capture of Constantinople in 1453, which ended her supremacy in the Levant; and by da Gama's voyage to India in 1498, which broke her monopoly of the Oriental trade: but for another three centuries she retained her panache and her pageantry, and she keeps her gilded reputation still.

She was never loved. She was always the outsider, always envied, always suspected, always feared. She fitted into no convenient category of nations. She was the lion who walked by herself. She traded indiscriminately with Christian and Muslim, in defiance of ghastly Papal penalties (she is the only Christian city marked on Ibn Khaldun's celebrated fourteenth-century map, together with such places as Gog, Oman, Stinking Land, Waste Country, Soghd, Tughuzghuz and Empty In The North Because of The Cold). She was the most expert and unscrupulous of money-makers, frankly dedicated to profit, even treating the Holy Wars as promising investments, and cheerfully accommodating the Emperor Baldwin of Jerusalem, when he wished to pawn his Crown of Thorns.

Venice's prices were high, her terms were unyielding, and her political motives were so distrusted that in the League of Cambrai most of the sixteenth-century Great Powers united to suppress "the insatiable cupidity of the Venetians and their thirst for domination" (and so perversely efficient was she that the news of their resolution was brought by her couriers from Blois to Venice in eight days flat). Even when, in the seventeenth and eighteenth centuries, she stood almost alone for Christendom against the triumphant Turks, Venice was never embraced by the nations. She was like a griffin or a phoenix, on the outside of a rookery.

And as the centuries passed, and she lost her supremacies, and the strain of the merchant princes was weakened, and she sapped her energies in endless Italian squabbles and embroilments, and became a mainland Power—as she sank into her eighteenth-century degeneracy, she became another kind of prodigy. During her last century of independence she was the gayest and worldliest of all cities, a perpetual masque and revelry, where nothing was too daring, too shameful or too licentious. Her carnivals were protracted and uninhibited. Her courtesans were honored. The domino and the Ace of Spades were her reigning symbols. The dissolute of the western world, the salacious and the mere fun-loving flocked to her theatres and gaming-tables, and respectable people all over Europe looked towards her as they might, from a safe distance, deplore the goings-on of a Sodom or a Gomorrah. No other nation ever died in such feverish hedonism. Venice whirled towards her fall, in the reign of the 120th Doge, in a fandango of high living and enjoyment, until at last Napoleon, brusquely deposing her ineffective Government, ended the Republic and handed the Serenissima contemptuously to the Austrians. *"Dust and ashes, dead and done with, Venice spent what Venice earned."*

This peculiar national history lasted a millennium, and the constitution of Venice was unchanged between 1310 and 1796. Nothing in the story of Venice is ordinary. She was born dangerously, lived grandly, and never abandoned her brazen individualism. "Those pantaloons!" is how a gentleman of the sixteenth-century French Court referred to the Venetians in an unguarded moment, and he was promptly slapped hard in the face by His Excellency the Venetian Ambassador. His contempt, anyway, was forced. You could not feel disdainful towards the Venetians, only resentful. Their system of government, for all its cruelties, was a brilliant success, and fostered in citizens of all classes an unparalleled love of country. Their navies were incomparable. The noblest artists of the day embellished Venice with their genius; the highest paid mercenaries competed for her commissions; the greatest Powers borrowed her money and rented her ships; and for two centuries the Venetians, at least in a commerical sense, "held the gorgeous east in fee." "Venice has preserved her independence during eleven centuries," wrote Voltaire just thirty years before the fall of the Republic, "and I flatter myself will preserve it for ever": so special was the Venetian position in the world, so strange but familiar, like Simeon Stylites on top of his pillar, in the days when Popes and Emperors sent their envoys to Syria to consult him.

Venice is still old. Since Napoleon's arrival, despite moments of heroism and sacrifice, she has been chiefly a museum, through whose clicking turnstiles the armies of tourism endlessly pass. When the Risorgimento triumphed in Italy, she joined the new Kingdom, and since 1866 has been just another Italian provincial capital: but she remains, as always, a phenomenon. She remains a city without wheels, a metropolis of waterways. She is still gilded and agate-eyed. Travellers still find her astonishing, exasperating, overwhelming, ruinously expensive, gaudy, and what one sixteenth-century Englishman called "decantated in majestie." The Venetians have long since become Italian citizens, but are still a race *sui generis,* comparable only, as Goethe said, to themselves. In essence, Venice was always a city-State, for all her periods of colonial expansion. There have perhaps been no more than three million true Venetians in all the history of the place: and this grand insularity, this isolation, this sense of queerness and crookedness has preserved the Venetian character uncannily, as though it was pickled like a rare intestine, or mummified in lotions.

PART II

NATIVE SON

In my opinion, if the Earthly Paradise where Adam dwelt with Eve were like Venice, Eve would have had a hard time to tempt him out of it with any fig. For it would have been another matter to lose Venice, where there are so many lovely things, than to lose that place where there are nothing but figs, melons and grapes.

PIETRO ARETINO (1492–1556)

Jacques Casanova

(De Seingalt)

·◄ 1725–1798 ►·

*Casanova epitomized, in Havelock Ellis's view, "the Venetian genius
. . . of sensuous enjoyment, of tolerant humanity, of unashamed earthli-
ness. Soldier, gambler, necromancer, adventurer, profligate and withal a
man of letters well aware of the refinements and elegancies of life,"
Casanova was denounced by a spy of the Venetian Inquisition in 1755 for
"impiety, imposture and licentiousness." Convinced that he was impris-
oned for life—although the sentence was for five years—Casanova
devised an escape and successfully executed it during the night of October 31–November 1, 1756. This remarkable exploit of human ingenuity
is recorded in Casanova's justly famous* Memoirs *along with his numerous amorous encounters and other fabulous adventures.*

MY ESCAPE FROM THE LEADS

To make the reader understand how I managed to escape from a place like
the Leads, I must explain the nature of the locality.

The Leads, used for the confinement of state prisoners, are in fact the
lofts of the ducal palace, and take their name from the large plates of lead
with which the roof is covered. One can only reach them through the gates
of the palace, the prison buildings, or by the Bridge of Sighs. . . .

I reasoned as follows:

I wish to regain my liberty at all hazards, I have in my cell an iron bar
by the sharpening one end of which I have converted it into a pike. My
pike is an admirable instrument, but I can make no use of it as my cell is
sounded all over (except the ceiling) every day. If I would escape, it is by
the ceiling; I must make a hole through it, and that I cannot do from this
side, for it would not be the work of a day. I must have someone to help

43

me; and not having much choice I have to pick out the monk, Father Balbi, with whom I correspond and who with the old nobleman occupies the adjoining cell. He was thirty-eight, and though not rich in common sense I judged the love of liberty—the first need of man—would give him sufficient courage to carry out any orders I might give. I must begin by telling him my plan in its entirety, and then I shall have to find a way to give him the bar. I had, then, two difficult problems before me.

My first step was to ask him if he wished to be free, and if he were disposed to hazard all in attempting his escape in my company. He replied that his mate and he would do anything to break their chains but, added he, "it is of no use to break one's head against a stone wall." He filled four pages with the impossibilities which presented themselves to his feeble intellect, for the fellow saw no chance of success on any quarter. I replied that I did not trouble myself with general difficulties, and that in forming my plan I had only thought of special difficulties, which I would find means to overcome, and I finished by giving him my word of honor to set him free, if he would promise to carry out exactly whatever orders I might give.

He gave me his promise to do so. I told him that I had a pike twenty inches long, and with this too he must pierce the ceiling of his cell next the wall which separated us, and he would then be above my head; his next step would be to make a hole in the ceiling of my cell and aid me to escape by it. "Here your task will end and mine will begin." . . .

The greatest relief of a man in the midst of misfortune is the hope of escaping from it. He sighs for the hour when his sorrows are to end; he thinks he can hasten it by his prayers; he will do anything to know when his torments shall cease. The sufferer, impatient and enfeebled, is mostly inclined to superstition. *"God,"* says he, "knows the time, and *God* may reveal it to me, it matters not how." Whilst he is in this state he is ready to trust in divination in any manner his fancy leads him, and is more or less disposed to believe in the oracle of which he makes choice.

I then was in this state of mind; but not knowing how to make use of the Bible to inform me of the moment in which I should recover my liberty, I determined to consult the divine *Orlando Furioso,* which I had read a hundred times, which I knew by heart, and which was my delight under The Leads. I idolized the genius of Ariosto, and considered him a far better fortune-teller than Virgil.

With this idea I wrote a question addressed to the supposed *Intelligence,* in which I asked in what canto of Ariosto I should find the day of my deliverance. I then made a reversed pyramid composed of the number formed from the words of the question, and by subtracting the number

44

nine I obtained, finally, *nine*. This told me that I should find my fate in the ninth canto. I followed the same method to find out the exact stanza and verse, and got *seven* for the stanza and *one* for the verse.

I took up the poem, and my heart beating as if I trusted wholly in the oracle, I opened it, turned down the leaf, and read:

Fra il fin d' ottobre, ei il capo di novembre.

The precision of the line and its appropriateness to my circumstances appeared so wonderful to me, that I will not confess that I placed my faith entirely in it; but the reader will pardon me if I say that I did all in my power to make the prediction a correct one. The most singular circumstance is that *between the end of October and the beginning of November,* there is only the instant of midnight, and it was just as the clock was striking midnight on the 31st of October that I escaped from my cell, as the reader will soon see. . . .

At eight o'clock without needing any help, my opening was made. I had broken up the beams, and the space was twice the size required. I got the plate of lead off in one piece. I could not do it by myself, because it was riveted. The monk came to my aid, and by dint of driving the bar between the gutter and the lead I succeeded in loosening it, and then, heaving at it with our shoulders, we beat it up till the opening was wide enough. On putting my head out through the hole I was distressed to see the brilliant light of the crescent moon then entering on its first quarter. This was a piece of bad luck which must be borne patiently, and we should have to wait till midnight, when the moon would have gone to light up the Antipodes. On such a fine night as this everybody would be walking in St. Mark's Place, and I dared not show myself on the roof as the moonlight would have thrown a huge shadow of me on the place, and have drawn towards me all eyes, especially those of *Messer-Grande* and his myrmidons, and our fine scheme would have been brought to nothing by their detestable activity. I immediately decided that we could not escape till after the moon set; in the meantime I prayed for the help of God, but did not ask Him to work any miracles for me. I was at the mercy of Fortune, and I had to take care not to give her any advantages; and if my scheme ended in failure I should be consoled by the thought that I had not made a single mistake. The moon would set at eleven and sunrise was at six, so we had seven hours of perfect darkness at our service; and though we had a hard task, I considered that in seven hours it would be accomplished. . . .

Our time had come. The moon had set. I hung half of the ropes by

Father Balbi's neck on one side and his clothes on the other. I did the same to myself, and with our hats on and our coats off we went to the opening.

I got out the first, and Father Balbi followed me. . . . Keeping on my hands and knees, and grasping my pike firmly I pushed it obliquely between the joining of the plates of lead, and then holding the side of the plate which I had lifted I succeeded in drawing myself up to the summit of the roof. The monk had taken hold of my waistband to follow me, and thus I was like a beast of burden who has to carry and draw along at the same time; and this on a steep and slippery roof.

After having surmounted with the greatest difficulty fifteen or sixteen plates we got to the top, on which I sat astride, Father Balbi imitating my example. Our backs were towards the little island of St. Giorgio, and about two hundred paces in front of us were the numerous cupolas of St. Mark's Church, which forms part of the ducal palace, for St. Mark's is really the Doge's private chapel, and no monarch in the world can boast of having a finer. My first step was to take off my bundle, and I told my companion to do the same. He put the rope as best he could upon his thighs, but wishing to take off his hat, which was in his way, he took hold of it awkwardly, and it was soon dancing from plate to plate to join the packet of linen in the gutter. My poor companion was in despair.

"A bad omen," he exclaimed; . . . .

I felt calmer now that I was no longer crawling on hands and knees, and I told him quietly that the accidents which had happened to him had nothing extraordinary in them, and that not even a superstitious person would call them omens, that I did not consider them in that light, and that they were far from damping my spirits.

"They ought rather," said I, "to warn you to be prudent, and to remind you that God is certainly watching over us, for if your hat had fallen to the left instead of to the right, we should have been undone; as in that case it would have fallen into the palace court, where it would have caught the attention of the guards, and have let them know that there was someone on the roof; and in a few minutes we should have been retaken."

After looking about me for some time I told the monk to stay still till I came back, and I set out, my pike in my hand, sitting astride the roof and moving along without any difficulty. For nearly an hour I went to this side and that, keeping a sharp look-out, but in vain; for I could see nothing to which a rope could be fastened, and I was in the greatest perplexity as to what was to be done. It was of no use thinking of getting down on the canal side or by the court of the palace, and the church offered only precipices which led to nothing. To get to the other side of the church towards the Canonica, I should have had to climb roofs so steep that I saw no prospect of success. The situation called for hardihood, but not the smallest piece of rashness.

It was necessary, however, either to escape, or to re-enter the prison, perhaps never again to leave it, or to throw myself into the canal. In such a dilemma it was necessary to leave a good deal to chance, and to make a start of some kind. My eye caught a window on the canal sides, and two-thirds of the distance from the gutter to the summit of the roof. It was a good distance from the spot I had set out from, so I concluded that the garret lighted by it did not form part of the prison I had just broken. It could only light a loft, inhabited or uninhabited, above some rooms in the palace, the doors of which would probably be opened by daybreak. I was morally sure that if the palace servants saw us they would help us to escape, and not deliver us over to the Inquisitors, even if they had recognised us as criminals of the deepest dye; so heartily was the State Inquisition hated by everyone.

It was thus necessary for me to get in front of the window, and letting myself slide softly down in a straight line I soon found myself astride on top of the dormer-roof. Then grasping the sides I stretched my head over, and succeeded in seeing and touching a small grating, behind which was a window of square panes of glass joined with thin strips of lead. I did not trouble myself about the window, but the grating, small as it was, appeared an insurmountable difficulty, failing a file, and I had only my pike.

I was thoroughly perplexed, and was beginning to lose courage, when an incident of the simplest and most natural kind came to my aid and fortified my resolution.

Philosophic reader, if you will place yourself for a moment in my position, if you will share the sufferings which for fifteen months had been my lot, if you think of my danger on the top of a roof, where the slightest step in a wrong direction would have cost me my life, if you consider the few hours at my disposal to overcome difficulties which might spring up at any moment, the candid confession I am about to make will not lower me in your esteem; at any rate, if you do not forget that a man in an anxious and dangerous position is in reality only half himself.

It was the clock of St. Mark's striking midnight, which, by a violent shock, drew me out of the state of perplexity I had fallen into. The clock reminded me that the day just beginning was All Saints' Day—the day of my patron saint (at least if I had one)—and the prophecy of my confessor came into my mind. But I confess that what chiefly strengthened me, both bodily and mentally, was the profane oracle of my beloved Ariosto: *Fra il fin d' ottobre, e il capo di novembre*.

The chime seemed to me a speaking talisman, commanding me to be up and doing, and promising me the victory. Lying on my belly I stretched my head down towards the grating, and pushing my pike into the sash which held it I resolved to take it out in a piece. In a quarter of an hour I succeeded, and held the whole grate in my hands, and putting it on one side I easily broke the glass window, though wounding my left hand.

With the aid of my pike, using it as I had done before, I regained the ridge of the roof, and went back to the spot where I had left Balbi. I found him enraged and despairing, and he abused me heartily for having left him for so long. He assured me that he was only waiting for it to get light to return to the prison.

"What did you think had become of me?"

"I thought you must have fallen over."

"And you can find no better way than abuse to express the joy you ought to feel at seeing me again?"

"What have you been doing all this time?"

"Follow me, and you shall see."

I took up my packets again and made my way towards the window. As soon as we were opposite to it I told Balbi what I had done, and asked him if he could think of any way of getting into the loft. For one it was easy enough, for the other could lower him by the rope; but I could not discover how the second of us was to get down afterwards, as there was nothing to which the rope could be fastened. If I let myself fall I might break my arms and legs, for I did not know the distance between the window and the floor of the room. To this chain of reasoning uttered in the friendliest possible tone, the brute replied thus:

"You let me down, and when I have got to the bottom you will have plenty of time to think how you are going to follow me."

I confess that my first indignant impulse was to drive my pike into his throat. My good genius stayed my arm, and I uttered not a word in reproach of his base selfishness. On the contrary, I straightway untied my bundle of rope and bound him strongly under the elbows, and making him lie flat down I lowered him feet foremost on the roof of the dormer-window. When he got there I told him to lower himself into the window as far as his hips, supporting himself by holding his elbows against the sides of the window. As soon as he had done so, I slid down the roof as before, and lying down on the dormer-roof with a firm grasp of the rope I told the monk not to be afraid but to let himself go. When he reached the floor of the loft he untied himself, and on drawing the rope back I found the fall was one of fifty feet—too dangerous a jump to be risked. The monk who for two hours had been a prey to terror, seated in a position which I

48

confess was not a very reassuring one, was now quite cool, and called out to me to throw him the ropes for him to take care of—a piece of advice you may be sure I took care not to follow.

Not knowing what to do next, and waiting for some fortunate idea, I made my way back to the ridge of the roof, and from there spied out a corner near a cupola, which I had not visited. I went towards it and found a flat roof, with a large window closed with two shutters. At hand was a tubful of plaster, a trowel, and a ladder which I thought long enough for my purpose. This was enough, and tying my rope to the first round I dragged this troublesome burden after me to the window. My next task was to get the end of the ladder (which was twelve fathoms long) into the opening, and the difficulties I encountered made me sorry that I had deprived myself of the aid of the monk.

I had set the ladder in such a way that one end touched the window, and the other went below the gutter. I next slid down to the roof of the window, and drawing the ladder towards me I fastened the end of my rope to the eighth round, and then let it go again till it was parallel with the window. I then strove to get it in, but I could not insert it farther than the fifth round, for the end of the ladder being stopped by the inside roof of the window, no force on earth could have pushed it any further without breaking either the ladder or the ceiling. There was nothing to be done but to lift it by the other end; it would then slip down by its own weight. I might, it is true, have placed the ladder across the window, and have fastened the rope to it, in which manner I might have let myself down into the loft without any risk; but the ladder would have been left outside to show . . . the guards where to look for us and possibly to find us in the morning.

I did not care to risk by a piece of imprudence the fruit of so much toil and danger, and to destroy all traces of our whereabouts the ladder must be drawn in. Having no one to give me a helping hand, I resolved to go myself to the parapet to lift the ladder and attain the end I had in view. I did so, but at such a hazard as had almost cost me my life. I could let go the ladder while I slackened the rope without any fear of its falling over, as it had caught to the parapet by the third rung. Then, my pike in my hand, I slid down beside the ladder to the parapet, which held up the points of my feet, as I was lying on my belly. In this position I pushed the ladder forward, and was able to get it into the window to the length of a foot, and that diminished by a good deal its weight. I now only had to push it in another two feet, as I was sure that I could get it in altogether by means of the rope from the roof of the window. To impel the ladder to the extent required I got on my knees, but the effort I had to use made me slip, and in an instant I was over the parapet as far as my chest, sustained only by my elbows.

I shudder still when I think of this awful moment, which cannot be conceived in all its horror. My natural instinct made me almost unconsciously strain every nerve to regain the parapet, and—I had nearly said miraculously—I succeeded. Taking care not to let myself slip back an inch, I struggled upwards with my hands and arms, while my belly was resting on the edge of the parapet. Fortunately the ladder was safe, for with that unlucky effort which had nearly cost me so dearly I had pushed it in more than three feet, and there it remained.

Finding myself resting on my groin on the parapet, I saw that I had only to lift up my right leg and to put up first one knee and then the other to be absolutely out of danger; but I had not yet got to the end of my trouble. The effort I made gave me so severe a spasm that I became cramped and unable to use my limbs. However, I did not lose my head, but kept quiet till the pain had gone off, knowing by experience that keeping still is the best cure for the false cramp. It was a dreadful moment! In two minutes I made another effort, and had the good fortune to get my knees on to the parapet, and as soon as I had taken breath I cautiously hoisted the ladder and pushed it half-way through the window. I then took my pike, and crawling up as I had done before, I reached the window, where my knowledge of the laws of equilibrium and leverage aided me to insert the ladder to its full length, my companion receiving the end of it. I then threw into the loft the bundles and the fragments that I had broken off the window, and I stepped down to the monk, who welcomed me heartily and drew in the ladder. Arm in arm we proceeded to inspect the gloomy retreat in which we found ourselves, and judged it to be about thirty paces long by twenty wide.

At one end were folding doors barred with iron. This looked bad, but putting my hand to the latch in the middle it yielded to the pressure, and the door opened. The first thing we did was to make the tour of the room, and in crossing it we stumbled against a large table surrounded by stools and armchairs. Returning to the part where we had seen windows, we opened the shutters of one of them, and the light of the stars only showed us the cupolas and the depths beneath them. I did not think for a moment of lowering myself down, as I wished to know where I was going, and I did not recognize our surroundings. I shut the window up, and we returned to the place where we had left our packages. Quite exhausted I let myself fall on the floor, and placing a bundle of rope under my head a sweet sleep came to my relief. I abandoned myself to it without resistance, and indeed, I believe if death were to have been the result, I should

50

have slept all the same, and I still remember how I enjoyed that sleep.

It lasted for three and half hours, and I was awakened by the monk's calling out and shaking me. He told me that it had just struck five. He said it was inconceivable to him how I could sleep in the situation we were in. But that which was inconceivable to him was not so to me. I had not fallen asleep on purpose, but had only yielded to the demands of exhausted nature, and, if I may say so, the extremity of my need. In my exhaustion there was nothing to wonder at, since I had neither eaten nor slept for two days, and the efforts I had made—efforts almost beyond the limits of mortal endurance—might well have exhausted any man. In my sleep my activity had come back to me, and I was delighted to see the darkness disappearing, so that we should be able to proceed with more certainty and quickness.

Casting a rapid glance around, I said to myself, "This is not a prison; there ought, therefore, to be some easy exit from it." We addressed ourselves to the end opposite to the folding-doors, and in a narrow recess I thought I made out a doorway. I felt it over and touched a lock, into which I thrust my pike, and opened it with three or four heaves. We then found ourselves in a small room and I discovered a key on a table, which I tried on a door opposite to us, which, however, proved to be unlocked. I told the monk to go for our bundles, and replacing the key we passed out and came into a galley containing presses full of papers. They were the state archives. I came across a short flight of stone stairs, which I descended, then another, which I descended also, and found a glass door at the end, on opening which I entered a hall well known to me: we were in the ducal chancery. I opened a window and could have got down easily but the result would have been that we should have been trapped in the maze of little courts around St. Mark's Church. I saw on a desk an iron instrument, of which I took possession; it had a rounded point and a wooden handle, being used by the clerks of the chancery to pierce parchments for the purpose of affixing the leaden seals. On opening the desk I saw the copy of a letter advising the *Proveditore of Corfu* of a grant of three thousand sequins for the restoration of the old fortress. I searched for the sequins but they were not there. *God* knows how gladly I would have taken them, and how I would have laughed the monk to scorn if he had accused me of theft! I should have received the money as a gift from Heaven, and should have regarded myself as its master by conquest.

Going to the door of the chancery, I put my bar into the keyhole, but finding immediately that I could not break it open, I resolved on making a hole in the door. I took care to choose the side where the wood had fewest knots, and working with all speed I struck as hard and as cleaving strokes as I was able. The monk, who helped me as well as he could with the punch I had taken from the desk, trembled at the echoing clamor of my pike, which must have been audible at some distance. I felt the danger myself, but it had to be risked.

In half an hour the hole was large enough—a fortunate circumstance, for I should have had much trouble in making it any larger without the aid of a saw. I was afraid when I looked at the edges of the hole, for they bristled with jagged pieces of wood which seemed made for tearing clothes and flesh together. The hole was at a height of five feet from the ground. We placed beneath it two stools, one beside the other, and when we had stepped upon them the monk with arms crossed and head foremost began to make his way through the hole, and taking him by the thighs, and afterwards by the legs, I succeeded in pushing him through, and though it was dark I felt quite secure, as I knew the surroundings. As soon as my companion had reached the other side I threw him my belongings, with the exception of the ropes, which I left behind, and placing a third stool on the two others, I climbed up, and got through as far as my middle, though with much difficulty, owing to the extreme narrowness of the hole. Then, having nothing to grasp with my hands, nor anyone to push me as I had pushed the monk, I asked him to take me, and draw me gently and by slow degrees towards him. He did so, I endured silently the fearful torture I had to undergo, as my thighs and legs were torn by the splinters of wood.

As soon as I got through I made haste to pick up my bundle of linen, and going down two flights of stairs I opened without difficuly the door leading into the passage whence opens the chief door to the grand staircase, and in another door of the closet of the *Savio alla scrittura.* The chief door was locked, and I saw at once that, failing a catapult or a mine of gunpowder, I could not possibly get through. The bar I still held seemed to say, "*Hic fines posuit.* My use is ended and you can lay me down." It was dear to me as the instrument of my freedom, and was worthy of being hung as an *ex voto* on the altar of liberty.

I sat down with the utmost tranquillity, and told the monk to do the same.

"My work is done," I said, "the rest must be left to God and fortune. . . . I do not know whether those who sweep out the palace will come here to-day, which is All Saints' Day, or to-morrow, All Soul's Day. If anyone comes, I shall run out as soon as the door opens, and do you follow after me; but if nobody comes, I do not budge a step, and if I die of hunger so much the worse for me."

At this speech of mine he became beside himself. He called me madman, seducer, deceiver, and liar. I let him talk, and took no notice. It struck six; only an hour had passed since I had my awakening in the loft.

My first task was to change my clothes. Father Balbi looked like a peasant, but he was in better condition than I, his clothes were not torn to shreds or covered with blood, his red flannel waistcoat and purple breeches were intact, while my figure could only inspire pity or terror, so bloodstained and tattered was I. I took off my stockings, and the blood gushed out of two wounds I give myself on the parapet, while the splinters in the hole in the door had torn my waistcoat, shirt, breeches, legs, and thighs. I was dreadfully wounded all over my body. I made bandages of handkerchiefs, and dressed my wounds as best I could, and then put on my fine suit, which on a winter's day would look old enough. Having tied up my hair, I put on white stockings, laced shirt, failing any other, and two others over it, and then stowing away some stockings and handkerchiefs in my pockets, I threw everything else into a corner of the room. I flung my fine cloak over the monk, and the fellow looked as if he had stolen it. I must have looked like a man who has been to a dance and has spent the rest of the night in a disorderly house, though the only foil to my unseasonable elegance of attire was the bandages round my knees.

In this guise, with my exquisite hat trimmed with Spanish lace and adorned with a white feather on my head, I opened a window. I was immediately remarked by some loungers in the palace court, who, not understanding what anyone of my appearance was doing there at such an early hour, went to tell the doorkeeper of the circumstance. He, thinking he must have locked somebody in the night before, went for his keys and came towards us. I was sorry to have let myself be seen at the window, not knowing that therein chance was working for our escape, and was sitting down listening to the idle talk of the monk, when I heard the jingling of keys. Much perturbed I got up and put my eye to a chink in the door, and saw a man with a great bunch of keys in his hand mounting leisurely up the stairs. I told the monk not to open his mouth, to keep well behind me, and to follow my steps. I took my pike, and concealing it in my right sleeve I got into a corner by the door, whence I could get out as soon as it was opened and run down the stairs. I prayed that the man might make no resistance, as if he did I should be obliged to fell him to the earth, and I determined to do so.

The door opened, and the poor man as soon as he saw me seemed turned to a stone. Without an instant's delay and in dead silence, I made haste to descend the stairs, the monk following me. Avoiding the appearance of a fugitive, but walking fast, I went by the Giants' Stairs, taking no notice of Father Balbi, who kept calling out, "To the church! to the church!"

The church door was only about twenty paces from the stairs, but the churches were no longer sanctuaries at Venice, and no one ever took refuge in them. The monk knew this, but fright had deprived him of his faculties. He told me afterwards that the motive which impelled him to go to the church was the voice of religion bidding him seek the horns of the altar.

"Why didn't you go by yourself?" said I.

"I did not like to abandon you;" but he should rather have said, "I did not like to lose the comfort of your company."

The safety I sought was beyond the borders of the Republic, and thitherward I began to bend my steps. Already there in spirit, I must needs be there in body also. I went straight towards the chief door of the palace, and looking at no one that might be tempted to look at me I got to the canal and entered the first gondola that I came across, shouting to the boatman on the poop:

"I want to go to Fusina; be quick and call another gondolier."

This was soon done, and while the gondola was being got off I sat down on the seat in the middle, and Balbi at the side. The old appearance of the monk, without a hat and with a fine cloak on his shoulders, with my unreasonable attire, was enough to make people take us for an astrologer and his man.

As soon as we had passed the custom-house, the gondoliers began to row with a will along the Giudecca Canal, by which we must pass to go to Fusina or to Mestre, which latter place was really our destination. When we had traversed half the length of the canal I put my head out, and said to the waterman on the poop:

"When do you think we shall get to Mestre?"

"But you told me to go to Fusina."

"You must be mad; I said Mestre."

The other boatman said that I was mistaken, and the fool of a monk, in his capacity of zealous Christian and friend of truth took care to tell me that I was in the wrong. I wanted to give him a hearty kick as a punishment for his stupidity, but reflecting that common sense comes not by wishing for it I burst into a peal of laughter, and agreed that I might have made a mistake, but that my real intention was to go to Mestre. To that they answered nothing, but a minute after the master boatman said he was ready to take me to England if I liked.

"Bravely spoken," said I, "and now for Mestre, ho!"

"We shall be there in three-quarters of an hour, as the wind and tide are in our favor."

Well pleased I looked at the canal behind us, and thought it had never seemed so fair, especially as there was not a single boat coming our way. It was a glorious morning, the air was clear and glowing with the first rays of the sun, and my two young watermen rowed easily and well; and as I thought over the night of sorrow, the dangers I had escaped, the abode where I had been fast bound the day before, all the chances which had been in my favor, and the liberty of which I now began to taste the sweets, I was so moved in my heart and grateful to my God that, well nigh choked with my emotion, I burst into tears.

My nice companion who had hitherto only spoken to back up the gondoliers, thought himself bound to offer me his consolations. He did not understand why I was weeping, and the tone he took made me pass from my sweet affliction to a strange mirthfulness which made him go astray once more, as he thought I had got mad. The poor monk, as I have said, was a fool, and whatever was bad about him was the result of his folly. I had been under the sad necessity of turning him to account, but though without intending to do so he had almost been my ruin. It was no use trying to make him believe that I had told the gondoliers to go to Fusina whilst I intended to go to Mestre; he said I could not have thought of that till I got on to the Grand Canal.

In due course we reached Mestre. There were no horses to ride post, but I found men with coaches who did as well, and I agreed with one of them to take me to Treviso in an hour and a quarter. The horses were put in in three minutes, and with the idea that Father Balbi was behind me I turned round to say "Get up," but he was not there. I told a groom to go and look for him, with the intention of reprimanding him sharply, even if he had gone for a necessary occasion, for we had no time to waste, not even thus. The man came back saying he could not find him, to my great rage and indignation. I was tempted to abandon him, but a feeling of humanity restrained me. I made inquiries all round; everybody had seen him, but not a soul knew where he was. I walked along the high street, and some instinct prompting me to put my head in at the window of a café I saw the wretched man standing at the bar drinking chocolate and making love to the girl. Catching sight of me, he pointed to the girl and said:

"She's charming," and then invited me to take a cup of chocolate, saying that I must pay, as he hadn't a penny. I kept back my wrath and answered:

"I don't want any, and do you make haste!" and caught hold of his arm in such sort that he turned white with pain. I paid the money and we went out. I trembled with anger. We got into our coach, but we had scarcely gone ten paces before I recognized an inhabitant of Mestre named Balbi Tommasi, a good sort of man, but reported to be one of the familiars of the Holy Office. He knew me, too, and coming up called out:

"I am delighted to see you here. I suppose you have just escaped. How did you do it?"

"I have not escaped, but have been set at liberty."

"No, no, that's not possible, as I was at M. Grimani's yesterday evening, and I should have heard it."

It will be easier for the reader to imagine my state of mind than for me to describe it. I was discovered by a man whom I believed to be a hired agent of the government, who had only to give a glance to one of the *sbirri* with whom Mestre swarmed to have me arrested. I told him to speak softly, and getting down I asked him to come to one side. I took him behind a house, and seeing that there was nobody in sight, a ditch in front, beyond which the open country extended, I grasped my pike, and took him by the neck. At this he gave a struggle, slipped out of my hands, leapt over the ditch, and without turning round set off to run at full speed. As soon as he was some way off he slackened his course, turned round and kissed his hand to me, in token of wishing me a prosperous journey. And as soon as he was out of my sight, I gave thanks to God that this man by his quickness had preserved me from the commission of a crime, for I would have killed him; and he, as it turned out, bore me no ill-will.

I was in a terrible position. In open war with all the powers of the Republic, everything had to give way to my safety, which made me neglect no means of attaining my ends.

With the gloom of a man who has passed through a great peril, I gave a glance of contempt towards the monk, who now saw to what danger he had exposed us, and I then got up again into the carriage. We reached Treviso without further adventure.

PART III

THE SPECTACLE

We have rediscovered the great law of town planning which radiates so delightfully through Venice.

The buildings people the sky; communications are precisely established, in cardinal roads and piazzas, with canals at another level. The pedestrian is master of the ground as he will be in the new town of our time.

LE CORBUSIER

Henry James

◄ 1843–1916 ►

Henry James made the first of fourteen Italian visits—"so much fewer than I wanted," he said—when he was twenty-six. His devotion to that "Paradise" from which "one returns to Purgatories at best" was undiminished by time. Venice was the first city he saw, but at that time Florence and Rome made the greater impression. In later years, after a stay of two months in 1881, he became enamored of Venice and especially its painters Tintoretto, Carpaccio and Bellini. "Never has the whole place seemed to me sweeter, dearer, diviner," he wrote of the city on his last visit. All but two of his twenty-two novels relate to Italy. In James's Portraits of Places *(1883)* and Italian Hours *(1892) can be found some of the finest evocations of the ambience of Venice that we possess in the English language.*

In almost one hundred years since James described it the view of the Grand Canal remains relatively unaltered in appearance except for further deterioration and in too few instances restoration. One of these has been the Ca' Rezzonico, now a museum of eighteenth-century Venice. The changes have been mainly in the use now made of the various palazzi and buildings. Some have been converted to hotels, offices, one to a university and several have become museums. One of the most popular of these contains Peggy Guggenheim's notable collection of modern art. Since James's days a third bridge, built in 1934, spans the Grand Canal near the railway station. The major innovation—and a disquieting one for many Venetians—is the rather severe modern facade of the new railway station at the end of the Grand Canal. One of the most disturbing changes is the increased congestion of motorized craft, public and private, which imperils the foundations of the city and pollutes the atmosphere.

THE GRAND CANAL

The *ricordi* of Venice that we prefer are gathered best where the gondola glides—best of all on the noble waterway that begins in its glory at the

Salute and ends in its abasement at the railway station. It is, however, the Piazzetta that introduces us most directly to the great picture by which the Grand Canal works its first spell, and to which a thousand artists, not always with a talent apiece, have paid their tribute. We pass into the Piazzetta to look down the great throat, as it were, of Venice, and the vision must console us for turning our back on St. Mark's. . . .

The classic Salute waits like some great lady on the threshold of her salon. She is more ample and serene, more seated at her door, than all the copyists have told us, with her domes and scrolls, her scolloped buttresses and statues forming a pompous crown, and her wide steps disposed on the ground like the train of a robe. This fine air of the woman of the world is carried out by the well-bred assurance with which she looks in the direction of her old-fashioned Byzantine neighbor; and the juxtaposition of two churches so distinguished and so different, each splendid in its sort, is a sufficient mark of the scale and range of Venice. However, we ourselves are looking away from St. Mark's—we must blind our eyes to that dazzle; without it indeed there are brightnesses and fascinations enough. We see them in abundance even while we look away from the shady steps of the Salute. These steps are cool in the morning, yet I don't know that I can justify my excessive fondness for them any better than I can explain a hundred of the other vague infatuations with which Venice sophisticates the spirit. Under such an influence fortunately one needn't explain—it keeps account of nothing but perceptions and affections. . . . It is from the Salute steps perhaps, of a summer morning, that this view of the open mouth of the city is most brilliantly amusing. The whole thing composes as if composition were the chief end of human institutions. The charming architectural promontory of the Dogana stretches out the most graceful of arms, balancing in its hand the gilded globe on which revolves the delightful satirical figure of a little weathercock of a woman. This Fortune, this Navigation, or whatever she is called—she surely needs no name—catches the wind in the bit of drapery of which she has divested her rotary bronze loveliness. On the other side of the Canal twinkles and glitters the long row of the happy palaces which are mainly expensive hotels. There is a little of everything everywhere, in the bright Venetian air, but to these houses belongs especially the appearance of sitting, across the water, at the receipt of custom, of watching in their hypocritical loveliness for the stranger and the victim. I call them happy, because even their sordid uses and their vulgar signs melt somehow, with their vague sea-stained pinks and drabs, into that strange gaiety of light and color which is made up of the reflection of superannuated things. The atmosphere plays over them like a laugh, they are of the essence of the sad old joke. They are almost as charming from other places as they are from their own balconies and share fully in that universal privilege of Venetian objects which consists of being both the picture and the point of view.

This double character, which is particularly strong in the Grand Canal, adds a difficulty to any control of one's notes. The Grand Canal may be practically, as in impression, the cushioned balcony of a high and well-loved palace—the memory of irresistible evenings, of the sociable elbow, of endless lingering and looking; or it may evoke the restlessness of a fresh curiosity, of methodical inquiry, in a gondola piled with references. There are no references, I ought to mention, in the present remarks, which sacrifice to accident, not to completeness. A rhapsody of Venice is always in order, but I think the catalogs are finished. I should not attempt to write here the names of all the palaces, even if the number of those I find myself able to remember in the immense array were less insignificant. There are many I delight in that I don't know, or at least don't keep, apart. Then there are the bad reasons for preference that are better than the good, and all the sweet bribery of association and recollection. These things, as one stands on the Salute steps, are so many delicate fingers to pick straight out of the row a dear little featureless house which, with its pale green shutters, looks straight across at the great door and through the very keyhole, as it were, of the church, and which I needn't call by a name—a pleasant American name—that everyone in Venice, these many years, has had on grateful lips. It is the very friendliest house in all the wide world, and it has, as it deserves to have, the most beautiful position. It is a real *porto di mare,* as the gondoliers say—a port within a port; it sees everything that comes and goes, and takes it all in with practiced eyes. Not a tint or a hint of the immense iridescence is lost upon it, and there are days of exquisite color on which it may fancy itself the heart of the wonderful prism. We wave to it from the Salute steps, which we must decidedly leave if we wish to get on, a grateful hand across the water.

*　*　*　*

If the long reach from this point to the deplorable iron bridge which discharges the pedestrian at the Accademia—or, more comprehensively, to the painted and gilded Gothic of the noble Palazzo Foscari—is too much of a curve to be seen at any one point as a whole, it represents the better the arched neck, as it were, of the undulating serpent of which the *Canalazzo* has the likeness. We pass a dozen historic houses, we note in our passage a hundred component "bits," with the baffled sketcher's sense, and with what would doubtless be, save for our intensely Venetian fatalism, the baffled sketcher's temper. It is the early palaces, of course, and also, to be fair, some of the late, if we could take them one by one, that give the Canal the best of its grand air. The fairest are often cheek-by-jowl with the foulest, and there are few, alas, so fair as to have been completely protected by their beauty. The ages and the generations have worked their will on them, and the wind and the weather have had much to say; but disfigured and dishonored as they are, with the bruises of their marbles and the patience of their ruin, there is nothing like them in the world, and the long succession of their faded, conscious faces makes of the quiet waterway they overhang a *promenade historique* of which the lesson, however often we read it, gives, in the depth of its interest, an incomparable dignity to Venice. We read it in the Romanesque arches, crooked today in their very curves, of the early middle-age, in the exquisite individual Gothic of the splendid time, and in the cornices and columns of a decadence almost as proud. These things at present are almost equally touching in their good faith; they have each in their degree so effectually parted with their pride. They have lived on as they could and lasted as they might, and we hold them to no account of their infirmities, for even those of them whose blank eyes today meet criticism with most submission are far less vulgar than the uses we have mainly managed to put them to. We have botched them and patched them and covered them with sordid signs; we have restored and improved them with a merciless taste, and the best of them we have made over to the pedlars. . . .

* * * *

Far-descended and weary, but beautiful in its crooked old age, with its lovely proportions, its delicate round arches, its carvings and its discs of marble, is the haunted Montecuculi Palace. Those who have a kindness for Venetian gossip like to remember that it was once for a few months the property of Robert Browning, who, however, never lived in it, and who died in the splendid Rezzonico, [later] the residence of his son and a wonderful cosmopolite "document," which, as it presents itself, in an admirable position, but a short way farther down the Canal, we can almost see, in spite of the curve, from the window at which we stand. This great seventeenth century pile, throwing itself upon the water with a peculiar florid assurance, a certain upward toss of its cornice which gives it the air of a rearing seahorse, decorates immensely—and within, as well as without—the wide angle that it commands.

The Spectacle

There is a more formal greatness in the high square Gothic Foscari, just below it, one of the noblest creations of the fifteenth century, a masterpiece of symmetry and majesty. Dedicated today to official uses—it is the property of the State—it looks conscious of the consideration it enjoys, and is one of the few great houses within our range whose old age strikes us as robust and painless. It is visibly "kept up"; perhaps it is kept up too much; perhaps I am wrong in thinking so well of it. These doubts and fears course rapidly through my mind—I am easily their victim when it is a question of architecture—as they are apt to do today, in Italy, almost anywhere, in the presence of the beautiful, of the desecrated or the neglected. We feel at such moments as if the eye of Mr. Ruskin were upon us; we grow nervous and lose our confidence. This makes me inevitably, in talking of Venice, seek a pusillanimous safety in the trivial and the obvious. I am on firm ground in rejoicing in the little garden directly opposite our windows—it is another proof that they really show us everything—and in feeling that the gardens of Venice would deserve a page to themselves. They are infinitely more numerous than the arriving stranger can suppose; they nestle with a charm all their own in the complications of most back views. Some of them are exquisite, many are large, and even the scrappiest have an artful understanding, in the interest of color, with the waterways that edge their foundations. On the small canals, in the hunt for amusement, they are the prettiest surprises of all. The tangle of plants and flowers crowds over the battered walls, the greenness makes an arrangement with the rosy sordid brick. Of all the reflected and liquefied things in Venice, and the number of these is countless, I think the lapping water loves them most. They are numerous on the *Canalazzo,* but wherever they occur they give a brush to the picture and in particular, it is easy to guess, give a sweetness to the house. Then the elements are complete—the trio of air and water and of things that grow. Venice without them would be too much a matter of the tides and the stones. . . .

If I may not go into those of the palaces this devious discourse has left behind, much less may I enter the great galleries of the Accademia which rears its blank wall; surmounted by the lion of St. Mark, well within sight of the windows at which we are still lingering. This wondrous temple of Venetian art—for all it promises little from without—overhangs, in a manner, the Grand Canal, but if we were so much as to cross its threshold we should wander beyond recall. It contains, in some of the most magnificent halls—where the ceilings have all the glory with which the imagination of Venice alone could over-arch a room—some of the noblest pictures in the world; and whether or not we go back to them on any particular occasion for another look, it is always a comfort to know that they are there, as the sense of them on the spot is a part of the furniture of the mind—the sense of them close at hand, behind every wall and under every cover, like the inevitable reverse of a medal, of the side exposed to the air that reflects, intensifies, completes the scene. In other words, as it was the inevitable destiny of Venice to be painted, and painted with passion, so the wide world of picture becomes, as we live there, and however much we go about our affairs, the constant habitation of our thoughts. The truth is, we are in it so uninterruptedly, at home and abroad, that there is scarcely a pressure upon us to seek it in one place more than in another. Choose your standpoint at random and trust the picture to come to you. This is manifestly why I have not, I find myself conscious, said more about the features of the *Canalazzo* which occupy the reach between the Salute and the position we have so obstinately taken up. It is still there before us, however, and the delightful little Palazzo Dario, intimately familiar to English and American travellers, picks itself out in the foreshortened brightness. The Dario is covered with the loveliest little marble plates and sculptured circles; it is made up of exquisite pieces—as if there had been only enough to make it small—so that it looks, in its extreme antiquity, a good deal like a house of cards that hold together by a tenure it would be fatal to touch. An old Venetian house dies hard indeed, and I should add that this delicate thing, with submission in every feature, continues to resist the contact of generations of lodgers. It is let out in floors (it used to be let as a whole) and in how many eager hands—for it is in great requisition—under how many fleeting dispensations have we not known and loved it? People are always writing in advance to secure it, as they are to secure the Jenkins's gondolier, and as the gondola passes we see strange faces at the windows—though it's ten to one we recognize them—and the millionth artist coming forth with his traps at the watergate. The poor little patient Dario is one of the most flourishing booths at the fair.

The faces at the window look out at the great Sansovino—the splendid pile that is now occupied by the Prefect. I feel decidedly that I don't object as I ought to the palaces of the sixteenth and seventeenth centuries. Their pretensions impose upon me, and the imagination peoples them more freely than it can people the interiors of the prime. Was not moreover this masterpiece of Sansovino once occupied by the Venetian post office, and thereby intimately connected with an ineffaceable first impression of the author of these remarks? . . . I am afraid to take the proper steps for finding out, lest I should learn that during these years I have misdirected my emotion. A better reason for the sentiment, at any rate, is that such a great house has surely, in the high beauty of its tiers, a refinement of its own. They make one think of colosseums and aqueducts and bridges, and they constitute doubtless, in Venice, the most pardonable specimen of the imitative. I have even a timid kindness for the huge Pesaro, far down the Canal, whose main reproach, more even than the coarseness of its forms, is its swaggering size, its want of consideration for the general picture, which the early examples so reverently respect. The Pesaro is as far out of the frame as a modern hotel, and the Corner della Regina close to it, oversteps almost equally the modesty of art. One more thing they and their kindred do, I must add, for which, unfortunately, we can patronize them less. They make even the most elaborate material civilization of the present day seem woefully shrunken and *bourgeois,* for they simply—I allude to the biggest palaces—can't be lived in as they were intended to be. The modern tenant may take in all the magazines, but he bends not the bow of Achilles. He occupies the place, but he doesn't fill it, and he has guests from the neighboring inns with ulsters and Baedekers. We are far at the Pesaro, by the way, from our attaching window, and we take advantage of it to go in rather a melancholy mood to the end. The long straight vista from the Foscari to the Rialto, the great middle stretch of the Canal, contains, as the phrase is, a hundred objects of interest, but it contains most the bright oddity of its general Deluge air. In all these centuries it has never got over its resemblance to a flooded city; for some reason or other it is the only part of Venice in which the houses look as if the waters had overtaken them. Everywhere else they reckon with them—have chosen them; here alone the lapping seaway seems to confess itself an accident.

There are persons who hold this long, gay, shabby, spotty perspective, in which, with its immense field of confused reflection, the houses have infinite variety, the dullest expanse in Venice. It was not dull, we imagine, for Lord Byron, who lived in the midmost of the three Mocenigo palaces, where the writing table is still shown at which he gave the rein to his passions. For other observers it is sufficiently enlivened by so delightful a creation as the Palazzo Loredan, once a masterpiece and at present the *Municipio,* not to speak of a variety of other immemorial bits whose beauty still has a degree of freshness. Some of the most touching relics of early Venice are here—for it was here she precariously clustered—peeping out of a submersion more pitiless than the sea. As we approach the Rialto indeed the picture falls off and a comparative commonness suffuses it. There is a wide paved walk on either side of the Canal, on which the waterman—and who in Venice is not a waterman?—is prone to seek repose. I speak of the summer days—it is the summer Venice that is the visible Venice. The big tarry barges are drawn up at the *fondamenta,* and the bare-legged boatmen, in faded blue cotton, lie asleep on the hot stones. If there were no color anywhere else there would be enough in their tanned personalities. Half the low doorways open into the warm interior of waterside drinking shops, and here and there, on the quay, beneath the bush that overhangs the door, there are rickety tables and chairs. Where in Venice is there not the amusement of character and of detail? The tone in this part is very vivid, and is largely that of the brown plebeian faces looking out of the patchy miscellaneous houses— the faces of fat undressed women and of other simple folk who are not aware that they enjoy, from balconies once doubtless patrician, a view the knowing ones of the earth come thousands of miles to envy them. The effect is enhanced by the tattered clothes hung to dry in the windows, by the sun-faded rags that flutter from the polished balustrades—these are ivory-smooth with time; and the whole scene profits by the general law that renders decadence and ruin in Venice more brilliant than any prosperity. Decay is in this extraordinary place golden in tint and misery *couleur de rose*. The gondolas of the correct people are unmitigated sable, but the poor market boats from the islands are kaleidoscopic.

The Bridge of the Rialto is a name to conjure with, but, honestly speaking, it is scarcely the gem of the composition. There are of course two ways of taking it—from the water or from the upper passage, where its small shops and booths abound in Venetian character; but it mainly counts as a feature of the Canal when seen from the gondola or even from the awful *vaporetto*. The great curve of its single arch is much to be commended, especially when, coming from the direction of the railway-station, you see it frame with its sharp compass line the perfect picture, the reach of the Canal on the other side. But the backs of the little shops make from the water a graceless collective hump, and the inside view is the diverting one. The big arch of the bridge—like the arches of all the bridges—is the waterman's friend in wet weather. The gondolas, when it rains, huddle beside the peopled barges, and the young ladies from the hotels, vaguely fidgeting, complain of the communication of insect life. Here indeed is a little of everything, and the jewellers of this celebrated precinct—they have their immemorial row—make almost as fine a show as the fruiterers. It is a universal market, and a fine place to study Venetian types. The produce of the islands is discharged there, and the fishmongers announce their presence. All one's senses indeed are vigorously attacked; the whole place is violently hot and bright, all odorous and noisy. The churning of the screw of the *vaporetto* mingles with the other sounds—not indeed that this offensive note is confined to one part of the Canal. But just here the little piers of the resented steamer are particularly near together, and it seems somehow to be always kicking up the water. As we go further down we see it stopping exactly beneath the glorious windows of the Ca' d'Oro. It has chosen its position well, and who shall gainsay it for having put itself under the protection of the most romantic façade in Europe? The companionship of these objects is a symbol; it expresses supremely the present and the future of Venice. Perfect, in its prime, was the marble Ca' d'Oro, with the noble recesses of its *loggie*. . . .

It is obvious that if the *vaporetti* have contributed to the ruin of the gondoliers, already hard pressed by fate, and to that of the palaces, whose foundations their waves undermine, and that if they have robbed the Grand Canal of the supreme distinction of its tranquillity, so on the other hand they have placed "rapid transit," in the New York phrase, in everybody's reach, and enabled everybody—save indeed those who wouldn't for the world—to rush about Venice as furiously as people rush about New York. The suitability of this consummation needn't be pointed out.

Even we ourselves, in the irresistible contagion, are going so fast now that we have only time to note in how clever and costly a fashion . . . the old *Fondaco dei Turchi* has been reconstructed and restored. It is a glare of white marble without, and a series of showy majestic halls within, where a thousand curious mementos and relics of old Venice are gathered and classified.* Of its miscellaneous treasures I fear I may perhaps frivolously prefer the series of its remarkable living Longhis, an illustration of manners more copious than the celebrated Carpaccio, the two ladies with their little animals and their long sticks. Wonderful indeed today are the museums of Italy, where the renovations and the *belle ordonnance* speak of funds apparently unlimited, in spite of the fact that the numerous custodians frankly look starved. What is the pecuniary source of all this civic magnificence—it is shown in a hundred other ways—and how do the Italian cities manage to acquit themselves of expenses that would be formidable to communities richer and doubtless less aesthetic? Who pays the bills for the expressive statues alone, the general exuberance of sculpture, with which every *piazzetta* of almost every village is patriotically decorated? Let us not seek an answer to the puzzling question, but observe instead that we are passing the mouth of the populous Cannaregio, next widest of the waterways . . . and at the

---

* Many relics of old Venice may now be seen in the Correr Museum in the Piazza San Marco.

corner of which the big colorless church of San Geremia stands gracefully enough on guard. The Cannaregio with its wide lateral footways and humpbacked bridges, makes on the feast of St. Giovanni, an admirable noisy, tawdry theatre for one of the prettiest and the most infantile of the Venetian processions.

The rest of the course is a reduced magnificence, in spite of interesting bits, of the battered pomp of the Pesaro and the Regina Corner, of the recurrent memories of royalty in exile which cluster about the Palazzo Vendramin Calergi, once the residence of the Comte de Chambord . . . in spite too of the big Papadopoli gardens, opposite the station, the largest private grounds in Venice, but of which Venice in general mainly gets the benefit in the usual form of irrepressible greenery climbing over walls and nodding at water. The rococo church of the Scalzi is here, all marble and malachite, all a cold, hard glitter and a costly, curly ugliness, and here too, opposite, on the top of its high steps, is San Simeone Profeta. . . . Thanks at any rate to the white church, domed and porticoed, on the top of its steps, the traveller emerging for the first time upon the terrace of the railway station seems to have a Canaletto before him. He speedily discovers indeed even in the presence of this scene of the final accents of the *Canalazzo*—there is a charm in the old pink warehouses on the hot *fondamenta*—that he has something much better. He looks up and down at the gathered gondolas; he has his surprise after all, his little first Venetian thrill; and as the terrace of the station ushers in these things we shall say no harm of it, though it is not lovely. It is the beginning of his experience, but it is the end of the Grand Canal.

Bernard Berenson

Bernard Berenson, the critic and aesthetician famous for his study of Italian renaissance painters, was intimately associated with Florence—he made his home outside that city—but he actually began his career, as an attributor of Italian paintings, in Venice, in 1888, *shortly after his graduation from Harvard. Much later, at the age of eighty-six, he wrote, "The Venetian painters and sculptors and architects were my first love, but Venice itself,* Venise la ville, *not so much. Now it is the town that fascinates and rejoices me at every step and in all effects of light and, I may say, in almost all weather." After* 1947 *Berenson visited Venice every year. At eighty-nine, his diary entry reads: "I feel as if it had taken me all these years from* 1888 *until now to learn to appreciate Venice fully. I may not say that for I have no doubt that if I remain really alive I shall probably appreciate it more and more."*

Berenson lived a long and engaged life. His intelligence, scholarship, conversation, wit, and his service to museums and collectors put him at the center of the art world, and he attracted to his home visitors from throughout Europe and America. Berenson was the author of many works, among them Florentine Painters of the Renaissance, Central Italian Painters of the Renaissance, North Italian Painters of the Renaissance. The Venetian Painters of the Renaissance, *from which this excerpt is taken, was Berenson's very first published work, in* 1894.

THE VENETIAN PAINTERS

Among the Italian schools of painting the Venetian has, for the majority of art-loving people, the strongest and most enduring attraction. In the course of the present brief account of the life of that school we shall perhaps discover some of the causes of our peculiar delight and interest in the Venetian painters, as we come to realize what tendencies of the human spirit their art embodied, and of what great consequence their example has been to the whole of European painting for the last three centuries.

The Venetians as a school were from the first endowed with exquisite tact in their use of color. Seldom cold and rarely too warm, their coloring never seems an afterthought, as in many of the Florentine painters, nor is it always suggesting paint, as in some of the Veronese masters. When the eye has grown accustomed to make allowance for the darkening caused by time, for the dirt that lies in layers on so many pictures, and for unsuccessful attempts at restoration, the better Venetian paintings present such harmony of intention and execution as distinguishes the highest achievements of genuine poets. Their mastery over color is the first thing that attracts most people to the painters of Venice. Their coloring not only gives direct pleasure to the eye but acts like music upon the moods, stimulating thought and memory in much the same way as a work by a great composer. . . .

* * * *

When it once reached the point where its view of the world naturally sought expression in painting, as religious ideas had done before, the Renaissance found in Venice clearer utterance than elsewhere, and it is perhaps this fact which makes the most abiding interest of Venetian painting. . . .

The growing delight in life with the consequent love of health, beauty, and joy were felt more powerfully in Venice than anywhere else in Italy. The explanation of this may be found in the character of the Venetian government, which was such that it gave little room for the satisfaction of the passion for personal glory and kept its citizens so busy in duties of state that they had small leisure for learning. Some of the chief passions of the Renaissance thus finding no outlet in Venice, the other passions insisted all the more on being satisfied. Venice moreover, was the only state in Italy which was enjoying, and for many generations had been enjoying, internal peace. This gave the Venetians a love of comfort, of ease, and of splendor, a refinement of manner, and humaneness of feeling which made them the first modern people in Europe. Since there was little room for personal glory in Venice, the perpetuators of glory, the Humanists, found at first scant encouragement there, and the Venetians were saved from that absorption in archaeology and pure science which overwhelmed Florence at an early date. This was not necessarily an advantage in itself, but it happened to suit Venice, where the conditions of life had for some time been such as to build up a love of beautiful things.

As it was, the feeling for beauty was not hindered in its natural development. Archaeology would have tried to submit it to the good taste of the past, a proceeding which rarely promotes good taste in the present. Too much archaeology and too much science might have ended in making Venetian art academic, instead of letting it become what it did, the product of a natural ripening of interest in life and love of pleasure. In Florence, it is true, painting had developed almost simultaneously with the other arts, and it may be due to this cause that the Florentine painters never quite realized what a different task from the architect's and sculptor's was theirs. At the time, therefore, when the Renaissance was beginning to find its best expression in painting, the Florentines were already too much attached to classical ideals of form and composition, in other words, too academic, to give embodiment to the throbbing feeling for life and pleasure.

Thus it came to pass that in the Venetian pictures of the end of the fifteenth century we find neither the contrition nor the devotion of those earlier years when the Church alone employed painting as the interpreter of emotion, nor the learning which characterized the Florentines. The Venetian masters of this time, although nominally continuing to paint the Madonna and saints, were in reality painting handsome, healthy, sane people like themselves, people who wore their splendid robes with dignity, who found life worth the mere living and sought no metaphysical basis for it. In short, the Venetian pictures of the last decade of the century seemed intended not for devotion, as they had been, nor for admiration, as they then were in Florence, but for enjoyment.

The Church itself, as has been said, had educated its children to understand painting as a language. Now that the passions men dared to avow were no longer connected with happiness in some future state only, but mainly with life in the present, painting was expected to give voice to these more human aspirations and to desert the outgrown ideals of the Church. In Florence, the painters seemed unable or unwilling to make their art really popular. Nor was it so necessary there, for Poliziano, Pulci, and Lorenzo dei Medici supplied the need of self-expression by addressing the Florentines in the language which their early enthusiasm for antiquity and their natural gifts had made them understand better than any other—the language of poetry. In Venice alone painting remained what it had been all over Italy in earlier times, the common tongue of the whole mass of the people. Venetian artists thus had the strongest inducements to perfect the processes which painters must employ to make pictures look real to their own generation; and their generation had an altogether firmer hold on reality than any that had been known since the triumph of Christianity. Here again the comparison of the Renaissance to youth must be borne in mind. The grasp that youth has on reality is not to be compared to that brought by age, and we must not expect to find in the Renaissance a passion for an acquaintance with things as they are such as we ourselves have; but still its grasp of facts was far firmer than that of the Middle Ages.

Painting, in accommodating itself to the new ideas, found that it could not attain to satisfactory representation merely by form and color, but that it required light and shadow and effects of space. Indeed, venial faults of drawing are perhaps the least disturbing, while faults of persepective, of spacing, and of color completely spoil a picture for people who have an everyday acquaintance with painting such as the Venetians had. We find the Venetian painters, therefore, more and more intent upon giving the space they paint its real depth, upon giving solid objects the full effect of the round, upon keeping the different parts of a figure within the same plane, and upon compelling things to hold their proper places one behind the other. As early as the beginning of the sixteenth century a few of the greater Venetian painters had succeeded in making distant objects less and less distinct, as well as smaller and smaller, and had succeeded also in giving some appearance of reality to the atmosphere. These are a few of the special problems of painting, as distinct from sculpture for instance, and they are problems which, among the Italians, only the Venetians and the painters closely connected with them solved with any success.

* * * *

The painters of the end of the fifteenth century who met with the greatest success in solving these problems were Giovanni and Gentile Bellini, Cima da Conegliano, and Carpaccio, and we find each of them enjoyable to the degree that he was in touch with the life of his day. . . . Venice knew the love of glory, and the passion was perhaps only the more intense because it was all dedicated to the State. There was nothing the Venetians would not do to add to its greatness, glory, and splendor. It was this which led them to make of the city itself that wondrous monument to the love and awe they felt for their republic, which still rouses more admiration and gives more pleasure than any other one achievement of the art impulse in man. They were not content to make their city the most beautiful in the world; they performed ceremonies in its honor partaking of all the solemnity of religious rites. Processions and pageants by land and by sea, free from the gross element of improvisation which charac- terized them elsewhere in Italy, formed no less a part of the functions of the Venetian State than the high mass in the Catholic church. Such a function, with doge and senators arrayed in gorgeous costumes no less prescribed than the raiments of ecclesiastics, in the midst of the fairy-like architecture of the Piazza or canals, was the event most eagerly looked forward to, and the one that gave most satisfaction to the Venetian's love of his State, and to his love of splendor, beauty, and gaiety. He would have had them every day if it were possible, and, to make up for their rarity, he loved to have representations of them. So most Venetian pictures of the beginning of the sixteenth century tended to take the form of magnificent processions, if they did not actually represent them. They are processions in the Piazza, as in Gentile Bellini's "Corpus Christi" picture, or on the water, as in Carpaccio's picture where St. Ursula leaves her home; or they represent what was a gorgeous but common sight in Venice, the reception or dismissal of ambassadors, as in several pictures of Carpaccio's St. Ursula series; or they show simply a collection of splendidly costumed people in the Piazza, as in Gentile's "Preaching of St. Mark." Not only the pleasure-loving Carpaccio, but the austere Cima, as he grew older, turned every biblical and saintly legend into an occasion for the picture of a pageant.*

But there was a further reason for the popularity of such pictures. The decorations which were then being executed by the most reputed masters in the Hall of Great Council in the Doge's Palace, were, by the nature of the subject, required to represent pageants. The Venetian State encouraged painting as did the Church, in order to teach its subjects it own glory in a way that they could understand without being led on to critical inquiry. Venice was not the only city, it is true, that used painting for political purposes; but the frescoes of Lorenzetti at Siena were admonitions to govern in accordance with the catechism, while the pictures in the Great Hall of the Doge's Palace were of a nature to remind the Venetians of their glory and also of their state policy. These mural paintings represented such subjects as the Doge bringing about a reconciliation between the Pope and the Emperor Barbarossa, an event which marked the first entry of Venice into the field of Continental politics, and typified as well its unchanging policy, which was to gain its own ends by keeping a balance of power between the allies of the Pope and the allies of his opponents. The first edition, so to speak, of these works had been executed at the end of the fourteenth century and in the beginning of the fifteenth. Towards the end of that century it no longer satisfied the new

---

* The paintings by Gentile Bellini and Carpaccio's St. Ursula series may be viewed in the Accademia; the city's gallery of great Venetian painting. —Ed.

feeling for reality and beauty, and thus had ceased to serve its purpose, which was to glorify the State. The Bellini, Alvise Vivarini, and Carpaccio were employed to make a second rendering of the very same subjects, and this gave the Venetians ample opportunity for finding out how much they liked pageant pictures. . . .

*   *   *   *

The councillors were not allowed to be the only people to enjoy fascinating pictures of gorgeous pageants and ceremonials. The Mutual Aid Societies—the *Scuole* as they were called—were not long in getting the masters who were employed in the Doge's Palace to execute for their own meeting places pictures equally splendid. The Schools of San Giorgio, St. Ursula, and Santo Stefano, employed Carpaccio, the Schools of San Giovanni and San Marco, Gentile Bellini, and other Schools employed minor painters. The works carried out for these Schools are of peculiar importance, both because they are all that remain to throw light upon the pictures in the Doge's Palace destroyed in the fire of 1576, and because they form a transition to the art of a later day. Just as the State chose subjects that glorified itself and taught its own history and policy, so the Schools had pictures painted to glorify their patron saints, and to keep their deeds and example fresh. Many of these pictures—most in fact— took the form of pageants; but even in such, intended as they were for almost domestic purposes, the style of high ceremonial was relaxed, and elements taken directly from life were introduced. In his "Corpus Christi," Gentile Bellini paints not only the solemn and dazzling procession in the Piazza, but the elegant young men who strut about in all their finery, the foreign loungers, and even the unfailing beggar by the portal of St. Mark's. In his "Miracle of the True Cross," he introduces gondoliers, taking care to bring out all the beauty of their lithe, comely figures as they stand to ply the oar, and does not reject even such an episode as a servingmaid standing in a doorway watching a Negro who is about to plunge into the canal. He treats this bit of the picture with all the charm and much of that delicate feeling for simple effects of light and color that we find in such Dutch painters as Vermeer van Delft and Peter de Hoogh. Episodes such as this in the works of the earliest great Venetian master must have acted on the public like a spark on tinder. They certainly found a sudden and assured popularity, for they play a more and more important part in the pictures executed for the Schools, many of the subjects of which were readily turned into studies of ordinary Venetian life. This was particularly true of the works of Carpaccio. Much as he loved pageants, he loved homelier scenes as well. His "Dream of St. Ursula" shows us a young girl asleep in a room filled with the quiet morning light. Indeed, it may be better described as the picture of a room with the light playing softly upon its walls, upon the flowerpots in the window, and upon the writing table and the cupboards. A young girl happens to be asleep in the bed, but the picture is far from being a merely economic illustration to this episode in the life of the saint. Again, let us take the work in the same series where King Maure dismisses the ambassadors. Carpaccio has made this a scene of a chancellery in which the most striking features are neither the king nor the ambassadors, but the effect of the light that streams through a side door on the left and a poor clerk laboring at his task. Or, again, take St. Jerome in his study, in the *Scuola* San Giorgio. He is nothing but a Venetian scholar seated in his comfortable, bright library, in the midst of his books, with his little shelf of bric-a-brac running along the wall. There is nothing in his look or surroundings to speak of a life of self-denial or of arduous devotion to the problems of sin and redemption. Even the "Presentation of the Virgin," which offered such a splendid chance for a pageant, Carpaccio, in one instance, turned into the picture of a simple girl going to her first communion. In other words, Carpaccio's quality is the quality of a painter of genre, of which he was the earliest Italian master. His genre differs from Dutch or French not in kind but in degree. Dutch genre is much more democratic, and, as painting, it is of a far finer quality, but it deals with its subject, as Carpaccio does, for the sake of its own pictorial capacities and for the sake of the effects of color and of light and shade.

* * * *

. . . Giorgione . . . combined the refined feeling and poetry of Bellini with Carpaccio's gaiety and love of beauty and color. Stirred with the enthusiasms of his own generation as people who had lived through other phases of feeling could not be, Giorgione painted pictures so perfectly in touch with the ripened spirit of the Renaissance that they met with success which those things only find that at the same moment wake us to the full sense of a need and satisfy it. Giorgione's life was short, and very few of his works—not a score in all—have escaped destruction. But these suffice to give us a glimpse into that brief moment when the Renaissance found its most genuine expression in painting. Its over-boisterous passions had quieted down into a sincere appreciation of beauty and of human relations. It would be really hard to say more about Giorgione than this, that his pictures are the perfect reflex of the Renaissance at its height.

His works, as well as those of his contemporaries and followers, still continue to be appreciated most by people whose attitude of mind and spirit has most in common with the Renaissance, or by those who look upon Italian art not merely as art but as the product of this period. For that is its greatest interest. Other schools have accomplished much more in mere painting than the Italian. A serious student of art will scarcely think of putting many of even the highest achievements of the Italians, considered purely as technique, beside the work of the great Dutchmen, the great Spaniard, or even the masters of today. Our real interest in Italian painting is at bottom an interest in that art which we almost instinctively feel to have been the fittest expression found by a period in the history of modern Europe which has much in common with youth. The Renaissance has the fascination of those years when we seemed so full of promise both to ourselves and to everybody else.

* * * *

Titian, in spite of a sturdier, less refined nature, did nothing for a generation after Giorgione's death but work on his lines. A difference in quality between the two masters shows itself from the first, but the spirit that animated each is identical. The pictures Titian was painting ten years after his companion's death have not only many of the qualities of Giorgione's, but something more, as if done by an older Giorgione, with better possession of himself, and with a larger and firmer hold on the world. At the same time, they show no diminution of spontaneous joy in life, and even an increased sense of its value and dignity. What an array of masterpieces might be brought to witness! In the "Assumption,"* for example, the Virgin soars heavenward, not helpless in the arms of angels, but borne up by the fullness of life within her, and by the feeling that the universe is naturally her own, and that nothing can check her course. The angels seem to be there only to sing the victory of a human being over his environment. They are embodied joys, acting on our nerves like the rapturous outburst of the orchestra at the end of "Parsifal." Or look at the "Bacchanals" in Madrid, or at the "Bacchus and Ariadne" in the National Gallery. How brim-full they are of exuberant joy! You see no sign of a struggle of inner and outer conditions, but life so free, so strong, so glowing, that it almost intoxicates. They are truly Dionysiac, Bacchanalian triumphs—the triumph of life over the ghosts that love the gloom and chill and hate the sun.

---

* The "Assumption" is on the high altar of the Frari Church.—Ed.

The Portraits Titian painted in these years show no less feeling of freedom from sordid cares, and no less mastery over life. Think of "The Man with the Glove" in the Louvre, of the "Concert" and "Young Englishman" in Florence, and of the Pesaro family in their altarpiece in the Frari at Venice—call up these portraits, and you will see that they are the true children of the Renaissance whom life has taught no meannesses and no fears. . . .

* * * *

It is as impossible to keep untouched by what happens to your neighbors as to have a bright sky over your own house when it is stormy everywhere else. Spain did not directly dominate Venice, but the new fashions of life and thought inaugurated by her nearly universal triumph could not be kept out. Her victims, among whom the Italian scholars must be reckoned, flocked to Venice for shelter, persecuted by a rule that cherished the Inquisition. Now for the first time Venetian painters were brought in contact with men of letters. As they were already, fortunately for themselves, too well acquainted with the business of their own art to be taken in tow by learning or even by poetry, the relation of the man of letters to the painter became on the whole a stimulating and at any rate a profitable one, as in the instance of two of the greatest, where it took the form of a partnership for mutual advantage. It is not to our purpose to speak of Aretino's gain, but Titian would scarcely have acquired such fame in his lifetime if that founder of modern journalism, Pietro Aretino, had not been at his side, eager to trumpet his praises and to advise him whom to court.

The overwhelming triumph of Spain entailed still another consequence. It brought home to all Italians, even to the Venetians, the sense of the individual's helplessness before organized power—a sense which, as we have seen, the early Renaissance, with its belief in the omnipotence of the individual, totally lacked. This was not without a decided influence on art. In the last three decades of his long career, Titian did not paint man as if he were as free from care and as fitted to his environment as a lark on an April morning. Rather did he represent man as acting on his environment and suffering from its reactions. He made the faces and figures show clearly what life had done to them. The great "Ecce Homo" and the "Crowning with Thorns" are imbued with this feeling no less than the equestrian portrait of Charles the Fifth. In the "Ecce Homo" we see a man with a godlike personality, humbled by the imperial majesty, broken by the imperial power, and utterly unable to hold out against them. In the "Crowning with Thorns" we have the same godlike being almost

brutalized by pain and suffering. In the portrait of the emperor we behold
a man whom life has enfeebled, one who has to meet a foe who may crush
him.

Yet Titian became neither soured nor a pessimist. Many of his late
portraits are even more energetic than those of his early maturity. He
shows himself a wise man of the world. "Do not be a grovelling
sycophant," some of them seem to say, "but remember that courtly
manners and tempered elegance can do you no harm." Titian, then, was
ever ready to change with the times, and on the whole the change was
towards a firmer grasp of reality, necessitating yet another advance in the
painter's mastery of his craft. Titian's real greatness consists in the fact
that he was as able to produce an impression of greater reality as he was
ready to appreciate the need of a firmer hold on life. In painting, as has
been said, a greater effect of reality is chiefly a matter of light and shadow,
to be obtained only by considering the canvas as an enclosed space, filled
with light and air, through which the objects are seen. There is more than
one way of getting this effect, but Titian attains it by the almost total
suppression of outlines, by the harmonizing of his colors, and by the
largeness and vigor of his brushwork. In fact, the old Titian was, in his
way of painting, remarkably like some of the best French masters of the
end of the nineteenth century. This makes him only the more attractive,
particularly when with handling of this kind he combined the power of
creating forms of beauty such as he has given us in the "Wisdom" of the
Venetian Ducal Palace, or in the "Shepherd and Nymph" of Vienna. The
difference between the old Titian, author of these works, and the young
Titian, painter of the "Assumption," and of the "Bacchus and Ariadne,"
is the difference between the Shakespeare of the *Midsummer Night's
Dream* and the Shakespeare of the *Tempest*. Titian and Shakespeare begin
and end so much in the same way by no mere accident. They were both
products of the Renaissance, they underwent similar changes, and each
was the highest and completest expression of his own age. This is not the
place to elaborate the comparison, but I have dwelt so long on Titian,
because, historically considered, he is the only painter who expressed
nearly all of the Renaissance that could find expression in painting. It is
this which makes him even more interesting than Tintoretto, an artist who
in many ways was deeper, finer, and even more brilliant.

* * * *

Tintoretto grew to manhood when the fruit of the Renaissance was ripe on
every bough. The Renaissance had resulted in the emancipation of the
individual, in making him feel that the universe had no other purpose than

his happiness. This brought an entirely new answer to the question. "Why should I do this or that?" It used to be, "Because self-instituted authority commands you." The answer now was, "Because it is good for men." . . . When ideas are fresh and strong, they are almost sure to find artistic embodiment, as indeed this whole epoch found in painting, and this particular period in the works of Tintoretto.

* * * *

Tintoretto stayed at home, but he felt in his own person a craving for something that Titian could not teach him. The Venice he was born in was not the Venice of Titian's early youth, and his own adolescence fell in the period when Spain was rapidly making herself mistress of Italy. The haunting sense of powers almost irresistible gave a terrible fascination to Michelangelo's works, which are swayed by that sense as by a demonic presence. Tintoretto felt this fascination because he was in sympathy with the spirit which took form in colossal torsos and limbs. To him these were not, as they were to Michelangelo's enrolled followers, merely new patterns after which to model the nude.

But beside this sense of overwhelming power and gigantic force, Tintoretto had to an even greater degree the feeling that whatever existed was for mankind and with reference to man. In his youth people were once more turning to religion, and in Venice poetry was making its way more than it had previously done, not only because Venice had become the refuge of men of letters, but also because of the diffusion of printed books. Tintoretto took to the new feeling for religion and poetry as to his birthright. Yet whether classic fable or Biblical episode were the subject of his art, Tintoretto colored it with his feeling for the human life at the heart of the story. His sense of power did not express itself in colossal nudes so much as in the immense energy, in the glowing health of the figures he painted, and more still in his effects of light, which he rendered as if he had it in his hands to brighten or darken the heavens at will and subdue them to his own moods.

He could not have accomplished this, we may be sure, if he had not had even greater skill than Titian in the treatment of light and shadow and of atmosphere. It was this which enabled him to give such living versions of Biblical stories and saintly legends. For, granting that an effect of reality were attainable in painting without an adequate treatment of light and atmosphere, even then the reality would look hideous, as it does in many modern painters who attempt to paint people of today in their everyday dress and among their usual surroundings. It is not realism which makes such pictures hideous, but the want of that toning down which the atmosphere gives to things in life, and of that harmonizing to which the light subjects all colors.

It was a great mastery of light and shadow which enabled Tintoretto to put into his pictures all the poetry there was in his soul without once tempting us to think that he might have found better expression in words. The poetry which quickens most of his works in the *Scuola di San Rocco* is almost entirely a matter of light and color. What is it but the light that changes the solitudes in which the Magdalen and St. Mary of Egypt are sitting into dreamlands seen by poets in their moments of happiest inspiration? What but light and color, the gloom and chill of evening, with the white-stoled figure standing resignedly before the judge, that give the "Christ before Pilate" its sublime magic? What, again, but light, color, and the star-procession of cherubs that imbue the realism of the "Annunciation" with music which thrills us through and through? . . .

Christ and the Apostles, the Patriarchs and Prophets, were the embodiment of living principles and of living ideals. Tintoretto felt this so vividly that he could not think of them otherwise than as people of his own kind, living under conditions easily intelligible to himself and to his fellow men. Indeed, the more intelligible and the more familiar the look and garb and surroundings of Biblical and saintly personages, the more would they drive home the principles and ideas they incarnated. So Tintoretto did not hesitate to turn every Biblical episode into a picture of what the scene would look like had it taken place under his own eyes, nor to tinge it with his own mood.

His conception of the human form was, it is true, colossal, although the slender elegance that was then coming into fashion, as if in protest against physical force and organization, influenced him considerably in his construction of the female figure; but the effect which he must always have produced upon his contemporaries, which most of his works still produce, is one of astounding reality as well as of wide sweep and power. Thus, in the "Discovery of the Body of St. Mark," in the Brera and in the "Storm Rising while the Corpse is being Carried through the Streets of Alexandria," in the Palace at Venice, the figures, although colossal, are so energetic and so easy in movement, and the effects of perspective and of light and atmosphere are so on a level with the gigantic figures, that the eye at once adapts itself to the scale, and you feel as if you too partook of the strength and health of heroes. . . .

* * * *

Paolo Veronese was the product of four or five generations of Veronese painters, the first two or three of which had spoken the language of the whole mass of the people in a way that few other artists had ever done. Consequently, in the early Renaissance, there were no painters in the North of Italy, and few even in Florence, who were not touched by the influence of the Veronese. But Paolo's own immediate predecessors were no longer able to speak the language of the whole mass of the people. There was one class they left out entirely, the class to whom Titian and Tintoretto appealed so strongly, the class that ruled, and that thought in the new way. Verona, being a dependency of Venice, did no ruling and certainly not at all so much thinking as Venice, and life there continued healthful, simple, unconscious, untroubled by the approaching storm in the world's feelings. But although thought and feeling may be slow in invading a town, fashion comes there quickly, Spanish fashions in dress and Spanish ceremonial in manners, reached Verona soon enough, and in Paolo Caliari we find all these fashions reflected, but health, simplicity and unconsciousness as well. This combination of seemingly opposite qualities forms his great charm for us today, and it must have proved as great an attraction to many of the Venetians of his own time, for they were already far enough removed from simplicity to appreciate to the full his singularly happy combination of ceremony and splendor with an almost childlike naturalness of feeling. Perhaps among his strongest admirers were the very men who most appreciated Titian's distinction and Tintoretto's poetry. But it is curious to note that Paolo's chief employers were the monasteries. His cheerfulness, and his frank and joyous worldliness, the qualities, in short, which we find in his huge pictures of feasts, seem to have been particularly welcome to those who were expected to make their meat and drink of the very opposite qualities. This is no small comment on the times, and shows how thorough had been the permeation of the spirit of the Renaissance when even the religious orders gave up their pretence to asceticism and piety.

* * * *

The building which occupies the center of the picture Venice leaves in the mind, the Salute, was not built until the seventeenth century. This was the picture that the Venetian himself loved to have painted for him, and that the stranger wanted to carry away. Canaletto painted Venice with a feeling for space and atmosphere, with a mastery over the delicate effects of mist peculiar to the city, that make his views of the Salute, the Grand Canal, and the Piazzetta still seem more like Venice than all the pictures of them that have been painted since. Later in the century Canaletto was followed by Guardi, who executed smaller views with more of an eye for the picturesque, and for what may be called instantaneous effects, thus anticipating both the Romantic and the Impressionist painters of our own century.

* * * *

Yet delightful as Longhi, Canaletto, and Guardi are, and imbued with the spirit of their own century, they lack the quality of force, without which there can be no impressive style. This quality their contemporary Tiepolo possessed to the utmost. His energy, his feeling for splendor, his mastery over his craft, place him almost on a level with the great Venetians of the sixteenth century, although he never allows one to forget what he owes to them, particularly to Veronese.* The grand scenes he paints differ from those of his predecessor not so much in inferiority of workmanship, as in a lack of that simplicity and candor which never failed Paolo, no matter how proud the event he might be portraying. Tiepolo's people are haughty, as if they felt that to keep a firm hold on their dignity they could not for a moment relax their faces and figures from a monumental look and bearing. They evidently feel themselves so superior that they are not pleasant to live with, although they carry themselves so well, and are dressed with such splendor, that once in a while it is a great pleasure to look at them. It was Tiepolo's vision of the world that was at fault, and his vision of the world was at fault only because the world itself was at fault. Paolo saw a world barely touched by the fashions of the Spanish court, while Tiepolo lived among people whose very hearts had been vitiated by its measureless haughtiness.

But Tiepolo's feeling for strength, for movement, and for color was great enough to give a new impulse to art. At times he seems not so much the last of the old masters as the first of the new. The works he left in Spain do more than a little to explain the revival of painting in that country under Goya; and Goya, in his turn, had a great influence upon many of the best French artists of our own times.

---

* An extraordinary series of paintings and frescoes by Veronese has been restored and can be seen in the San Sebastiano Church, which also has works from his earlier and later periods. The Church is a veritable Veronese museum.—Ed.

Charles Eliot Norton

◄ 1827–1908 ►

Charles Eliot Norton, a pre-eminent American scholar of his era, was a professor of the history of art at Harvard, an editor of the North American Review, *and a founder of the* Nation. *He corresponded with John Ruskin and edited a two-volume editon of their letters. Among Norton's notable works are a prose translation of Dante and* Historical Studies of Church-Building in the Middle Ages *(1880), in which he offered three noble examples: the cathedrals of Venice, Siena, and Florence. These illustrated his favorite thesis—which he shared with Ruskin—that "into a supreme masterpiece of architecture the physical and moral character of a whole race is built, and therefore finds therein its fullest expression."*

ST. MARK'S CATHEDRAL

The design of St. Mark's, both in its general plan and in its details, was not copied from any existing edifice. It gave evidence, in its conception, of a quality characteristic of Venetian art at all times and in all departments—the quality of independent and original treatment of elements derived from foreign sources. This is a distinguishing trait of the artistic races of the world, and this it is which gives Venice a higher rank in the history of the arts than that which any other medieval Italian city can claim. Florence, indeed, at times presses her hard; but even the Florentine artists were less inspired by the spirit which remodels traditional types of beauty into new forms, adapted to give expression to the special genius of a people of definite originality, than the great masters of Venetian architecture and painting. Whatever Venice touched she stamped with her own impress. She studied under Byzantine teachers, but was not content merely to copy their works. She partook of the inheritance of Roman tradition, but improved upon and modified its rules. She felt the strong influence of the Gothic spirit—no other Italian city felt it so strongly, but, instead of yielding her own originality to the powerful compulsion of the Northern style, she accepted its principles, not as ultimate canons of a fixed system, but as vital and plastic elements for her own invention to work with; and created a fresh and beautiful Gothic style of her own.

The architect of St. Mark's is unknown, but that he was a Venetian is evident from the exhibition of this prime trait of Venetian genius in his work. Constantino le and Rome furnished him with separate elements of his design, which he fused into a composition neither Byzantine nor Romanesque, unexampled hitherto, only to be called Venetian. Adopting the Greek cross for his ground plan, he placed over the point of intersection of its arms a central dome, forty-two feet in diameter, connected by pendentives with four great arches that sprang from four piers of vast dimensions. Over each arm of the cross rose a similar but somewhat smaller cupola; each cupola, including the central one, having a range of small windows at its base, which seemed to lighten the pressure upon its supports. Through the piers ran archways in both directions, so as to open a narrow aisle on each side of the nave and transept. The level of the eastern arm of the cross was raised above that of the body of the church to give space to a crypt beneath it, where, below the high altar, the relics of St. Mark were laid in their secret repose. A semicircular apse terminated the eastern end of the church, stretching out beyond the aisles, which were closed externally by a flat wall, but shaped within into small, also semicircular, apses. The material of the structure was brick, but the whole surface of the walls, within and without, was to be covered with precious incrustations of mosaic or of marble.

The form of the cross, the domes, the incrusted decoration, were all borrowed from the East, and all had their prototypes in Byzantine buildings. But the crypt and the apses and many of the details were of Romanesque character; and the diverse elements of the two styles mingled here in harmonious combination.

How far the adorning of the church with mosaic and marble had advanced at the time of its dedication in 1094 cannot be told; but the work was not of a nature to be speedily accomplished, and the twelfth century may have been drawing to its close before the completion of the elaborate and splendid covering of the walls. The consistent and steady carrying-out of a system of decoration so costly and so magnificent is a proof of the interest of the Venetians in the work and of the reality of that piety which was one of the constant boasts of the republic.

The church was properly the Chapel of the Doges,* and, as such, under

---

* St. Mark's became the Cathedral Church of Venice in 1807.

their immediate charge; but though successive doges devoted large sums to its construction and adornment, the chief cost was doubtless defrayed by the offerings of the citizens, to whom, year by year, it became more and more an object of pride, and who saw in it the image of the faith and the power of the State itself. It became by degrees the center of Venetian life, the glory of Venice. And thus while the mosaics of its vaults and domes display the religious conceptions of the age and the sentiment and skill of a long succession of nameless artists, in like manner the slabs of marble and alabaster that cover pier and wall, the multitudinous carvings, and the priceless columns of marble exhibit no less plainly the persistent zeal of seagoing trades and men-at-arms in contributing for the adornment of their church the gains of their commerce or the spoils of their conquests. From far and near—from the ruins of Aquileia and from the desolate palace of Spalato, from the temples of ancient cities along the coast of Italy and Asia Minor, from Athens and Constantinople, from the islands of the Ægean, from Sicily and Africa—were brought shafts and capitals, fragments of sculpture, blocks of colored stone, to be offered for the work of the church. It is a most striking indication of the prevalence of a genuine artistic spirit at Venice, not only that these objects should have been so widely sought, but that the successive master builders should have had the genius to make such use of this medley of materials, supplied to them irregularly and without order, as to produce not a mere variegated patchwork of carved and colored ornament, but a skillful, harmonious composition, in which each detail seems to be calculated in relation to the general effect with hardly less intention and appropriateness than if all had been so designed from the beginning. Their success, however, lay in the fact that they worked upon a principle wholly diverse from those which controlled the builders of Gothic structures—a principle which subordinated the effects of pure line and constructive form to those of color. The church was designed to afford broad, unbroken masses of wall for colored surface decoration, and the elaborate multiplicities of form peculiar to Gothic architecture were altogether unattempted.

There have been no such colorists in architecture as the Venetians. It was as special a gift to them as the perfect sense of form was to the Athenians. Gifts such as these, limited to single races, to defined epochs, are not to be accounted for by any enumeration of external conditions. Their sources lie concealed in undiscoverable regions. But their influence is to be traced in all the most characteristic expressions of the race, and may be perceived often in remote and varied fields of thought and of action. They appear not merely in art and manners and language, but their subtle influence penetrates into those relations of private or public conduct in which the imagination claims an interest. Of all the legacies of Athens to the world, none, perhaps, is more precious than the teaching of the intellectual value of form and proportion; of the many heirlooms that Venice has bequeathed, one of the best is the doctrine of the refined and noble use of color.

Though the original plan of the main building seems to have been that of the simple Greek cross, yet, not long after its walls were erected, an addition to it was begun, by which the western arm was to be enclosed within an *atrium*, or vestibule, upon its northern side and western end, and on its southern side with a chapel dedicated to St. John the Baptist and an apartment for the sacred treasury of the church. This addition, in the course of the twelfth century, gave to the building that magnificent facade which is the most striking and original characteristic of its exterior. Upon the adornment of this facade the resources of Venetian wealth and art were lavished. It was enriched not only with precious marbles, but with carvings and mosaics, till it was made the most splendid composition of colored architecture that Europe has beheld. No building so costly or so sumptuous had been erected since the fall of the Empire; and none more impressive, in proportion to its size, none more picturesque, has been built in later times. And yet it is this unique facade, to which the hand of time has given the last touch of beauty, in the hue which only years can bestow, that, at this moment, as these pages are going through the press, is threatened with destruction, under the name of restoration. Italy plays the part in these days of the serving maid of Aladdin, and over and over again is cheated into giving up her old magical treasure by the allurement of bright new brass. Florence, Perugia, Siena, Rome—all have suffered irreparably in loss of beauty and in historic dignity through the wanton work of that modern spirit of vulgarity which has neither reverence for the past nor regard for the future. But there has been nothing worse than this proposal to ruin "those golden walls that East and West once joined to build." The protest against this special desecration now making itself heard in Europe may be effectual to prevent it, but there is need of constant vigilance and effort to protect the most venerable monuments from the rude hand of the professional despoiler.

The church was not merely picturesque, but pictorial. The system of mosaic decoration with which arches, vaults, and domes were covered was intended not merely for ornament, but as a series of pictures for religious instruction. The scriptures were here displayed in imperishable painting before the eyes of those who could not read the written word. The church became thus not only a sanctuary wherein to pray, to confess, to be absolved, but also a schoolhouse for the teaching of the faithful. It was like "a vast illuminated missal," its pages filled with sacred designs painted on gold. . . .

The scheme of its pictorial decoration includes the story of the race of man, his fall and redemption; the life and passion of the Saviour, and the works of his apostles and saints.

The ceiling of the *atrium*, or forecourt, of the temple was naturally, according to the order of thought of its designers, occupied with subjects from the Old Dispensation; and there appears to have been an obvious and impressive intention, as has been pointed out by Mr. Ruskin, in the conclusion of the series with the miracle of the fall of manna. It was to direct the thoughts of the disciple to the saying "Your fathers did eat manna and are dead," and to bring to his remembrance that living bread whereof "if any man eat, he shall live forever." Entering the central door of the church, he would see before him, dim in the distance of the eastern end, the mighty figure of the Saviour throned in glory. . . .

Then, turning and looking upward to the wall above the door by which he had entered, the worshipper would behold the same figure, with the Virgin on one side and St. Mark on the other, Christ himself holding open upon his knee the Book of Life, on the pages of which is written "I am the door; by me if any man enter in, he shall be saved;" and above, on the molding of red marble around the mosaic, were the words "I am the gate of life; enter through me ye who are mine." . . .

At the beginning of the twelfth century St. Mark's was essentially complete. But such a building was not erected by contract, with the stipulation that it should be finished at a certain date. It was not, indeed, regarded as a work that admitted to definite conclusion, but rather as one to be continually in hand, to be made more excellent from generation to generation, the constant care of the State and of the people, an object of unceasing interest and of endless increase in beauty and adornment. There was never a time when some one of the arts was not adding to its embellishment.

Of much that was done no record remains; but the history of the building can in part be traced from its own walls, in part from written records. During the twelfth century the Campanile was carried up above all the other towers of Venice, and from that time has been the most conspicuous signal of the city by sea or by land. It stands, after the common Italian fashion, detached from the church, with whose low domes and enriched arcades its own simple and stern vertical lines are a vigorous and picturesque contrast.* For at least two centuries (1125–

---

* The original Campanile was begun in 912. The wooden summit was shattered by

1350) the structures annexed to the main body of the church, and forming a part of it as seen from without, including the baptistery, the treasury, and the fore-court, or vestibule, were slowly advancing towards completion and receiving their rich casing of marble and mosaic. All this work corresponded in general style with that of the church, and was in harmony with its general design. But meanwhile a great change was going on in the taste of the Venetians. The influences of the East were losing ground before those of the West, and the Byzantine elements in Venetian architecture were giving place to those of Gothic art. It was about the end of the fourteenth century, or perhaps in the early years of the fifteenth, that the incongruous but picturesque and fanciful crowd of pinnacles and tabernacles, of crockets, finials, and canopies with pointed arches, which is in such striking opposition to the older and simpler forms of the building, was set up on the church. These architectural decorations enhance the impression of variety and wealth of adornment, they give a strange and complex character to the facade, but they serve no constructive purpose: they are mere external decoration; and though their effect is brilliant and surprising, it is not in keeping with the scheme of the earlier builders. Intended but to increase the richness of the front, they have, indeed, a real significance as marking a change in the moral temper of Venice and a loss of fineness in her perceptions of fitness and of beauty. She was growing luxurious, sensual, and prodigal. A century earlier she had known how to use the forms of Gothic architecture with dignity, and with imagination all the more powerful for being held firmly in restraint. But this ornamentation of St. Mark's indicated by its wantonness the beginning of a new epoch of Venetian art, in which architecture, sculpture, and painting, after having long united their powers to express the sentiment and faith of a high-spirited community, were to become the ministers to its ostentation and the servants of the luxury and display of private citizens.

The moral history of Venice for five hundred years is indelibly recorded on the walls on the church, the decoration of which had been the chief task of her arts; the arts are incorruptible witnesses, and form and color are undeniable indications of spiritual conditions. The testimony of mosaics and marbles concerning the character and aims of the Venetians corresponds with and is confirmed by the less instinctive evidence of the

lightning in 1489 and restored in stone by the architect Bartolomeo Bon. On July 14, 1902, the structure calmly subsided into a pile of rubble. It was rebuilt, almost exactly, and completed April 25, 1912, one thousand years after the original Campanile's foundation was begun—*Ed*.

inscriptions set in the walls or engraved on the monuments of the dead buried within the church.

St. Mark's, the Chapel of the Doges, was used, not for strictly religious services and ceremonies alone, but served as the gathering place of the people when great affairs were to be determined, and the doge saw fit to summon the citizens to hear and to decide by their vote what course should be followed. There was no other place so fitting for public transactions of importance, for which the blessing and guidance of Heaven were to be sought by the powerful intercession of the saint. Here, too, each doge, upon his election by the council, was presented before an assemblage of the people, called together by the ringing of the bells, that the choice might be confirmed by the voices of the common citizens. "We have chosen this man doge, if so it please you," were the words with which their consent was asked, and it was seldom that the people had reason not to be pleased with the choice. . . .

* * * *

The story of St. Mark's is an epitome of the story of Venice. So long as Venice lived, St. Mark's was the symbol and expression of her life. Among the noble works of men, few more beautiful, few more venerable, adorn the face of the world. It is the chief monument of one of the communities which in its time did most to elevate and refine mankind. For a long period the Venetians served as the advance guard of modern civilization, and their history can never cease to be of interest to the student of political institutions and of the highest forms of human society.

BERNARD BERENSON ON ST. MARK'S:*

Art histories and serious guide books call St. Mark's in Venice over-whelmingly Byzantine. I am not sure to what extent the cultivated public has taken in and made its own the significance of San Marco. Not only is it entirely Byzantine, despite later ornamental accretions, but it is the most typical, the most complete and the most satisfactory Byzantine edifice now in existence. . . .

In calling San Marco the most complete Byzantine edifice I do not except St. Sophia, which makes scarcely any aesthetic appeal on the outside. Inside St. Sophia is no doubt more breathtaking as space, but less

---

*   From the diary entry for June 25–28, 1954, published in *The Passionate Sightseer*.

harmonious, and in its present God-abandoned state it has become a dreary, cold museum. . . .

San Marco is excitingly rich outside as inside. The bare, naked structure is scarcely visible from Piazza or Piazzetta. One must look for it from within the courtyard of the Doge's Palace, or round the back from the Canal and through the free passage to the sacristy. Wherever you descry the design and the brick masonry, you perceive an unadulterated Byzantine structure. Within, the raw bones of the structure lie hidden under every kind of Byzantine panelling of varied marbles, within columns of porphyry and other rare stones, some with capitals as of plaited straw, others as of daintily patterned bronze, still others like tops of windswept pine trees, all brought from the Byzantine world if not from Constantinople itself. . . .

The facade and sides, particularly the northern one, are covered over with early and late Byzantine reliefs representing subjects and features, sacred and profane. Even the rare Byzantine-Sassanian motive of Alexander the Great's ascent into heaven is among them. They form a compendious collection of Byzantine sculpture. On the southwest corner of the balcony there is a fine museum piece in the shape of a prophyry head of a Byzantine emperor who, during a rebellion, had his nose cut off. On the south side there are the two groups of the Emperor Diocletian and his imperial colleagues embracing each other. To enumerate these sculptures one by one, outside and inside the basilica, to describe and date them, would fill a bulky catalogue. . . .

The mosaics above the balcony, except for the one on the extreme left, have disappeared. We find them reproduced in Gentile Bellini's painting of the Corpus Christi procession at the Accademia, as they still existed at the end of the fifteenth century. If there were the will to put them back, it would not be difficult to do.

Of the mosaics inside the basilica the best are in the cupolas, and on the walls of the right transept. In the cupolas the human figures represent saints but at the same time function as ribs of the structure. On the walls the narrative compositions are spaced with such wide intervals between the different groups, and the figures in the groups so vertical, that they avoid the aspect of illustrative cartoons on the walls as we find them in the sixteenth-century mosaics in the nave. . . .

In the choir itself the columns of the tabernacle are pre-Byzantine and the Pala d'Oro is not only the most gorgeous and most radiant enamel work, but the most exquisite as illustration, surpassing anything and everything of its own kind in Byzantine art and leaving far behind all other medieval enamel work. . . .

John Ruskin

-◄ 1819–1900 ►-

"Torcello," excerpted from The Stones of Venice *recaptures the haunting quality of this deserted island, the original settlement of the peoples of* Venetiae, *a part of the Roman Empire. They had fled to the marshlands of the coast to escape barbaric invasions. By* 638 *Torcello was consecrated by the arrival of the Bishop of Altinum and the building of the Cathedral, Santa Maria Assunta, here described by John Ruskin from its campanile. In the middle of the nineteenth century Ruskin could say: "Thirteen hundred years ago, the grey moorland looked as it does this day" and the same can be said at this date, except for the addition of a small museum of antiquities, and several other tourist's lures, among them lace vendors from Torcello's nearby sister island, Burano, and the* Locanda Cipriani, *a beautiful little inn and restaurant, in which Ernest Hemingway wrote* Across the River and into the Trees.

TORCELLO

Seven miles to the north of Venice, the banks of sand, which near the city rise little above low-water mark, attain by degrees a higher level, and knit themselves at last into fields of salt morass, raised here and there into shapeless mounds, and intercepted by narrow creeks of sea. One of the feeblest of these inlets, after winding for some time among buried fragments of masonry, and knots of sunburnt weeds whitened with webs of fucus, stays itself in an utterly stagnant pool beside a plot of greener grass covered with ground ivy and violets. On this mound is built a rude brick campanile, of the commonest Lombardic type, which if we ascend towards evening (and there are none to hinder us, the door of its ruinous staircase swinging idly on its hinges), we may command from it one of the most notable scenes in this wide world of ours.

Far as the eye can reach, a waste of wild sea moor, of a lurid ashen grey;

91

not like our northern moors, with their jet-black pools and purple heath, but lifeless, the color of sackcloth, with the corrupted seawater soaking through the roots of its arid weeds, and gleaming hither and thither through its snaky channels. No gathering of fantastic mists, nor coursing of clouds across it; but melancholy clearness of space in the warm sunset, oppressive, reaching to the horizon of its level gloom. To the very horizon, on the northeast; but to the north and west, there is a blue line of higher land along the border of it, and above this, but farther back, a misty band of mountains, touched with snow. To the east, the paleness and roar of the Adriatic, louder at momentary intervals as the surf breaks on the bars of sand; to the south, the widening branches of the calm lagoon, alternately purple and pale green, as they reflect the evening clouds or twilight sky; and almost beneath our feet, on the same field which sustains the tower we gaze from, a group of four buildings, two of them little larger than cottages (though built of stone, and one adorned by a quaint belfry), the third an octagonal chapel, of which we can see but little more than the flat red roof with its rayed tiling, the fourth a considerable church with nave and aisles, but of which, in like manner, we can see little but the long central ridge and lateral slopes of roof, which the sunlight separates in one glowing mass from the green field beneath and grey moor beyond. There are no living creatures near the buildings, nor any vestige of village or city round about them. They lie like a little company of ships becalmed on a far-away sea.

Then look farther to the south. Beyond the widening branches of the lagoon, and rising out of the bright lake into which they gather, there are a multitude of towers, dark, and scattered among square-set shapes of clustered palaces, a long and irregular line fretting the southern sky.

Mother and daughter—you behold them, both in their widowhood— Torcello and Venice.

Thirteen hundred years ago, the grey moorland looked as it does this day, and the purple mountains stood as radiantly in the deep distances of evening; but on the line of the horizon, there were strange fires mixed with the light of sunset, and the lament of many human voices mixed with the fretting of the waves on their ridges of sand. The flames rose from the ruins of Altinum; the lament from the multitude of its people, seeking, like Israel of old, a refuge from the sword in the paths of the sea. . . .

The inlet which runs nearest to the base of the campanile is not that by which Torcello is commonly approached. Another, somewhat broader, and overhung by alder copse, winds out of the lagoon up to the very edge of the little meadow which was once the Piazza of the city, and there, stayed by a few grey stones which present some semblance of a quay, forms its boundary at one extremity. Hardly larger than an ordinary English farmyard, and roughly enclosed on each side by broken palings and hedges of honeysuckle and briar, the narrow field retires from the water's edge, traversed by a scarcely traceable footpath, for some forty or fifty paces, and then expanding into the form of a small square, with buildings on three sides of it, the fourth being that which opens to the water. Two of these, that on our left and that in front of us as we approach from the canal, are so small that they might well be taken for the outhouses of the farm, though the first is a conventual building, and the other aspires to the title of the "Palazzo Publico," both dating as far back as the beginning of the fourteenth century; the third, the octagonal church of Santa Fosca, is far more ancient than either, yet hardly on a larger scale. Though the pillars of the portico which surrounds it are of pure Greek marble, and their capitals are enriched with delicate sculpture, they, and the arches they sustain, together only raise the roof to the height of a cattle shed; and the first strong impression which the spectator receives from the whole scene is, that whatever sin it may have been which has on this spot been visited with so utter a desolation, it could not at least have been ambition. Nor will this impression be diminished as we approach, or enter, the larger church, to which the whole group of buildings is subordinate. It has evidently been built by men in flight and distress who sought in the hurried erection of their island church such a shelter for their earnest and sorrowful worship as, on the one hand, could not attract the eyes of their enemies by its splendor, and yet, on the other, might not awaken too bitter feelings by its contrast with the churches which they had seen destroyed. There is visible everywhere a simple and tender effort to recover some of the form of the temples which they had loved, and to do honor to God by that which they were erecting, while distress and humiliation prevented the desire, and prudence precluded the admission, either of luxury or ornament or magnificence of plan. The exterior is absolutely devoid of decoration, with the exception only of the western entrance and the lateral door, of which the former has carved sideposts and architrave, and the latter, crosses of rich sculpture; while the massy stone shutters of the windows, turning on huge rings of stone, which answer the double purpose of stanchions and brackets, cause the whole building rather to resemble a refuge from Alpine storm than the cathedral of a populous city; and, internally, the two solemn mosaics of the eastern and western extremities—one representing the Last Judgment, the other the Madonna, her tears falling as her hands are raised to bless—and the noble range of pillars which enclose the space between, terminated by the high throne for the pastor and the semicircular raised seats for the superior clergy, are expressive at once of the deep sorrow and the sacred courage of men who had no home left them upon earth, but who looked for one to come, of men "persecuted but not forsaken, cast down but not destroyed."

*   *   *   *

. . . Nothing is more remarkable than the finish and beauty of all the portions of the building, which seem to have been actually executed for the place they occupy in the present structure: the rudest are those which they brought with them from the mainland; the best and most beautiful, those which appear to have been carved for their island church: of these, the new capitals already noticed, and the exquisite panel ornaments of the chancel screen, are the most conspicuous; the latter form a low wall across the church, between six small shafts . . . and serve to enclose a space raised two steps above the level of the nave, destined for the singers. . . . The bas-reliefs on this low screen are groups of peacocks and lions, two face to face on each panel, rich and fantastic beyond description, though not expressive of very accurate knowledge either of leonine or pavonine forms. And it is not until we pass to the back of the stair of the pulpit, which is connected with the northern extremity of this screen, that we find evidence of the haste with which the church was constructed. . . .

The pulpit is not the only place where this rough procedure has been permitted; at the lateral door of the church are two crosses, cut out of slabs of marble, formerly covered with rich sculpture over their whole surfaces, of which portions are left on the surface of the crosses; the lines of the original design being, of course, just as arbitrarily cut by the incisions between the arms, as the patterns upon a piece of silk which has been shaped anew. The fact is, that in all early Romanesque work, large surfaces are covered with sculpture for the sake of enrichment only; sculpture which indeed had always meaning, because it was easier for the sculptor to work with some chain of thought to guide his chisel, than without any; but it was not always intended, or at least not always hoped, that this chain of thought might be traced by the spectator. All that was proposed appears to have been the enrichment of surface, so as to make it delightful to the eye; and this being once understood, a decorated piece of marble became to the architect just what a piece of lace or embroidery is to a dressmaker, who takes of it such portions as she may require, with little regard to the places where the patterns are divided. And though it may appear, at first sight, that the procedure is indicative of bluntness and rudeness of feeling, we may perceive, upon reflection, that it may also indicate the redundance of power which sets little price upon its own exertion. When a barbarous nation builds its fortress walls out of fragments of the refined architecture it has overthrown, we can read nothing but its savageness in the vestiges of art which may thus chance to have been preserved; but when the new work is equal, if not superior, in execution, to the pieces of the older art which are associated with it, we may justly conclude that the rough treatment to which the latter have been subjected is rather a sign of the hope of doing better things than of want of feeling for those already accomplished. And, in general, this careless fitting of ornament is, in very truth, an evidence of life in the school of builders, and of their making a due distinction between work which is to be used for architectural effect, and work which is to possess an abstract perfection; and it commonly shows also that the exertion of design is so easy to them, and their fertility so inexhaustible, that they feel no remorse in using somewhat injuriously what they can replace with so slight an effort. . . .

There is one more circumstance which we ought to remember as giving peculiar significance to the position which the episcopal throne occupies in this island church, namely, that in the minds of all early Christians the Church itself was most frequently symbolized under the image of a ship, of which the bishop was the pilot. Consider the force which this symbol would assume in the imaginations of men to whom the spiritual Church had become an ark of refuge in the midst of a destruction hardly less terrible than that from which the eight souls were saved of old, a destruction in which the wrath of man had become as broad as the earth, and as merciless as the sea, and who saw the actual and literal edifice of the Church raised up, itself like an ark in the midst of the waters. No marvel if, with the surf of the Adriatic rolling between them and the shores of their birth, from which they were separated forever, they should have looked upon each other as the disciples did when the storm came down on the Tiberias Lake, and have yielded ready and loving obedience to those who ruled them in His name, who had there rebuked the winds and commanded stillness to the sea. And if the stranger would yet learn in what spirit it was that the dominion of Venice was begun, and in what strength she went forth conquering and to conquer, let him not seek to estimate the wealth of her arsenals, or number of her armies; nor look upon the pageantry of her palaces, nor enter into the secrets of her councils; but let him ascend the highest tier of the stern ledges that sweep round the altar of Torcello, and then, looking as the pilot did of old along the marble ribs of the goodly temple-ship, let him re-people its veined deck with the shadows of its dead mariners, and strive to feel in himself the strength of heart that was kindled within them.

Theophile Gautier

◄ 1811–1872 ►

Theophile Gautier was prompted, on first seeing Venice in 1850 to call it "one of the most marvelous prospects which the human eye can behold." The French poet, painter, critic and man of letters wrote a number of notable books about his journeys to Russia, Spain and Italy. The latter, Voyage en Italie, *written for "La Presse," is chiefly devoted to Venice.*

STREETS OF STONE

The streets of Venice are rarely mentioned, although they exist in great numbers, and writers describe the quaintness of the canals and gondolas alone. The absence of horses and carriages gives to Venetian streets a peculiar appearance. By their narrowness they resemble the streets of Oriental cities. As the area of the islands is limited, and the houses generally very high, the narrow lanes which separate them look like saw-cuts in enormous blocks of stone. Certain *calles* in Granada and certain London alleys very closely approximate them.

The Frezzaria is one of the most animated streets of the city. It is quite six to eight feet wide, and is therefore analogous to the Rue de la Paix in Paris. It is in this street chiefly that are to be found the goldsmiths who manufacture those delicate little golden chains as tenuous as hairs, which are called *jaserons,* and which are one of the characteristic curiosities of Venice. With the exception of these chains and a few rough gems set in silver for sale to country people, which an artist may think picturesque, these shops have nothing remarkable. The fruiterers' shops have splendid stalls. The heaps of blooming peaches, the quantities of golden, amber-colored, transparent grapes colored with the richest tints, shining like gems, and the grains of which, strung in the form of necklaces and bracelets, would admirably adorn the neck and arms of some antique Maenad, are beautifully fresh and admirably grouped. The tomatoes mingle their brilliant scarlet with the golden tints and the watermelon shows its rosy pulp through the cleft in its green skin. All these lovely fruits, brightly lighted by gas jets, show well against the vine leaves upon which they are laid. It is impossible to regale one's eyes more agreeably, and often, without being hungry, I purchased peaches and grapes through sheer love of color. I recall also certain fishmongers' stalls covered with little fishes so white, so silvery, so pearly, that I felt like swallowing them raw, after the manner of the ichthyophagists of the Southern seas, for fear of spoiling their tints. I could understand, on seeing them, the barbarous custom of ancient banquets, which consisted in watching the death of muraenas in crystal vases in order to enjoy the opal tints which they assumed in their death throes.

In the evening these streets are extremely animated and brilliant. The stalls are illuminated *a giorno,* and the narrowness of the street prevents the light being scattered. The cook shops and the pastry shops, the *osteria,* the taverns, the numerous cafes, bloom and blaze; there is a constant going and coming of people. Every shop, without a single exception, has its miniature chapel adorned with a Madonna, in front of which are placed lighted lamps or tapers and pots of artificial or natural flowers. Sometimes it is a statuette in colored plaster, sometimes a smoky painting, sometimes a Greek image with a Byzantine gold background, or a simple modern engraving. The Madonna replaces in devout Italy the Lares of antiquity. This form of the worship of the Virgin, so touching and poetic, has but few, if any, dissenters in Venice, and the followers of Voltaire would, so far, be ill-satisfied with the progress of enlightenment in the ancient city of the doges. . . .

Next to the Frezzaria, the street which leads from the Campo San Moisè to the Campo Santa Maria del Giglio is one of those which offer to a stranger the greatest number of points worthy of observation. Many lanes open into it as into an artery, for it connects the banks of the Grand Canal with the Piazza San Marco. The shops remain open longer than elsewhere, and as it is nearly straight, *forestieri* traverse it without being afraid of losing their way; a very easy thing to do in Venice, the maze of streets, complicated by canals and blind alleys, being so perplexing that it has been found necessary to mark by a succession of stones, on which are cut arrows indicating the way, the road from the Piazza to the railway station, situated at the other end of the city, near the Church of the Scalzi.

How often have I enjoyed losing myself at night in the labyrinth out of which a Venetian alone can find his way! After having followed a score of streets, traversed some thirty lanes, crossed ten canals, ascended and descended as many bridges, plunged at hazard into *sottoportici,* I have found myself just where I started from. These walks, for which I chose moonlight nights, enabled me to see Venice in its secret aspect, and from numerous picturesque and unexpected points of view.

Sometimes I came upon a great palace half in ruins, faintly showing in the shadows, thanks to a silvery beam; the panes left in its broken windows gleaming suddenly like scales or mirrors; now a bridge tracing its black arch against a stretch of bluish water over which floated a light mist; farther on a trail of red fire, falling from a lighted house upon the oily darkness of a sleeping canal; at other times a deserted square on which stood out quaintly the top of a church covered with statues which in the obscurity looked like spectres; or else a tavern where were gesticulating like demons gondoliers and *facchini,* their shadows projected upon the window; or else a half-opened watergate through which a mysterious figure sprang into a gondola.

Once I thus reached a really sinister lane behind the Grand Canal. The high houses, originally covered with the red tint which is usually found upon old Venetian buildings, had a fierce and truculent aspect. Rain, damp, neglect, and the absence of light at the bottom of this narrow cut had little by little killed the color of the facades and made the wash run. A faint reddish tint still marked the walls and looked like blood insufficiently cleansed off after the commission of a crime. Oppression, chilliness, terror, stole out from these sanguinolent walls; a sickly odor of saltpeter and well water, a moldy smell reminiscent of prisons, cloisters, and cellars, seized me as I entered it. At the blind windows there was no gleam of light, no appearance of life. The low doors, studded with rusty nails, their iron knockers worn by time, seemed incapable of ever opening. Nettles and wall plants grew on the thresholds and seemed not to have been trodden for a long time back by any human foot. . . .

If Gozzi, . . . who believed himself the victim of the hatred of wizards and hobgoblins whose tricks he had discovered and whose secrets he had told in his fairy pieces, ever traversed this solitary lane, he must have met with some of the amazing misadventures reserved, apparently, for the poet of *Turandot, The Love of the Three Oranges* and the *Blue Monster.* But Gozzi, who felt the invisible world, must certainly have always avoided Barristers' Street at the hour of twilight.

*   *   *   *

I delayed my departure from week to week, from day to day, and always had some good reason for remaining. In vain did light vapors begin to rise in the morning over the lagoon, or sudden showers compel me to take refuge in a church; in vain when I wandered in the moonlight on the Grand Canal did the chill night air force me sometimes to close the window of the gondola. . . . I was always remembering a palazzo, a church, or a picture which I had not seen. I must visit, before leaving Venice, the white church of Santa Maria Formosa, made illustrious by the famous Santa Barbara, so splendidly posed, so heroically beautiful, which Palma Vecchio painted; and the palazzo of Bianca Capello, with its remembrances of a love legend thoroughly Venetian and full of romantic charm; the strange and splendid church of San Zaccaria, in which there is a marvelous altarpiece brilliant with gold by Antonio Vivarini. . . .

Sometimes it was something else—an island I had forgotten, Mazzorbo or Torcello, which has a curious Byzantine basilica and Roman antiquities, or a picturesque façade on an unfrequented canal which I must sketch—a thousand reasons of this kind, every one excellent, but which were not the real ones, although I did my best to believe they were. I yielded, in spite of myself, to the melancholy which seizes upon the most determined traveller when he is to leave, perhaps forever, a country he has long desired to see, a place where he has spent beautiful days and lovelier nights. . . .

As the moment of departure approached, it became dearer to me, its full value revealed itself as I was about to lose it. I reproached myself with not having turned my stay to better account; I bitterly regretted a few hours of laziness, a few cowardly concessions to the enervating influence of the sirocco. It seemed to me that I might have seen more, taken more notes, made more sketches, trusted less to my memory; and yet, heaven knows that I conscientiously fulfilled my duty as a tourist. I was to be met with everywhere, in churches, in galleries, at the Academy of the Fine Arts, on the Piazza San Marco, in the Palace of the Doges, in the Library. My weary gondoliers begged for rest. I scarcely took time to swallow an ice at the Cafe Florian or a soup of mussels and a *pasticcio* of *polenta* at the Gasthoff San Gallo or at the tavern of the Black Hat. In six weeks I had worn out three pairs of eyeglasses, a pair of opera glasses, and lost a telescope. Never did anyone indulge in such an orgy of sightseeing; I looked at things fourteen hours a day without a stop. If I had dared, I would have continued my visiting by torchlight.

During the last few days it became a regular fever with me. I made a general round, a review, on the dead run, with the quick, sharp glance of a man who knows the thing he looks at and goes straight to what he wants. Like painters who ink the drawings which they do not wish rubbed out, I strengthened by a new remembrance the thousand sketches in my memory. I saw again the beautiful Ducal Palace, built purposely for a stage scene in a drama or an opera, with its great rose-colored walls, its white lacework, its two stories of pillars, its Arab trefoils; wonderful San Marco, the Saint Sophia of the West, the colossal reliquary of Venetian civilization, a gilded cavern, diapered with mosaics, a vast heaping up of jasper, porphyry, alabaster, and fragments of antiquity, a pirate cathedral enriched with the spoils of the universe; the Campanile, which bears so high within the heavens the golden angel, protector of Venice, and guards at its feet Sansovino's Loggetta carved like a gem; the Clock Tower, gold and blue, on which, on a great dial, meander the black and white hours; the Library, Athenian in its elegance, crowned with graceful mythological statues, sweet remembrance of neighboring Greece; and the Grand Canal, bordered by a double row of Gothic, Moorish, Renaissance, and rococo palaces, whose ever varying façades amaze one by the inexhaustible fancy and the perpetual invention of the details, which it would take more than a man's whole life to study; a splendid gallery in which is exhibited the genius of Sansovino, Scamozzi, Pietro Lombardo, Palladio, Longhena, Bergamasco, Rossi, Tremignon, and other wondrous architects, to say nothing of the unknown and humble workmen of the Middle Ages, who are not less admirable. I went in my gondola from the Dogana Point to Quintavalle Point in order to fix forever in my memory that fairy sight which painting is as powerless to render as are words, and I devoured with desperate attention the mirage of the Fata Morgana about to vanish forever so far as I was concerned. . . .

Every monument, every church, every gallery calls for a volume, and I can scarcely afford a page. Yet I have spoken only of what is visible; I have avoided removing the dust from the old chronicles, reviving forgotten remembrances, peopling with their former inhabitants the deserted palaces—for that would have been a life work.

Mary McCarthy

"Venice Preserved" is a selection from one of eight incisive essays in Miss McCarthy's Venice Observed. *Her commentaries cover a wide range of subjects and illuminate varied aspects of the Venetian pageant that would appear to contradict her own statement "that nothing can be said here (including this statement) that has not been said before."*

VENICE PRESERVED

No stones are so trite as those of Venice, that is, precisely, so well worn. It has been part museum, part amusement park, living off the entrance fees of tourists, ever since the early eighteenth century, when its former sources of revenue ran dry. The carnival that lasted half a year was not just a spontaneous expression of Venetian license; it was a calculated tourist attraction. Francesco Guardi's early "views" were the postcards of that period. In the Venetian preserve, a thick bitter-sweet marmalade, tourism itself became a spicy ingredient, suited to the foreign taste; legends of dead tourists now are boiled up daily by gondoliers and guides. Byron's desk, Gautier's palace, Ruskin's boarding house, the room where Browning died, Barbara Hutton's plate-glass window—these memorabilia replace the Bucintoro or Paolo Sarpi's statue as objects of interest. The Venetian crafts have become sideshows—glass-blowing, bead-stringing, lace-making; you watch the product made, like pink spun sugar at a circus, and bring a sample home, as a souvenir. Venetian manufactures today lay no claim to beauty or elegance, only to being "Venetian."

And there is no use pretending that the tourist Venice is not the real Venice, which is possible with other cities—Rome or Florence or Naples. The tourist Venice *is* Venice: the gondolas, the sunsets, the changing light, Florian's, Quadri's, Torcello, Harry's Bar, Murano, Burano, the pigeons, the glass beads, the vaporetto. Venice is a folding picture-post-card of itself. And though it is true (as is sometimes said, sententiously) that nearly two hundred thousand people live their ordinary working lives in Venice, they too exist in it as tourists or guides. Nearly every Venetian is an art-appreciator, a connoisseur of Venice, ready to talk of Tintoretto or to show you, at his own suggestion, the spiral staircase (said to challenge the void), to demonstrate the Venetian dialect or identify the sound of the Marangona, the bell of the Campanile, when it rings out at midnight.

A count shows the Tiepolo on the ceiling of his wife's bedroom; a dentist shows his sitting room, which was formerly a ridotto. Everything has been catalogued, with a pride that is more in the knowledge than in the thing itself. "A fake," genially says a gentleman, pointing to his Tintoretto. "Réjane's," says a house owner, pointing to the broken-down bed in the apartment she wants to let. The vanity of displaying knowledge can outweigh commercial motives or the vanity of ownership. "Eighteenth century?" you say hopefully to an antique dealer, as you look at a set of china. "No, nineteenth," he answers with firmness, losing the sale. In my apartment, I wish everything to be Venetian, but "No," says the landlady, as I ask about a cabinet: "Florentine." We stare at a big enthroned Madonna in the bedroom—very bad. She would like me to think it a Bellini and she measures the possibility against the art knowledge she estimates me to possess. "*School* of Giovanni Bellini," she announces, nonchalantly, extricating herself from the dilemma.

A Venetian nobleman has made a study of plants peculiar to Venice and shows slides on a projector. He has a library of thirty thousand volumes, mainly devoted to Venetian history. In the public libraries, in the wintertime the same set of loungers pores over Venetian archives or illustrated books on Venetian art; they move from the Correr library, when it closes, to the heatless Marciana, where they sit huddled in their overcoats, and finally to the Querini-Stampaglia, which stays open until late at night. . . .

Almost any Venetian, even a child, will abandon whatever he is doing in order to show you something. They do not merely give directions; they lead, or in some cases follow, to make sure you are still on the right way. Their great fear is that you will miss an artistic or "typical" sight. A sacristan, who has already been tipped, will not let you leave until you have seen the last Palma Giovane. The "pope" of the Chiesa dei Greci calls up to his housekeeper to throw his black hat out the window and settles it firmly on his broad brow so that he can lead us personally to the Archaeological Museum in the Piazza San Marco; he is afraid that, if he does not see to it, we shall miss the Greek statuary there.

The Spectacle

This is Venetian courtesy. Foreigners who have lived here a long time dismiss it with the observation: "They have nothing else to do." But idleness here is alert, on the *qui vive* for the opportunity of sightseeing; nothing delights a born Venetian so much as a free gondola ride. When the funeral gondola, a great black-and-gold ornate hearse, draws up beside a *fondamenta,* it is an occasion for aesthetic pleasure. My neighborhood was especially favored in this way, because across the *campo* was the Old Men's Home. Everyone has noticed the Venetian taste in shop displays, which extends down to the poorest bargeman, who cuts his watermelons in half and shows them, pale pink, with green rims against the green side canal, in which a pink palace with oleanders is reflected. *Che bello, che magnifico, che luce, che colore!* —they are all *professori delle Belle Arti.* And throughout the Veneto, in the old Venetian possessions, this internal tourism, this expertise, is rife. In Bassano, at the Civic Museum, I took the Mayor for the local art critic until he interrupted his discourse on the jewel tones ("like Murano glass") in the Bassani pastorals to look at his watch and cry out: "My citizens are calling me." . . .

When the Venetians stroll out in the evening, they do not avoid the Piazza San Marco, where the tourists are, as the Romans do with Doney's on the Via Veneto. The Venetians go to look at the tourists, and the tourists look back at them. It is all for the ear and eye, this city, but primarily for the eye. Built on water, it is an endless succession of reflections and echoes, a mirroring. Contrary to popular belief, there are no back canals where a tourist will not meet himself, with a camera, in the person of the other tourist crossing the little bridge. And no word can be spoken in this city that is not an echo of something said before. *"Mais c'est aussi cher que Paris"* exclaims a Frenchman in a restaurant, unaware that he repeats Montaigne. The complaint against foreigners, voiced by a foreigner, chimes querulously through the ages, in unison with the medieval monk who found St. Mark's Square filled with "Turks, Libyans, Parthians, and other monsters of the sea." Today it is the Germans we complain of, and no doubt they complain of the Americans, in the same words.

Nothing can be said here (including this statement) *that has not been said before.* One often hears the Piazza described as an open-air drawing room; the observation goes back to Napoleon, who called it "the best drawing room in Europe." A friend likens the ornamental coping of St. Mark's to sea foam, but Ruskin thought of this first: ". . . at last, as if in ecstasy, the crests of the arches break into a marbly foam, and toss themselves far into the blue sky in flashes and wreaths of sculptured

105

spray. . . ." Another friend observes that the gondolas are like hearses; I
was struck by the novelty of the fancy until I found it, two days later, in
Shelley: "that funereal bark." Now I find it everywhere. A young man,
boarding the vaporetto, sighs that "Venice is so urban," a remark which
at least *sounds* original and doubtless did when Proust spoke of the
"always urban impression" made by Venice in the midst of the sea. And
the worst of it is that nearly all these clichés are true. It is true, for
example, that St. Mark's at night looks like a painted stage flat; this is a
fact which everybody notices and which everybody thinks he has discovered for himself. I blush to remember the sound of my own voice, clear in
its own conceit, enunciating this proposition in the Piazza, nine years
ago.

"I envy you, writing about Venice," says the newcomer. "I pity you,"
says the old hand. One thing is certain. Sophistication, that modern kind
of sophistication that begs to differ, to be paradoxical, to invert, is not a
possible attitude in Venice. In time, this becomes the beauty of the place.
One gives up the struggle and submits to a classic experience. One
accepts the fact that what one is about to feel or say has not only been said
before by Goethe or Musset but is on the tip of the tongue of the tourist
from Iowa who is alighting in the Piazzetta with his wife in her furpiece
and jewelled pin. Those Others, the existential enemy, are here identical
with oneself. After a time in Venice, one comes to look with pity on the
efforts of the newcomer to disassociate himself from the crowd. He has
found a "little" church—has he?—quite off the beaten track, a real gem,
with inlaid colored marbles on a soft dove grey, like a jewel box. He
means Santa Maria dei Miracoli. As you name it, his face falls. It is so
well known, then? Or has he the notion of counting the lions that look
down from the window ledges of the palazzi? They remind him of cats.
Has anybody ever noticed how many cats there are in Venice or compared
them to the lions? On my table two books lie open with chapters on the
Cats of Venice. My face had fallen too when I came upon them in the
house of an old bookseller, for I too had dared think that I had hold of an
original perception.

The cat = the lion. Venice is a kind of pun on itself, which is another
way of saying that it is a mirror held up to its own shimmering image—
the central conceit on which it has evolved. The Grand Canal is in the
shape of a fish (or an eel, if you wish to be more literal); on the Piazzetta,
St. Theodore rides the crocodile (or the fish, if you perfer). Dolphins and
scallop shells carry out the theme in decoration. It becomes frozen in the
state ceremonial; the Doge weds the Adriatic in a mock, i.e., a punning,
marriage. The lion enters the state myth in the company of the Evangelist

and begets litter on litter of lions—all allusions, half jesting, half literary, to the original one: the great War Lion of the Arsenal gate whose Book ("Peace be with you") is ominously closed, the graduated lions from Greece below him, in front of the Arsenal, like the three bears in the story, the King of Beasts with uplifted tail in *trompe-l'oeil* on the Scuola di San Marco, the red, roaring lions on the left of St. Mark's who play hobby-horse for children every day, the lion of Chioggia, which Venetians say is only a cat, the doggy lion of the Porta della Carta being honored by the Doge Foscari. . . . From St. Mark's Square, they spread out, in varying shapes and sizes, whiskered or clean-shaven, through Venice and her ancient territories, as far as Nauplia in the Peloponnesus. But St. Mark's lion is winged, i.e., a monster, and this produces a whole crop of monsters, basilisks and dragons, with their attendant saints and slayers, all dear to Venetian artists. St. Jerome, thanks to his tame lion, becomes a favorite saint of the Venetians.

The twinning continues. The great pink church of the Frari is echoed on the other side of the city by the great pink church of the Dominicans, the other preaching order. And in St. Mark's shelter, near the Pietra del Bando, four small identical brothers, called the Moors, in porphyry embrace two and two, like orphans. The famous Venetian *trompe-l'oeil,* marble simulating brocade or flat simulating round, is itself a sort of twinning or unending duplication, as with a repeating decimal.

Venice is a game (see how many lions you can count; E. V. Lucas found 75 on the Porta della Carta alone), a fantasy, a fable, a city of Methuselahs, in which mortality has almost been vanquished. Titian, according to the old writers, was carried off by the plague in his hundredth year. How many Venetian painters can you count who, like him, passed three score and ten before they were gathered to their fathers? Jacopo Bellini (70 years), Gentile Bellini (78), Giovanni Bellini (86), Lorenzo Lotto (76), Tintoretto (76), Palma Il Giovane (84), Tiepolo (80), G. D. Tiepolo (77), Pietro Longhi (83), Alessandro Longhi (80), Piazzetta (71), Canaletto (71), Guardi (81). And among the sculptors and architects, Pietro Lombardo (65), Sansovino (93), Alessandro Vittoria (83), Palladio (72), Longhena (84). This makes Venice, the nourisher of old men, appear as a dream, the Fountain of Youth which Ponce de Leon sought in the New World. It brings us back to the rationalist criticism of Venice, as a myth that ought to be exploded.

"Those Pantaloons," a French ambassador called the Venetian statesmen in the early seventeenth century, when the astuteness of their diplomacy was supposed to be the wonder of Europe. The capacity to arouse contempt and disgust in the onlooker was a natural concomitant, not only of Venice's prestige, but of the whole fairy tale she wove about herself; her Council of Ten, her mysterious three Inquisitors, her dungeons, her punishments, "swift, silent, and sure." Today, we smile a little at the fairy tale of Venetian history, at the doge under his golden umbrella, as we smile at the nuns entertaining their admirers in Guardi's picture in the Ca' Rezzonico, at the gaming tables and the masks; it is the same smile we give to the all-woman regatta, to the graduated lions, to Carpaccio's man-eating dragon. If we shiver as we pass through the Leads or as we slip our hand into the Bocca del Leone, it is a histrionic shiver, partly self-induced, like the screams that ring out from the little cars in an amusement-park tunnel as they shoot past the waxworks. For us, Venetian history is a curio; those hale old doges and warriors seem to us a strange breed of sea-animal who left behind them the pink, convoluted shell they grew to protect them, which is Venice.

The old historians took a different line and tended to view Venice as an allegory in which vice and reckless greed (or undemocratic government) met their just reward. They held up Venice as a cautionary example to other nations. But we cannot feel this moral indignation or this solemn awe before the Venetian spectacle. In Ravenna or Mantua, we can sense the gloom of history steal over us like a real shadow. These cities are truly sad, and they compel belief in the crimes and tragedies that were enacted in them. Venice remains a child's pageant, minute and ingenious, brightened with touches of humorous "local color," as in the pageant pictures of Gentile Bellini and Carpaccio. Or, with Tintoretto and Veronese, it swells into a bepearled myth. The sumptuous Apotheoses of the rooms of the Doge's Palace, the blues and golds and nacreous flesh tones, discredit the reality of the Turkish disasters that were befalling the Republic at the time they were painted, just as Giorgione's idylls discredit the reality of the League of Cambrai. With the eighteenth-century painters, the pneumatic goddess is deflated. The pictures of Canaletto and Guardi and Longhi take us back again into playland, with toy boats (the gondolas) and dominos and masks and lacy shawls, while the pictures of Tiepolo with their chalky tones take us to a circus, in which everyone is a clown or a trapeze artist, in white theatrical make-up and theatrical costuming. Napoleon was at the gates, but it is hard to believe it. It was hard for the Venetians, at the time. For them, their "liberation" from the oligarchy was simply another pageant, another procession, with allegorical figures in costume before the old stage flat of St. Mark's, which was hung with garlands and draperies. At the opera that night, the fall of the Republic was celebrated by a ballet danced by the workers of the Arsenal; the patricians were there, in silks and laces and brocades, gold and silver lamés, diamonds and pearls, and, in honor of the occasion, gondoliers were admitted free.

Everything that happens in Venice has this inherent improbability, of which the gondola, floating, insubstantial, at once romantic and haunting, charming and absurd, is the symbol. "Why don't they put outboard motors on them?" an American wondered, looking on the practical side. But a dream is only practical in unexpected ways; that is, it is *resourceful,* like the Venetians. "It is another world," people say, noting chiefly the absence of the automobile. And it *is* another world, a palpable fiction, in which the unexpected occurs with regularity; that is why it hovers on the brink of humor.

A prominent nobleman this autumn, rushing to the sickbed of a friend, slipped getting into his motorboat and fell into the Grand Canal. All Venice laughed. But if the count had had his misadventure in Padua, on *terra ferma,* if he had fallen getting out of his car, everyone would have condoled with him. Traffic lights are not funny, but it is funny to have one in Venice over a canal intersection. The same with the Venetian fire brigade. The things of *this* world reveal their essential absurdity when they are put in the Venetian context. In the unreal realm of the canals, as in a Swiftian Lilliput, the real world, with its contrivances, appears as a vast folly.

PART IV

SPECTATORS

So, o'er the lagoon
We glided; and from that funereal bark
I leaned, and saw the city, and could mark
How from their many isles, in evening's gleam,
Its temples and its palaces did seem
Like fabrics of enchantment piled to heaven.

PERCY BYSSHE SHELLY

Thomas Coryat

-◄ 1577?–1617 ►-

Thomas Coryat, an Oxford-educated traveller touring the world on foot, reached Venice in 1608, a little more than one hundred years after the first English professional voyager, Sir Richard Guildford (1455–1506), who wrote of "the rychisse, the suptuos buyldyngs, and relygyous houses with all other things maketh a cytie glorious, surmonteth in Venyse above all places ever I sawe" in his Pilgrimage *to the Holy Land. Earlier, in 1372–1373 and again in 1378 Chaucer came to Italy on diplomatic missions but left no record of a visit to Venice. Later, John Milton, who travelled and studied in Italy for two years, 1638–40, was in Venice April–May, 1639, but all that is known of his visit is that he purchased a number of books which he shipped to England, among them a history of Venice, in Latin. The cavalcade of English literary travellers' accounts begins in earnest with* Coryat's Crudities *published in 1611, from which "The Queene of Christendome" has been selected.*

THE QUEENE OF CHRISTENDOME, 1608

Such is the rarenesse of the situation of Venice, that it doth even amaze and drive into admiration all strangers that upon their first arrival behold the same. For it is built altogether upon the water in the innermost gulf of the Adriatic Sea which is commonly called *Gulfo di Venetia,* and is distant from the main Sea about the space of three miles. From the which it is divided by a certain great bank called *litto maggior,* which is at the least fifty miles in length. This bank is so necessary a defence for the City, that it serveth instead of a strong wall to repulse and reverberate the violence of the furious waves of the Sea. For were not this bank inter-posed like a bulwark betwixt the City and the Sea, the waves would utterly overwhelm and deface the City in a moment. The form of this aforesaid bank is very strange to behold. For nature herself the most cunning mistress and architect of all things hath framed it crooked in form of a bow, and by the Art of man there are five *Ostia,* that is mouths, or gaps made therein, whereof each maketh a haven, and yieldeth passage to the ships to sail forth and back to Venice. The names of them are Malamocco (which is the fairest) a place well furnished with houses, and much inhabited with people, Brondolo, Chioggia, Saint Erasmo, Castella. Now that whole space which is betwixt this bank and the continent . . . is the same which we call *Gulfo di Venetia,* or the lakes of the Adriatic sea, in which space are to be seen many fennes, marshes, and other dry places, whereof some are covered altogether with reeds and flags, others do show like fair little green Islands, which are the very places that yielded harbor to diverse companies of people, who in the time of the Huns' Goths', and Vandals' devastation and depopulation of Italy repaired thither with their whole families as to a safe refuge and sanctuary for the better security of their lives.

The first place of Venice that was inhabited is that which now they call the Rialto, which word is derived from *rivus altus,* that is, a deep river, because the water is deeper there than about the other Islands. And the first that dwelt in the same Rialto was a poor man called Joannes Bonus, who got his living there by fishing. . . .

The city is divided in the midst by a goodly fair channel, which they call *Canal Il Grande.* The same is crooked and made in the form of a Roman S. It is in length a thousand and three hundred paces, and in breadth at the least forty, in some places more. The six parts of the City whereof Venice consisteth are situated on both sides of this *Canal Il Grande.* The names of them are these: St. Marco, Castello, Cannaregio that lie on one side of it, and those on the other side are called St. Polo, St. Croce, Dorsoduro. Also both the sides of this channel are adorned with many sumptuous and magnificent palaces that stand very near to the water, and make a very glorious and beautiful show. For many of them are of a great height three or four stories high, most being built with brick and some few with fair free stone. Besides, they are adorned with a great multitude of stately pillars made partly of white stone and partly of Istrian marble. Their roofs do much differ from those of our English buildings. For they are all flat and built in that manner as men may walk upon them, as I have often observed, which form of roofing is generally used in all those Italian cities that I saw, and in some places of France, especially in Lyons, where I could not see as much as one house but had a flat roof. . . .

Many things I observed in these Venetian palaces, that make them very conspicuous and passing fair; amongst the rest these two things especially. Every palace of any principal note hath a pretty walk or open gallery betwixt the wall of the house and the brink of the river's bank, the edge or extremity whereof is garnished with fair pillars that are finely arched at the top. This walk serveth for men to stand in without their houses and behold things. Suetonius calleth these kind of open galleries *Podia*. Truly, they yield no small beauty to their buildings.

Again, I noted another thing in these Venetian Palaces that I have very seldom seen in England, and it is very little used in any other country that I could perceive in my travels, saving only in Venice and other Italian cities. Somewhat above the middle of the front of the building, or (as I have observed in many of their palaces) a little beneath the top of the front, they have right opposite unto their windows a very pleasant little terrace, that jutteth or butteth out from the main building: the edge whereof is decked with many pretty little turned pillars, either of marble or free stone to lean over. These kind of terraces or little galleries of pleasure Suetonius calleth Meniana. They give great grace to the whole edifice, and serve only for this purpose, that people may from that place as from a most delectable prospect contemplate and view the parts of the city round about them in the cool evening.

Withall I perceived another thing in their buildings, which as it is the rarest thing that ever I saw in my life, so I hold it convenient to be mentioned in this discourse. The foundations of their houses are made after a very strange manner. For whereas many of them are situated in the water, whensoever they lay the foundation of any house, they remove the water by certain devices from the place where they lay the first fundamental matter. Most commonly they drive long stakes into the ground, without the which they do *aggerere molem,* that is, raise certain heaps of sand, mud, clay, or some other such matter to repell the water. Then they ram in great piles of wood, which they lay very deep, upon the which they place their brick or stone, and so frame the other parts of the building. These foundations are made so exceedingly deep, and contrived with so great labour that I have heard they cost them very near the third part of the charge of the whole edifice. But all the houses of the city are not founded with this difficulty. For those that are built upon the middle of the islands, or any other part thereof, saving only upon the brinks, or in the very water itself, are founded in that manner as other houses are upon the main land. These kind of foundations thus made upon piles I have both read and heard to be contrived in the like manner both at the noble town of Amsterdam in Holland and at Stockholm the metropolitan city of Suethland, most of the buildings of which cities are founded like to these of the Venetian houses.

But to return again to the *Canal Il Grande* wherehence I digressed, it is said there are in the city of Venice at the least a hundred and twenty goodly palaces, the greatest part whereof is built upon the sides of this great channel. So that if you will take a view of the fairest palaces that the whole city yieldeth, you must behold these palaces of the *Canal Il Grande,* either from the Rialto bridge or passing in a little boat which they call a gondola through the Channel itself. . . .

* * * *

There are many notable things to be considered in this Piazza of St. Mark. . . . Most memorable is the Tower of St. Mark, which is a very fair building, made all of brick till towards the top, being distant from St. Mark's Church about eighty feet: It is from the bottom to the top about some two hundred and eighty feet and hath such an exceeding deep foundation that some do think the very foundation cost almost as much as the rest of the building from the ground to the top. This tower is square, being of an equal breadth in every side, namely forty feet broad. The whole top is covered with pieces of brass, made in form of tiles that are gilt. Such is the height of this tower that in a fair season it is to be seen by sea from Istria and Croatia, which is at the least one hundred miles from Venice: the stairs are made after such a strange manner that not only a man, or woman, or child may with great ease ascend to the top of it, but also a horse, as it is commonly reported in the city. But I think this will seem such a paradox and incredible matter to many, that perhaps they will say I may lie by authority (according to the old proverb) because I am a traveller. Indeed I confess I saw no horse ascend the stairs; but I heard it much reported in Venice, both by many of my countrymen, and by the Venetians themselves; neither it is unlikely to be true. For these stairs are not made as other common stairs, by which a man can ascend by no more then a foot higher from stair to stair till he commeth to the highest; but these are made flat, and ascend so easily by little and little in height, that a man can hardly be weary, and scarce perceive any pains or difficulty in the ascent. For that whole space which begins from the entrance of the stair at the corner of the tower within, till you ascend to the next corner, which perhaps containeth about some twenty foot at the least, is esteemed but one stair. When you have ascended almost as high as you can, you shall leave the stairs, and enter into a void loft, and from that you are conveyed by a short ladder into a little square gallery butting out from the tower, and made in the form of a terrace, being supported with fair round pillars of alabaster. From every side of this square gallery you have the fairest and goodliest prospect that is (I think) in all the world. For therehence may you see the whole model and form of the city, a sight that doth in my opinion far surpass all the shows under the cope of heaven. There you may have a synopsis, that is, a general view of little Christendom (for so do many entitle this city of Venice) or rather of the Jerusalem of Christendom. For so me thinks may a man not improperly call this glorious city of Venice: not in respect of the religion thereof, or the situation, but of the sumptuousness of their buildings, for which we read Jerusalem in former times was famed above all the eastern cities of the world. There you may behold all their sumptuous palaces adorned with admirable variety of beautiful pillars: the Church of St. Mark which is but a little way therehence distant, with the duke's stately palace adjoining it, being one of the principal wonders of the Christian world; the lofty Rialto, the Piazza of Saint Stephen which is the most spacious and goodly place of the City except St. Mark's; all the six parts of the city. For into so many it is divided, as I have before said; their streets, their Churches, their Monasteries, their market places, and all their other public buildings of rare magnificence; also many fair gardens replenished with diversity of delicate fruits, as oranges, citrons, lemons, apricots, musk melons, angurias, and what not; together with their little islands bordering about the city wonderfully frequented and inhabited with people, being in number fifty or there about; also the Alpes that lead into Germany two ways, by the City of Trent, and the Grisons country; and those that lead into France through Savoy, the Appennines, the pleasant Euganean hills, with a little world of other most delectable objects: Therefore whosoever thou art that means to see Venice, in any case forget not to go up to the top of Saint Mark's tower before thou commest out of the city. For it will cost thee but a *gazet,* which is not fully an English penny. On the top of the tower is erected a brazen angel fairly gilt, which is made in that sort that he seemeth to bless the people with his hand. . . .

I have taken occasion to mention some notable particulars of their women, I will insist farther upon that matter, and make relation of their courtesans also, as being a thing incident and very proper to this discourse, especially because the name of a courtesan of Venice is famed over all Christendom. . . .

The woman that professes this trade is called in the Italian tongue *Cortezana,* which word is derived from the Italian word *cortesia* that signifieth courtesie, because these kind of women are said to receive courtesies of their favourites, which word . . . signifieth properly a sociable woman, and is by Demosthenes, Athenaeus, and divers other prose writers often taken for a woman of a dissolute conversation. As for the number of these Venetian courtesans it is very great. For it is thought there are of them in the whole city and other adjacent places, as Murano,

Malamocco, etc. at the least twenty thousand, whereof many are esteemed so loose that they are said to open their quivers to every arrow, a most ungodly thing without doubt that there should be a tolleration of such licentious wantons in so glorious, so potent, so renowned a city. For me thinks that the Venetians should be daily afraid least their winking at such uncleanness should be an occasion to draw down upon them God's curses and vengeance from heaven, and to consume their city with fire and brimstone, as in times past he did Sodom and Gomorrha. But they not fearing any such thing do grant large dispensation and indulgence unto them, and that for these two causes. First, they think that the chastity of their wives would be the sooner assaulted, and so consequently they should be capricornified, (which of all the indignities in the world the Venetian cannot patiently endure) were it not for these places of evacuation. But I marvel how that should be true though these courtesans were utterly rooted out of the city. For the gentlemen do even coop up their wives always within the walls of their houses for fear of these inconveniences, as much as if there were no courtesans at all in the city. So that you shall very seldom see a Venetian gentleman's wife but either at the solemnization of a great marriage or at the Christening of a Jew, or late in the evening rowing in a gondola. The second cause is for that the revenues which they pay unto the Senate for their tolleration do maintain a dozen of their galleys (as many reported unto me in Venice) and so save them a great charge. The consideration of these two things hath moved them to tolerate for the space of these many hundred years these kind of ladies. . . .

So infinite are the allurements of these amorous Calypsoes, that the fame of them hath drawn many to Venice from some of the remotest parts of Christendom to contemplate their beauties and enjoy their pleasing dalliances. And indeed such is the variety of the delicious objects they minister to their lovers, that they want nothing tending to delight. For when you come into one of their palaces (as indeed some few of the principallest of them live in very magnificent and portly buildings fit for the entertainment of a great prince) you seem to enter into the Paradise of Venus. For their fairest rooms are most glorious and glittering to behold. The walls round about being adorned with most sumptuous tapistry and gilt leather. Besides you may see the picture of the noble courtesan most exquisitely drawn. As for herself, she comes to thee decked like the queen and goddess of love. . . . Also the ornaments of her body are so rich, that except thou dost even geld thy affections (a thing hardly to be done) or carry with thee Ulysses herb called Moly which is mentioned by Homer, that is, some antidote against those venereous titillations, she will very near benumb and captivate thy senses. For thou shalt see her decked with many chains of gold and oriental pearl like a second Cleopatra (but they are very litle), diverse gold rings beautified with diamonds and other costly stones, jewels in both her ears of great worth, a gown of damask (I speak this of the nobler courtesans) either decked with a deep gold fringe or laced with five or six gold laces each two inches broad. Her petticoat of red chamlet edged with rich gold fringe, stockings of carnasion silk, her breath and her whole body, the more to enamour thee, most fragrantly perfumed. . . . Moreover she will endevour to enchant thee partly with her melodious notes that she warbles out upon her lute, which she fingers with as laudable a stroak as many men that are excellent professors in the noble science of Music, and partly with that heart-tempting harmony of her voice. Also thou wilt find the Venetian *Cortezana* (if she be a selected woman indeed) a good rhetorician and a most elegant discourser, so that if she cannot move thee with all these foresaid delights, she will assay thy constancy with her Rhetorical tongue. And to the end she may minister unto thee the stronger temptations to come to her lure, she will show thee her chamber of recreation, where thou shalt see all manner of pleasing objects, as many fair painted coffers wherewith it is garnished round about, a curious milk white canopy of needlework, a silk quilt embroidered with gold, and generally all her bedding sweetly perfumed. And amongst other amiable ornaments she will show thee one thing only in her chamber tending to mortification, a matter strange amongst so many *irritamenta malorum,* even the picture of our Lady by her bed side, with Christ in her arms, placed within a cristal glass. . . .

Moreover I will tell thee this news which is most true that if thou shouldest wantonly converse with her, and not give her that *salarium iniquitatis,* which thou hast promised her, but perhaps cunningly escape from her company, she will either cause thy throat to be cut by her Ruffiano, if he can after catch thee in the city, or procure thee to be arrested (if thou art to be found) and clapped up in prison, where thou shalt remain till thou hast paid her all thou didst promise her. . . .

There is one most notable thing more to be mentioned concerning these Venetian courtesans, with the relation whereof I will end this discourse of them. If any of them happen to have any children (as indeed they have but a few, for according to the old proverb the best carpenters make the fewest chips) they are brought up either at their own charge or in a certain house of the city appointed for no other use but only for the bringing up of the courtesan's bastards, which I saw eastward above St. Mark's street near to the seaside. In the south wall of which building that looketh towards the sea, I observed a certain iron grate inserted into a hollow piece of the wall, betwixt which grate and a plain stone beneath it there is a convenient little space to put in an infant. Hither doth the mother or somebody for her bring the child shortly after it is born into the world; and if the body of it be no greater but that it may conveniently without any hurt to the infant be conveighed in at the aforesaid space, they put it in there without speaking at all to anybody who is in the house to take charge thereof. From thenceforth the mother is absolutely discharged of her child. But if the child be grown to that bigness that they cannot conveigh it through that space, it is carried back again to the mother, who taketh charge of it herself, and bringeth it up as well as she can. Those that are brought up in this aforesaid house, are removed therehence when they come to years of discretion, and many of the females if they be fair do imitate their mothers in their gainful faculty and get their living by prostituting their bodies to their favourites.

Thus have I described unto thee the Venetian courtesans, but because I have related so many particulars of them, as few Englishmen that have lived many years in Venice can do the like, or at the least if they can, they will not upon their return into England, I believe thou wilt cast an aspersion of wantonness upon me and say that I could not know all these matters without mine own experience. I answer thee that although I might have known them without my experience, yet for my better satisfaction, I went to one of their noble houses (I will confess) to see the manner of their life, and observe their behaviour.

* * * *

Having now so amply declared unto thee things of this thrice-renowned and illustrious city, I will briefly mention most of the other particulars thereof, and so finally shut up this narration: There are reported to be in Venice and the adjacent islands two hundred churches in which are one hundred forty-three pair of organs, fifty-four monasteries, twenty-six nunneries, fifty-six tribunals or places of judgment, seventeen hospitals, six companies or *scuole*; one hundred sixty-five marble statues of worthy personages, partly equestrian, partly pedestrial, which are erected in sundry places of the city to the honour of those that either at home have prudently administred the commonweale or abroad valiantly fought for the same. Likewise of brass there are twenty-three, whereof one is that of Bartholomew Coleon. Also there are twenty-seven public clocks, ten brasen gates, one hundred fourteen towers for bells to hang in, ten brasen horses, one hundred fifty-five wells for the common use of the citizens, one hundred eighty-five most delectable gardens, ten thousand gondolas, four-hundred fifty bridges partly stony, partly timber, one hundred twenty palaces, whereof one hundred are very worthy of that name, one hundred seventy-four courts; and the total number of souls living in the city and about the same is thought to be about five hundred thousand, something more or less. For sometimes there is a catalogue made of all the persons in the city of what sex or age soever they be. . . .

So at length I finish the treatise of this incomparable city, this most beautiful queene, this untainted virgin, this paradise, this temple, this rich diadem and the most flourishing garland of Christendom, of which the inhabitants may as proudly vaunt, as I have read the Persians have done of their Ormus, who say that if the world were a ring, then should Ormus be the gem thereof. The same (I say) may the Venetians speak of their city, and much more truly. The sight whereof hath yielded unto me such infinite and unspeakable contentment (I must needs confess) that even as Albertus Marquesse of Guasto said were he put to his choice to be lord of four of the fairest cities of Italy or the Arsenal of Venice, he would prefer the Arsenal. In like manner, I say that had there been an offer made unto me before I took my journey to Venice, either that four of the richest manors of Somersetshire (wherein I was born) should be gratis bestowed upon me if I never saw Venice, or neither of them if I should see it; although certainly those manors would do me much more good in respect of a state of livelihood to live in the world then the sight of Venice, yet notwithstanding I will ever say while I live that the sight of Venice and her resplendent beauty, antiquities, and monuments, hath by many degrees more contented my mind and satisfied my desires, then those four lordships could possibly have done.

Thus much of the glorious city of Venice.

John Evelyn

John Evelyn, author of over thirty works on such subjects as numismatics, the natural sciences, and gardening, is best known for his lifelong Diary unfailingly maintained for sixty-six years, 1640–1706. The Englishman arrived in Venice in May, 1645, proceeded directly to the Black Eagle, an inn near the Rialto, then one of the better quarters of the city, and stayed until March, 1646. The record he kept is regarded as "the first fairly complete picture of Italy that we possess" in the English language.

DIARY, 1645–1646

On the Po, we embarked in a stout vessell, and thro' an artificial chanell, very strait, we entered the Adice, which carried us by breake of day into the Adriatic, and so sailing prosperously by Chioza, (a towne upon an island in this Sea,) and Palestina, we came over against Malamocco (the chiefe port and ankerage where our English merchantmen lie that trade to Venice,) about 7 at night, after we had stayed at least 2 hours for permission to land, our bill to health being deliver'd according to costome. So soone as we came on shore we were conducted to the Dogana, where our portmanteaus were visited, and then we got to our lodging, which was at honest Signor Paulo Rhodomante's at the Black Eagle near the Rialto, one of the best quarters of the towne. . . .

The next morning, finding myself extreamly weary and beaten with my journey, I went to one of their bagnios, where you are treated after the Eastern manner, washing with hot and cold water, with oyles; and being rubbed with a kind of strigil of seal's-skin, put on the operator's hand like a glove. This bath did so open my pores that is cost me one of the greatest colds I ever had in my life, for want of necessary caution in keeping myselfe warme for some time after; for coming out I im'ediately began to visit the famous places of the Citty; and Travellers who come into Italy do nothing but run up and down to see sights, and this Citty well deserved our admiration, being the most wonderfully placed of any in the world, built on so many hundred islands, in the very Sea, and at good distance from the Continent. It has no fresh water except what is reserv'd in cisterns from raine, and such as is daily brought from *terra ferma* in boates, yet there was no want of it, and all sorts of excellent provisions were very cheape.

'Tis said that when the Huns overran Italy some meane fishermen and others left the maine land and fled for shelter to these despicable and muddy islands, which in processe of time, by industry, are growne to the greatnesse of one of the most considerable States, considered as a Republic, and having now subsisted longer than any of the foure ancient Monarchies, flourishing in greate state, wealth, and glory, by the conquest of greate territories in Italy, Dacia, Greece, Candy, Rhodes, and Sclavonia, and at present challenging the empire of all the Adriatiq Sea, which they yearly espouse by casting a gold ring into it with greate pomp and ceremony on Ascension Day: the desire of seeing this was one of the reasons that hastened us from Rome.

The Doge, having heard masse in his robes of state (which are very particular, after the Eastern fashion,) together with the Senat in their gownes, imbark'd in their gloriously painted, carved, and gilded Bucentora, inviron'd and follow'd by innumerable gallys, gondolas, and boates, filled with spectators, some dressed in masquerade, trumpets, musiq, and canons; having rowed about a league into the Gulph, the Duke at the prow casts a gold ring and cup into the Sea, at which a loud acclamation is ecchoed from the greate guns of the Arsenal and at the Liddo. We then return'd. . . .

The first publiq building I went to see was the Rialto, a brige of one arch over the grand Canall, so large as to admit a gally to row under it, built of good marble, and having on it, besides many pretty shops, three ample and stately passages for people without any inconvenience, the two outmost nobly balustred with the same stone; a piece of Architecture much to be admir'd. It was evening, and the Canall where the Noblesse go to take the air, as in our Hide-park, was full of ladys and gentlemen. There are many times dangerous stops by reason of the multitude of gondolas ready to sink one another; and indeede they affect to leane them on one side, that one who is not accostom'd to it would be afraid of over-setting. Here they were singing, playing on harpsicords and other musick, and serenading their mistresses; in another place racing and other pastimes upon the water, it being now exceeding hot.

Next day I went to their Exchange, a place like ours frequented by merchants, but nothing so magnificent: from thence my guide led me to the Fondigo di Todeschi, which is their magazine, and here many of the merchants, especialy Germans, have their lodging and diet as in a college. The outside of this stately fabric is painted by Giorgione da Castelfranco, and Titian himselfe.

Hence I pass'd thro' the Merceria, which is one of the most delicious streets in the world for the sweetnesse of it, and is all the way on both sides tapistred as it were with cloth of gold, rich damasks and other silks, which the shops expose and hang before their houses from the first floore, and with the variety that for neere halfe the yeare spent cheifly in this Citty I hardly remember to have seene the same piece twice expos'd; to this add the perfumes, apothecaries shops, and the innumerable cages of nightingales which they keepe, that entertaine you with their melody from shop to shop, so that shutting your eyes you would imagine yourselfe in the country, when indeede you are in the middle of the Sea. It is almost as silent as the middle of a field, there being neither rattling of coaches nor trampling of horses. This streete, pav'd with brick and exceedingly cleane, brought us thro' an arch into the famous Piazza of St.Marc.

Over this Porch stands that admirable Clock, celebrated next to that of Strasburg for its many movements; amongst which, about 12 and 6, which are their houres of Ave Maria when all the towne are on their knees, come forth the 3 Kings led by a starr, and passing by the image of Christ in his Mother's armes do their reverence, and enter into the clock by another doore. At the top of this turret another automaton strikes the quarters; an honest merchant told me that one day walking in the Piazza, he saw the fellow who kept the Clock struck with this hammer so forceably, as he was stooping his head neere the bell to mend something amisse at the instant of striking, that being stunn'd he reel'd over the battlements and broke his neck. The buildings in this Piazza are all arch'd, on pillars, pav'd within with black and white polish'd marble even to the shops, the rest of the fabric as stately as any in Europ, being not only marble but the architecture is of the famous Sansovini. . . .

The next day, by favour of the French Ambassador I had admittance with him to see the Reliquary call'd here Tresoro di San Marco, which very few even of travellers are admitted to see. It is a large chamber full of presses. There are twelve breast-plates, or pieces of pure golden armour studded with precious stones, and as many crownes dedicated to St. Mark by so many noble Venetians who had recovered their wives taken at sea by the Saracens; many curious vases of achats; the cap or cornet of the Dukes of Venice, one of which had a rubie set on it esteemed worth

200,000 crownes; two unicorns hornes; numerous vases and dishes of achat set thick with precious stones and vast pearles; divers heads of Saints inchas'd in gold; a small ampulla or glasse with our Saviour's blood; a greate morcell of the real crosse; one of the nailes; a thorn; a fragment of the column to which our Lord was bound when scorged; the standard or ensigne of Constantine; a piece of St. Luke's arme; a rib of St. Stephen; a finger of Mary Magdalene; numerous other things which I could not remember; but a priest, first vesting himselfe in his sacerdotals with the stole about his neck, shew'd us the Gospel of St. Mark (their tutelar patron) written by his own hand, and whose body they shew buried in the Church, brought hither from Alexandria many years ago. . . .

It was now Ascension Weeke, and the greate Mart or Faire of the whole yeare was now kept, every body at liberty and jollie. The noblemen stalking with their ladys on *choppines;* these are high-heel'd shoes, particularly affected by these proude dames, or, as some say, invented to keepe them at home, it being very difficult to walke with them; whence one being asked how he like the Venetian dames, replied, that they were *mezzo carne, mezzo ligno,* half flesh, half wood, and he would have none of them. The truth is, their garb is very odd, as seeming allwayes in masquerade; their other habits also totaly different from all nations. They weare very long crisped haire, of severall strakes and colours, which they make so by a wash, dischevelling it on the brims of a broade hat that has no head, but an hole to put out ther heads by; they drie them in the sunn, as one may see them at their windows. In their tire they set silk flowers and sparkling stones, their peticoates coming from their very arme-pits, so that they are neere three quarters and an half apron; their sleeves are made exceeding wide, under which their shift sleeves as wide, and commonly tucked up to the shoulder, shewing their naked armes, thro' false sleeves of tiffany, girt with a bracelet or two, with knots of points richly tagged about their shoulders and others places of their body, which they usually cover with a kind of yellow vaile of lawn very transparent. Thus attir'd they set their hands on the heads of two matron-like servants or old women, to support them, who are mumbling their beades. 'Tis ridiculous to see how these ladys crawle in and out of their gondolas by reason of their *choppines,* and what dwarfs they appeare when taken downe from their wooden scaffolds; of these I saw near thirty together, stalking half as high again as the rest of the world, for courtezanes or the citizens may not weare *choppines,* but cover their bodies and faces with a vaile of a certaine glittering taffeta or lustreè, out of which they now and then dart a glaunce of their eye, the whole face being otherwise entirely hid with it; nor may the com'on misses take this habit, but go abroad barefac'd. To the corners of these virgin-vailes hang broad but flat tossells of curious Point de Venize; the married women go in black vailes. The nobility weare the same colour, but of fine cloth lin'd with taffeta in Summer, with fur of the bellies of squirrells in the Winter, which all put on at a certaine day girt with a girdle emboss'd with silver; the vest not much different from what our Bachelors of Arts weare in Oxford, and a hood of cloth made like a sack, cast over their left shoulder, and a round cloth black cap fring'd with wool which is not so comely; they also weare their collar open to shew the diamond button of the stock of their shirt. I have never seene pearle for color and bignesse comparable to what the ladys wear, most of the noble families being very rich in jewells, especially pearles, which are always left to the son or brother who is destined to marry, which the eldest seldome do. The Doge's vest is of crimson velvet, the Procurator's, &c. of damasc, very stately. Nor was I lesse surprised with the strange variety of the severall nations which were seen every day in the streets and piazzas; Jews, Turks, Armenians, Persians, Moores, Greekes, Sclavonians, some with their targets and boucklers, and all in their native fashions, negotiating in this famous Emporium, which is allways crowded with strangers. . . .

* * * *

The Arsenal is thought to be one of the best furnish'd in the world. We entred by a strong port always guarded, and ascending a spacious gallery saw armes of back, breast, and head, for many thousands; in another were saddles, over them ensignes taken from the Turks. Another Hall is for the meeting of the Senat; passing a graff are the smiths forges, where they are continualy at work on ankers and iron work. Neere it is a well of fresh water, which they impute to two rhinoceros's horns which they say lie in it and will preserve it from ever being empoison'd. Then we came to where the carpenters were building their magazines of oares, masts, &c. for an hundred gallys and ships, which have all their aparell and furniture neere them. Then the founderie, where they cast ordinance; the forge is 450 paces long, and one of them has thirteen furnaces. There is one cannon weighing 16,573 lbs. cast whilst Henry the Third dined, and put into a gally built, rigg'd, and fitted for launching within that time. They have also armes for 12 galeasses, which are vessels to rowe, of almost 150 foote long and 30 wide, not counting prow or poop, and contain 28 banks of oares, each 7 men, and to carry 1300 men, with 3 masts. In another a magazin for 50 gallys, and place for some hundreds more. Here stands the Bucentaur, with a most ample deck, and so contriv'd that the slaves are not seene, having on the poop a throne for the Doge to sit, when he gos in triumph to espouse the Adriatic. Here is also a gallery of 200 yards long for cables, and over that a magazine of hemp. Over against these are their saltpetre houses, and a large row of cells or houses to protect their gallies from the weather. Over the gate as we go out, is a roome full of greate and small guns, some of which discharge six times at once. Then there is a court full of can'on, bullets, chaines, grapples, granados, &c. and over that armes for 800,000 men, and by themselves armes for 400 taken from some that were in a plot against the State; together with weapons of offence and defence for 62 ships; 32 pieces of ordance on carriages taken from the Turks, and one prodigious mortar-piece. In a word, 'tis not to be reckoned up what this large place containes of this sort. There were now 23 gallys, and 4 gally-grossi of 100 oares of a side. The whole Arsenal is wall'd about and may be in compasse about 3 miles, with 12 towres for the watch, besides that the sea invirons it. The workmen, who are ordinarily 500, march out in military order, and every evening receive their pay thro' a small hole in the gate where the Governor lives.

The next day I saw a wretch executed who had murther'd his master, for which he had his head chop'd off by an axe that slid down a frame of timber, between the two tall columns in St. Mark's Piazza at the sea brink; the executioner striking on the axe with a beatle, and so the head fell off the block. . . .

* * * *

1646. In January Sign. Molino was chosen Doge of Venice, but the extreame snow that fell, and the cold, hindered my going to see the solemnity, so as I stirred not from Padoa till Shrovetide, when all the world repaire to Venice to see the folly and madnesse of the Carnevall; the women, men, and persons of all conditions disguising themselves in antiq dresses, with extravagant musiq and a thousand gambols, traversing the streetes from house to house, all places being then accessible and free to enter. Abroad, they fling eggs fill'd with sweete water, but sometimes not over sweete. They also have a barbarous costome of hunting bulls about the streetes and piazzas, which is very dangerous, the passages being generally narrow. The youth of the several wards and parishes contend in other masteries and pastimes, so that 'tis impossible to recount the universal madnesse of this place during this time of licence. The greate banks are set up for those who will play at bassett; the comedians have liberty, and the operas are open; witty pasquils are thrown about, and the mountebanks have their stages at every corner. The diversion which cheifely tooke me up was three noble operas, where were excellent voices and musiq, the most celebrated of which was the famous Anna Rencha, whome we invited to a fish dinner after foure daies in Lent, when they had given over at the theater. Accompanied with an eunuch whom she brought with her, she entertain'd us with rare musiq, both of them singing to an harpsichord. It growing late, a gentleman of Venice came for her to shew her the gallys, now ready to sayle for Candia. This entertainment produced a second, given us by the English Consul of the merchants, inviting us to his house, where he had the Genoeze, the most celebrated base in Italy, who was one of the late opera band. This diversion held us so late at night, that conveying a gentlewoman who had supped with us to her gondola at the usual place of landing, we were shot at by two carbines from out another gondola in which was a noble Venetian and his courtezan unwilling to be disturb'd, which made us run in and fetch other weapons, not knowing what the matter was, till we informed of the danger we might incur by pursuing it farther.

* * * *

I was conducted to the Ghetta, where the Jewes dwell together as in a tribe or ward, where I was present at a marriage. The bride was clad in white, sitting in a lofty chaire, and cover'd with a white vaile; then two old Rabbies joyned them together, one of them holding a glasse of wine in his hand, which in the midst of the ceremony, pretending to deliver to the woman, he let fall, the breaking whereof was to signify the frailty of our nature, and that we must expect disasters and crosses amidst all enjoyments. This don, we had a fine banquet, and were brought into the bride-chamber, where the bed was dress'd with flowers, and the counter pan strewed in workes. At this ceremony we saw divers very beautifull Portuquez Jewesses with whom we had some converstation. . . .

Having pack'd up my purchases of books, pictures, castes, treacle, &c. (the making and extraordinary ceremonie whereof I had ben curious to observe, for 'tis extremely pompous and worth seeing) I departed from Venice. . . .

Johann Wolfgang Von Goethe

◄ 1749–1832 ►

Goethe, whose genius probed the entire range of human potential and left over one hundred volumes of poetry, drama and essays in science, fulfilled a lifelong desire to see Venice for the first time "on the evening of the 28th of September, by five o'clock German time," in 1786 and stayed until April, 1787. During Goethe's second residence in the city, from March 31 to May 22, 1790, he wrote the major part of 103 Venetian Epigrams, first published in the same year. The description of his Italian travels, Die Italienische Reise, *was published almost thirty years after the journey.*

LETTERS, 1786

Now it stood written on my page in the Book of Fate, that on the evening of the 28th of September, by 5 o'clock, German time, I should see Venice for the first time, as I passed from the Brenta into the Lagoon and that, soon afterwards, I should actually enter and visit this strange island-city, this heaven-like republic. So now, Heaven be praised, Venice is no longer to me a bare and a hollow name, which has so long tormented me,—*me,* the mental enemy of mere verbal sounds. . . .

I am well lodged at the sign of the *Queen of England,* not far from the square of St. Mark, which is, indeed, the chief advantage of the spot. My windows look upon a narrow canal between lofty houses, a bridge of one arch is immediately below me, and directly opposite is a narrow, bustling alley. Thus am I lodged, and here I shall remain until I have made up my packet for Germany, and until I am satiated with the sight of the city. I can now really enjoy the solitude for which I have longed so ardently, for nowhere does a man feel himself more solitary than in a crowd, where he must push his way unknown to every one. Perhaps in Venice there is only one person who knows me, and he will not come in contact with me all at once.

* * * *

Sept. 29 *(Michaelmas-Day). Evening.*

So much has already been told and printed about Venice, that I shall not be circumstantial in my description, but shall only say how it struck *me*. Now, in this instance again, that which makes the chief impression upon me, is the people,—a great mass, who live an involuntary existence determined by the changing circumstances of the moment.

It was for no idle fancy that this race fled to these islands; it was no mere whim which impelled those who followed to combine with them; necessity taught them to look for security in a highly disadvantageous situation, that afterwards became most advantageous, endowing them with talent, when the whole northern world was immersed in gloom. Their increase and their wealth were a necessary consequence. New dwellings arose close against dwellings, rocks took the place of sand and marsh, houses sought the sky, being forced like trees inclosed in a narrow compass, to seek in height what was denied them in breadth. Being niggards of every inch of ground, as having been from the very first compressed into a narrow compass, they allowed no more room for the streets than was just necessary to separate a row of houses from the one opposite, and to afford the citizens a narrow passage. Moreover, water supplied the place of street, square, and promenade. The Venetian was forced to become a new creature; and thus Venice can only be compared with itself. The large canal, winding like a serpent, yields to no street in the world, and nothing can be put by the side of the space in front of St. Mark's square—I mean that great mirror of water, which is encompassed by Venice.

I hastened to fix my first impression of the whole, and without a guide, and merely observing the cardinal points, threw myself into the labyrinth of the city, which though everywhere intersected by larger or smaller canals, is again connected by bridges. The narrow and crowded appearance of the whole cannot be conceived by one who has not seen it. In most cases one can quite or nearly measure the breadth of the street, by stretching out one's arms, and in the narrowest, a person would scrape his elbows if he walked with his arms akimbo. Some streets, indeed, are wider, and here and there is a little square, but comparatively all may be called narrow.

I easily found the grand canal, and the principal bridge—the Rialto, which consists of a single arch of white marble. Looking down from this, one has a fine prospect—the canal full of ships, which bring every necessary from the continent, and put it chiefly at this place to unload, while between them is a swarm of gondolas. Today, especially, being

Michaelmas, the view was wonderfully animated; but to give some notion of it, I must go back a little.

The two principal parts of Venice, which are divided by the grand canal, are connected by no other bridge than the Rialto, but several means of communication are provided, and the river is crossed in open boats at certain fixed points. Today a very pretty effect was produced, by the number of well-dressed ladies, who, their features concealed beneath large black veils, were being ferried over in large parties at a time, in order to go to the church of the Archangel, whose festival was being solemnized. I left the bridge and went to one of the points of landing, to see the parties as they left the boats. I discovered some very fine forms and faces among them.

After I had become tired of this amusement. I seated myself in a gondola, and, quitting the narrow streets with the intention of witnessing a spectacle of an opposite description, went along the northern part of the grand canal, into the lagoon and then entered the Giudecca canal, going as far as the square of St. Mark. Now was I also one of the birds of the Adriatic sea, as every Venetian feels himself to be whilst reclining in his gondola. I then thought with due honor of my good father, who knew of nothing better than to talk about the things I now witnessed. And will it not be so with me likewise? All that surrounds me is dignified—a grand venerable work of combined human energies, a noble monument, not of a ruler, but of a people. And if their lagoon is gradually filling up, if unwholesome vapors are floating over the marsh, if their trade is declining and their power has sunk, still the great place and the essential character will not for a moment be less venerable to the observer. Venice succumbs to time, like everything that has a phenomenal existence.

* * * *

Sept. 30.

Towards evening I again rambled, without a guide, into the remotest quarters of the city. The bridges here are all provided with stairs, that gondolas, and even larger vessels, may pass conveniently under the arches. I sought to find my way in and out of this labyrinth, without asking anybody, and, on this occasion also, only guiding myself by the points of the compass. One disentangles one's self at last, but it is a wonderful complication, and my manner of obtaining a sensible impression of it is the best. I have now been to the remotest points of the city and observed the conduct, mode of life, manners, and character of the inhabitants; and in every quarter they are different. Gracious Heaven! What a poor good sort of animal man is, after all!

Most of the smaller houses stand immediately on the canals, but there are here and there quays of stone, beautifully paved, along which one may take a pleasant walk between the water, and the churches and palaces. Particularly cheerful and agreeable is the long stone quay on the northern side, from which the islands are visible, especially Murano, which is a Venice on a small scale.

October 8, 1786

Yesterday I set out early with my tutelary genius, for the Lido, the tongue of land which shuts in the lagoon and divides it from the sea. We landed and walked straight across the isthmus. I heard a loud hollow murmur—it was the sea! I soon saw it: it crested high against the shore as it retired—it was about noon, and time of ebb. I have then at last seen the sea with my own eyes and followed it on its beautiful bed, just as it quitted it. I wished the children had been there to gather the shells; childlike I myself picked up plenty of them; however, I attempted to make them useful; I tried to dry in them some of the fluid of the cuttle fish, which here dart away from you in shoals.

On the Lido, not far from the sea, is the burial place of Englishmen and a little further on of the Jews: both alike are refused the privilege of resting in consecrated ground. I found here the tomb of Smith, the noble English consul, and of his first wife. It is to him that I owe my first copy of Palladio; I thanked him for it here in his unconsecrated grave. And not only unconsecrated, but half buried is the tomb. The Lido is at best but a sandbank: The sand is carried from it backwards and forwards by the wind and thrown up in heaps in encroaching on every side. In a short time the monument, which is tolerably high, will no longer be visible.

But the *sea*—it is a grand *sight!* I will try and get a sail upon it some day in a fishing boat: the gondolas never venture out so far.

* * * *

Oct. 8, 1786.

On the seacoast I found also several plants, whose characters similar to others I already knew, enabled me to recognize pretty well their properties. They are all alike, fat and strong—full of sap and clammy—and it is evident that the old salt of the sandy soil, but still more the saline atmosphere, gives them these properties. Like aquatic plants they abound in sap, and are fleshy and tough, like mountainous ones; those whose leaves show a tendency to put forth prickles, after the manner of thistles, have them extremely sharp and strong. I found a bush with leaves of this kind. It looked very much like our harmless coltsfoot, only here it is armed with sharp weapons, the leaves like leather, as also are the seed-vessels, and the stalk very thick and succulent. I bring with me seeds and specimens of the leaves.

The fishmarket, with its numberless marine productions, afforded me much amusement. I often go there to contemplate the poor captive inhabitants of the sea.

* * * *

Venice, Oct. 9, 1786.

A delicious day from morning to night! I have been towards Chioggia as far as Pelestrina, where are the great structures, called *Murazzi,* which the Republic has caused to be raised against the sea. They are of hewn stone and properly are intended to protect from the fury of the wild element the tongue of land called the Lido, which separates the lagoon from the sea.

The lagoon is the work of old nature. First of all, the land and tide, the ebb and flow, working against one another, and then the gradual sinking of the primal waters were together the causes why at the upper end of the Adriatic, we find a pretty extensive range of marshes which, covered by the flood-tide, are partly left bare by the ebb. Art took possession of the highest spots, and thus arose Venice, formed out of a group of a hundred isles and surrounded by hundreds more. Moreover, at an incredible expense of money and labor, deep canals have been dug through the marshes in order that at the time of high water ships of war might pass to the chief points. What human industry and wit contrived and executed of old, skill and industry must now keep up. The Lido, a long narrow strip of land, separates the lagoon from the sea, which can enter only at two points—at the castle and at the opposite end near Chioggia. The tide flows in usually twice a day, and with the ebb again carries out the waters twice and always by the same channel and in the same direction. The flood covers the lower parts of the morass, but leaves the higher, if not dry, yet visible.

The case would be quite altered were the sea to make new ways for itself, to attack the tongue of land and flow in and out whereever it chose. Not to mention that the little villages on the Lido, Pelestrina, and others would be overwhelmed, the canals of communication would be choked up, and while the water involved all in ruin, the Lido would be changed into an island, and the islands which now lie behind it be converted into necks and tongues of land. To guard against this it was necessary to protect the Lido as far as possible, lest the furious element should capriciously attack and overthrow what man had already taken possession of, and with a certain end and purpose given shape and use to.

In extraordinary cases when the sea rises above measure, it is especially necessary to prevent it entering at more than two points. Accordingly the rest of the sluicegates being shut, with all its violence it is unable to enter and in a few hours submits to the law of the ebb, and its fury lessens.

Otherwise Venice has nothing to fear; the extreme slowness with which the sealine retires, assures to her thousands of years yet, and by prudently deepening the canals from time to time, they will easily maintain their possessions against the inroads of the water.

I could only wish that they kept their streets a little cleaner: a duty which is as necessary as it is easy of performance, and which in fact becomes of great consequence in the course of centuries. Even now in the principal thoroughfares it is forbidden to throw anything into the canals: the sweepings even of the streets may not be cast into them. No measures, however, are taken to prevent the rain, which here falls in sudden and violent torrents, from carrying off the dirt which is collected in piles at the corner of every street, and washing it into the lagoon—nay, what is still worse, into the gutters for carrying off the water, which consequently are often so completely stopped up, that the principal squares are in danger of being under water. Even in the smaller piazza of St. Mark's, I have seen the gullies which are well laid down there, as well as in the greater square, choked up and full of water.

When a rainy day comes, the filth is intolerable; everyone is cursing and scolding. In ascending and descending the bridges one soils one's mantle and great coat, which is here worn all the year long, and as one goes along in shoes and silk stockings, one gets splashed, and then scolds, for it is not common mud, but mud that adheres and stains that one is here splashed with. The weather soon becomes fine again, and then no one thinks of cleaning the streets.

Venice, Oct. 9, 1786.

I now turn with my narrative once more to the sea. I there saw yesterday the haunts of the sea-snails, the limpets, and the crab, and was highly delighted with the sight. What a precious glorious object is a living thing—how wonderfully adapted to its state of existence, how true, how *real*. What great advantages do I not derive now from my former studies of nature, and how delighted am I with the opportunity of continuing them! But as the present is a matter that admits of being communicated to my friends, I will not seek to excite their sympathy merely by exclamations.

The stoneworks which have been built against the inroads of the sea consist first of all of several steep steps; then comes a slightly inclined plane, then again they rise a step, which is once more succeeded by a greatly ascending surface, and last of all comes a perpendicular wall with an overhanging coping—over these steps—over these planes the raging sea rises until in extraordinary cases it even dashes over the highest wall with its projecting head.

The sea is followed by its inhabitants, little periwinkles good to eat, . . . limpets, and whatever else has the power of motion. But scarcely have these little creatures taken possession of the smooth walls, ere the sea retires again, swelling and cresting as it came. At first the crowd knows not where they are, and keep hoping that the briny flood will soon return to them but it still keeps away; the sun comes out and quickly dries them up, and now begins the retreat. It is on these occasions that the crabs seek their prey. Nothing more wonderful or comical can be seen than the maneuvers of these little creatures, with their round bodies and two long claws (for the other spider-feet are scarcely worth noticing). On these stilted forelegs, as it were, they stride along watching the limpets, and as soon as one moves itself under its shell on the rock, a crab comes up and inserting the point of his claw in the tiny interstice between the shell and the rock turns it over, and so manages to swallow the oyster. The limpets, on the other hand, proceed cautiously on their way, and by suction fasten themselves firmly to the rocky surface as soon as they are aware of the proximity of their foe. In such cases the crab deports himself amusingly enough; round and round the pulpy animal who keeps himself safe beneath his roof will he go with singular politeness; but not succeeding with all his coaxing and being unable to overcome its powerful muscle, he leaves in despair this intended victim and hastens after another who may be wandering less cautiously on his way.

I never saw a crab succeed in his designs, although I have watched for hours the retreat of the little troop as they crawled down the two planes and the intermediate steps.

George Sand

·◄ 1804–1876 ►·

George Sand and Alfred de Musset, the French poet, went to Italy in December, 1833, staying for five months, to July, 1834, with the express idea of using Venice as a setting for a novel. The relationship having ended disastrously, it was Sand who wrote the novel, Consuelo, *in 1842. In view of Sand's notoriety, her American translator felt constrained to explain that in his opinion, the prejudices "excited against the author . . . have arisen as much from the bold and uncompromising manner in which she has asserted and maintained the rights of humanity, and especially of her own sex, as from any offenses against the laws of society, of which she may have been accused." In addition to having dealt with problems which are only now being frankly probed, her deep romantic love of nature as she found it in Venice is shown in her* Lettres d'un Voyageur, *from which "April in Venice" is taken. Among her numerous novels were two others about Venice,* Les Maitres Mosaistes *and* L'Usoque.

APRIL IN VENICE, 1834

My friend, you have no idea of what Venice is. She has not quitted the mourning garb she assumed in winter, when you saw her ancient pillars of Greek marble, which in color and form you compared to dry bones. At present, spring has breathed upon her, as though her breath were emerald dust. The base of her palaces, where oysters clustered in the stagnant moss, is now covered with the most tender green, and gondolas float between two banks of this verdure, soft as velvet, and the noise of the water dies away languishingly, mingled with the foam of the gondola's track. All the balconies are filled with vases of flowers; and the flowers of Venice, brought to light in this warm clayey soil, blossoming in this damp atmosphere, have a freshness, a richness of tissue, and a languor of attitude which makes them resemble the women of this climate, whose

139

beauty is brilliant and evanescent as their own. The double flowering bramble climbs round every pillar, and suspends its garlands of white rosettes, from the black arabesques of the balconies. The vanilla iris, the Persian tulip, so beautifully striped with pure red and white that it seems formed from the material in which the ancient Venetians used to dress; Greek roses, and pyramids of gigantic campanulas are heaped in the vases which cover the balustrades. Sometimes there is quite an arbor of honeysuckle crowning the balcony from one end to the other, and two or three cages hidden in the foliage contain nightingales that sing day and night, as though they were in the open country. These tame nightingales are a luxury peculiar to Venice. The women there have a remarkable talent for bringing up and educating, so to speak, these poor harmonious prisoners, and know how, by every species of delicacy and kindness, to soften the *ennui* of their captivity. In the night, the birds call to and answer one another from each side of the canal. If a serenade passes, they are quiet and listen, and as soon as it has passed by, they recommence their song and seem vying to surpass the melody they have just heard. At every street corner, the Madonna shelters her mysterious lamp under a jasmine canopy; and the *traghetti,* shaded by trellises, diffuse, all along the Grand Canal, the perfume of the vine in flower, perhaps the sweetest odor among plants.

These *traghetti* are the stations for the public gondolas. Those which are established on the shores of the Grand Canal are the rendezvous of the porters who come to smoke and talk with the gondoliers. These often present very theatrical-looking groups. Whilst one, lying on his gondola, alternately smiles and yawns at the stars, another on the shore, with open breast, and air of mockery, his hat thrust back upon a forest of long crisp curled hair, throws his great shadow on the wall. He is the hero of the *traghetto.*

Towards sunset I was in the public garden. As usual, there was very little company there. The elegant Venetian ladies dread the heat, and dare not go out in full daylight, but they also dread the cold, and never venture out in the night. There are three or four days in each season which seem expressly made for them, and then they raise the covers of their gondolas, but they rarely put their foot to the ground.

They are a species set apart, beings so frail and delicate, that one ray of sunlight would wither their beauty, or one breath of the breeze expose their very existence. All civilized men seek those places by preference where they may meet the fair sex; the theatres, the *conversazioni,* the cafés, and the sheltered enclosure of the Piazzetta, about seven o'clock in the evening. Therefore few remain in the gardens, but grumbling old men, stupid smokers, or melancholy victims to bile. You may class me amongst whichever you like of these three classes.

Gradually, I found myself quite alone; the elegant cafe, which extends itself to the lagoons, extinguished its tapers placed in lilies and marine flowers made of the crystal of Murano.

The last time you saw this garden, it was damp and sad enough! . . . But the spring! As you say, who can resist the influence of the month of April? And at Venice, my dear friend, it is yet more impossible.

Even the stones are being clothed with verdure; those infected marshes which our gondolas so carefully avoided, two months since, are now watery meadows covered by cresses, seaweeds, reeds and flags, and all sorts of marine mosses, exhaling a peculiar perfume, beloved by those to whom the sea is a cherished memory; and harboring thousands of sea-gulls, . . . and the lesser bustard. The petrel incessantly hovers over these floating meadows, where the ebb and flow bring the waters of the Adriatic every day, teeming with myriads of insects, coral, and shells.

Instead of the icy-cold alleys from which we so hastily fled, on the evening before your departure, and which I had never since had the courage to revisit, a half-warm sand, patches of Easter daisies, and groves of sumach and sycamores were just opening to the soft breezes from the Grecian shore. The little promontory, planted in the English fashion, is so beautiful, so thickly grown, so rich in flowers, perfume, and prospect, that I asked myself if it were not the promised land my dreams had revealed to me. But no, the promised land is pure from all sorrow, and this is already watered with my tears.

The sun had just sunk behind the Vicentine mountains. Blue mists were covering the whole heaven above Venice.

The tower of St. Mark, the cupolas of Santa Maria, and little groves of pinnacles and minarets which rise from all quarters of the town were defined like so many black points upon the vivid background of the horizon. The color of the heavens changed through a wonderful gradation of softening tints, from crimson to blue; and the water, calm and limpid, faithfully reflected the rainbow tints of color. Below the town, the waves looked exactly like a large mirror of red copper. Never had I seen Venice so beautiful, so fairylike. This black shadow thrown between the sky and the glowing waters, as though in a lake of fire, seemed one of those sublime aberrations of architecture which the poet of the Apocalypse saw, in his visions, floating on the shores of Patmos, when he dreamed his new Jerusalem, and compared her to a bride.

Little by little the bright colors faded, the outlines became more massive, the depths more mysterious. Venice assumed the aspect of an immense fleet, then of a lofty wood of cypresses, into which the canals flowed like high roads of silver sand. At such moments I delight in contemplating the distance. When the outlines become vague, when every object is trembling in the mist, when my imagination may disport in an immense field of conjecture and caprice, when, by merely half closing the eyes, one can in fancy destroy a city, turn it into a forest, a camp, or a cemetery, when I can metamorphose the high roads, white with dust, into peaceful rivers, and the rivulets, winding so serpent-like down the dark verdure of the hills, into rapid torrents, then it is that I really enjoy Nature, I play with her, I reign over her, with one glance I possess her and people her with my own fantasies.

* * * *

The absence of horses and carriages and the resonance of the canal make Venice the most delightful city for unceasing songs and serenading. One must be an enthusiast indeed to fancy that the gondolier choruses are better than those of the opera at Paris, as I have heard asserted by some individuals of a particularly happy temperament, but it is quite certain that one of those choruses, heard from afar under the arcades of these Moorish palaces, looking so white in the moon's rays, gives more pleasure even than better music executed under a colonnade formed of painted canvas. These rough uncultivated dilettanti shout in tune and time; and the calm marble echoes prolong these rude and grave harmonies, like the winds over the sea. The magic of acoustic effect, and the desire to hear some sort of harmony in the silence of these enchanted nights, make one listen with indulgence, and almost I may say with gratitude, to the humblest melody which floats by, and is lost in the distance. . . . Fairy days of Venice. . . . No one has ever said enough of the beauty of the heavens, and the delights of the night at Venice. The lagoon is so calm, that in fine evenings, the stars do not even tremble on its surface. When you are in the midst, it is so blue, so quiet that the outline of the horizon cannot be distinguished, and the waves and the heavens form an azure veil, where reverie loses itself and sleeps. The atmosphere is so transparent, so pure that thousands more stars may be seen than in our North of France. I have seen here nights, when the silvery luster of the stars occupied more space in the firmament than the blue of the atmosphere. It was a galaxy of diamonds giving almost as good a light as the moon at Paris. . . . Here Nature, more powerful in her influence, perhaps, imposes too much silence on the mind; she sends all thought to sleep, but agitates the heart, and dominates the senses. One must not even dream, unless one is a man of genius, of writing poems during these voluptuous nights: one must love or sleep.

As for sleeping, there is a most delicious spot: the platform of white marble which descends from the Viceroy's gardens to the canal. When the ornamented gate is shut on the garden-side, one can go in a gondola to these steps, still warm from the rays of the setting sun, and remain without being interrupted by an inopportune stroller, unless he be endowed with the faith so much needed by St. Peter. Many hours have I passed there alone, thinking of nothing, whilst Catullo and his gondola slumbered in the midst of the waters, within call.

When the breath of midnight passes over the linden trees, and scatters their blossoms over the waters, when the perfume of wallflowers and geraniums rises in gusts, as though the earth gave forth her sighs of fragrance to the moon; when the cupolas of Santa Maria raise towards heaven their alabaster hemispheres and their turban-crowned minarets; when all is white, the water, the sky, the marble, the three elements of Venice, and when from the tower of St. Mark a giant sound hovers over my head, then I begin to feel life through every pore, and evil be to him who should then come to make an appeal to my soul! I vegetate, I repose, I forget. Who would not do the same in my place? . . . I defy anyone, no matter who, to prevent me from sleeping happily when I see Venice, so impoverished, so oppressed, so miserable, still so beautiful, so calm, in spite of men and of time. Behold her, round me, admiring herself in the lagoons with the air of a sultana; and this populace of fishermen, sleeping on the pavement, winter as well as summer, with no other pillow than one of granite, no other mattress than a tattered cloak; is not such a populace a great example of philosophy? When it has no longer wherewithal to purchase a pound of rice, it sings a chorus to drive away the pangs of hunger; thus braving masters and misery, as it used to brave cold, heat, and the sudden tempest. It would require many years of slavery to imbrute entirely this careless frivolous character, so accustomed for many years to be nourished with *fêtes* and diversions. Existence is still so easy at Venice!

Charles Dickens

·◁ 1812–1870 ▷·

Dickens visited Venice in 1844 and 1853. When he woke in the Hotel Danieli and saw the quay, the Riva degli Schiavoni, for the first time, the most popular English author of his day said that "no words can describe the freshness of the air . . . the sparkling of the water under the rays of the sun that shine in the clear blue sky." Elsewhere he wrote: "Nothing in the world that you have heard about Venice equals the magnificence and wonderful reality . . . that exceeds the most extravagant dream; the wildest visions of The Arabian Nights *are nothing to the Piazza San Marco, and the first impression of the inside of the church . . . opium couldn't build such a place, and enchantment couldn't shadow it forth in vision . . . I've never before visited a place that I am afraid to describe." In* Pictures from Italy *Dickens described Venice as "An Italian Dream."*

AN ITALIAN DREAM, 1844

It was now quite night, and we were at the waterside. There lay here, a black boat, with a little house or cabin in it of the same mournful color. When I had taken my seat in this, the boat was paddled, by two men, towards a great light, lying in the distance on the sea.

Ever and again, there was a dismal sigh of wind. It ruffled the water, and rocked the boat, and sent the dark clouds flying before the stars. I could not but think how strange it was, to be floating away at that hour: leaving the land behind, and going on, towards this light upon the sea. It soon began to burn brighter; and from being one light became a cluster of tapers, twinkling and shining out of the water, as the boat approached towards them by a dreamy kind of track, marked out upon the sea by posts and piles.

We had floated on, five miles or so, over the dark water, when I heard it rippling in my dream, against some obstruction near at hand. Looking out attentively, I saw, through the gloom, a something black and massive—like a shore, but lying close and flat upon the water, like a raft—which we were gliding past. The chief of the two rowers said it was a burial-place.

Full of the interest and wonder which a cemetery lying out there, in the lonely sea, inspired, I turned to gaze upon it as it should recede in our path, when it was quickly shut out from my view. Before I knew by what, or how, I found that we were gliding up a street—a phantom street; the houses rising on both sides, from the water, and the black boat gliding on beneath their windows. Lights were shining from some of these case-ments, plumbing the depth of the black stream with their reflected rays, but all was profoundly silent.

So we advanced into this ghostly city, continuing to hold our course through narrow streets and lanes, all filled and flowing with water. Some of the corners, where our way branched off, were so acute and narrow, that it seemed impossible for the long slender boat to turn them; but the rowers, with a low melodious cry of warning, sent it skimming on without a pause. Sometimes, the rowers of another black boat like our own, echoed the cry, and slackening their speed (as I thought we did ours) would come flitting past us like a dark shadow. Other boats, of the same sombre hue, were lying moored, I thought, to painted pillars, near to dark mysterious doors, that opened straight upon the water. Some of these were empty; in some, the rowers lay asleep; towards one, I saw some figures coming down a gloomy archway from the interior of a palace: gaily dressed, and attended by torchbearers. It was but a glimpse I had of them, for a bridge, so low and close upon the boat seemed ready to fall down and crush us; one of the many bridges that perplexed the dream: blotted them out, instantly. On we went, floating towards the heart of this strange place—with water all about us where never water was elsewhere—clusters of houses, churches, heaps of stately buildings growing out of it—and, everywhere, the same extraordinary silence. Presently, we shot across a broad and open stream; and passing, as I thought, before a spacious paved quay, where the bright lamps with which it was illuminated showed long rows of arches and pillars, of ponderous construction and great strength, but as light to the eye as garlands of hoar-frost or gossamer—and where, for the first time, I saw people walking—arrived at a flight of steps leading from the water to a large mansion, where, having passed through corridors and galleries innumerable, I lay down to rest; listening to the black boats stealing up and down below the window on the rippling water, till I fell asleep.

The glory of the day that broke upon me in this dream; its freshness, motion, buoyancy; its sparkles of the sun in water; its clear blue sky and rustling air; no waking words can tell. But, from my window, I looked down on boats and barks; on masts, sails, cordage, flags; on groups of busy sailors, working at the cargoes of these vessels; on wide quays, strewn with bales, casks, merchandise of many kinds; on great ships, lying near at hand in stately indolence; on islands, crowned with gorgeous domes and turrets: and where golden crosses glittered in the light, atop of wondrous churches, springing from the sea! Going down upon the margin of the green sea, rolling on before the door, and filling all the streets, I came upon a place of such surpassing beauty, and such grandeur, that all the rest was poor and faded, in comparison with its absorbing loveliness.

It was a great piazza, as I thought; anchored, like all the rest, in the deep ocean. On its broad bosom, was a palace, more majestic and magnificent in its old age, than all the buildings of the earth, in the high prime and fullness of their youth. Cloisters and galleries: so light, they might have been the work of fairy hands: so strong that centuries had battered them in vain: wound round and round this palace, and enfolded it with a cathedral, gorgeous in the wild luxuriant fancies, of the East. At no great distance from its porch, a lofty tower, standing by itself and rearing its proud head, alone, into the sky, looked out upon the Adriatic Sea. Near to the margin of the stream were two ill-omened pillars of red granite; one having on its top a figure with a sword and shield; the other, a winged lion. Not far from these again, a second tower: richest of the rich in all its decorations: even here, where all was rich: sustained aloft, a great orb, gleaming with gold and deepest blue: the Twelve Signs painted on it, and a mimic sun revolving in its course around them: while above, two bronze giants hammered out the hours upon a sounding bell. An oblong square of lofty houses of the whitest stone, surrounded by a light and beautiful arcade, formed part of this enchanted scene; and, here and there, gay masts for flags rose, tapering, from the pavement of the unsubstantial ground.

I thought I entered the cathedral, and went in and out among its many arches: traversing its whole extent. A grand and dreamy structure, of immense proportions; golden with old mosaics; redolent of perfumes; dim with the smoke of incense; costly in treasure of precious stones and metals, glittering through iron bars; holy with the bodies of deceased saints; rainbow-hued with windows of stained glass; dark with carved woods and colored marbles; obscure in its vast heights, and lengthened distances; shining with silver lamps and winking lights; unreal, fantastic, solemn, inconceivable throughout. I thought I entered the old palace; pacing silent galleries and council-chambers, where the old rulers of this mistress of the waters looked sternly out, in pictures, from the walls, and where her high-prowed galleys, still victorious on canvas, fought and conquered as of old. I thought I wandered through its halls of state and triumph—bare and empty now!—and musing on its pride and might, extinct: for that was past; all past: heard a voice say, "Some tokens of its ancient rule, and some consoling reasons for its downfall, may be traced here, yet!"

I dreamed that I was led on, then, into some jealous rooms, communicating with a prison near the palace; separated from it by a lofty bridge crossing a narrow street; and called, I dreamed, the Bridge of Sighs.

But first I passed two jagged slits in a stone wall; the lions' mouths—now toothless—where, in the distempered horror of my sleep, I thought denunciations of innocent men to the old wicked Council, had been dropped through, many a time, when the night was dark. So, when I saw the council-room to which such prisoners were taken for examination, and the door by which they passed out, when they were condemned—a door that never closed upon a man with life and hope before him—my heart appeared to die within me.

It was smitten harder though, when, torch in hand, I descended from the cheerful day into two ranges, one below another, of dismal, awful, horrible stone cells. They were quite dark. Each had a loophole in its massive wall, where, in the old time, every day, a torch was placed—I dreamed—to light the prisoner within, for half an hour. The captives, by the glimmering of these brief rays, had scratched and cut inscriptions in the blackened vaults. I saw them. For their labor with a rusty nail's point, had outlived their agony and them, through many generations.

One cell, I saw, in which no man remained for more than four-and-twenty hours; being marked for dead before he entered it. Hard by, another, and a dismal one, whereto, at midnight, the confessor came—a monk brown-robed, and hooded—ghastly in the day, and free bright air, but in the midnight of that murky prison, Hope's extinguisher, and Murder's herald. I had my foot upon the spot, where, at the same dread hour, the shriven prisoner was strangled; and struck my hand upon the guilty door—low browed and stealthy—through which the lumpish sack was carried out into a boat; and rowed away, and drowned where it was death to cast a net.

Around this dungeon stronghold, and above some part of it: licking the rough walls without, and smearing them with damp and slime within: stuffing dank weeds and refuse into chinks and crevices, as if the very stones and bars had mouths to stop: furnishing a smooth road for the removal of the bodies of the secret victims of the State—a road so ready that it went along with them, and ran before them, like a cruel officer— flowed the same water that filled this dream of mine, and made it seem one, even at the time.

Descending from the palace by a staircase, called, I thought, the Giant's—I had some imaginary recollection of an old man abdicating, coming, more slowly and more feebly, down it, when he heard the bell, proclaiming his successor—I glided off, in one of the dark boats, until we came to an old arsenal guarded by four marble lions. To make my dream more monstrous and unlikely, one of these had words and sentences upon its body, inscribed there, at an unknown time, and in an unknown language; so that their purport was a mystery to all men. . . .

In the luxurious wonder of so rare a dream, I took but little heed of time, and had but little understanding of its flight. But there were days and nights in it; and when the sun was high, and when the rays of lamps were crooked in the running water, I was still afloat, I thought: plashing the slippery walls and houses with the cleavings of the tide, as my black boat, borne upon it, skimmed along the streets.

Sometimes, alighting at the doors of churches and vast palaces, I wandered on, from room to room, from aisle to aisle, through labyrinths of rich altars, ancient monuments; decayed apartments where the furniture, half awful, half grotesque, was moldering away. Pictures were there, replete with such enduring beauty and expression; with such passion, truth and power that they seemed so many young and fresh realities among a host of specters. I thought these often intermingled with the old days of the city with its beauties, tyrants, captains, patriots, merchants, courtiers, priests; nay, with its very stones, and bricks, and public places, all of which lived again, about me, on the walls. Then, coming down some marble staircase where the water lapped and oozed against the lower steps, I passed into my boat again, and went on in my dream.

Floating down narrow lanes, where carpenters, at work with plane and chisel in their shops, tossed the light shaving straight upon the water, where it lay like weed, or ebbed away before me in a tangled heap. Past open doors, decayed and rotten from long steeping in the wet, through which some scanty patch of vine shone green and bright, making unusual shadows on the pavement with its trembling leaves. Past quays and terraces, where women, gracefully veiled, were passing and repassing, and where idlers were reclining in the sunshine, on flagstones and on flights of steps. Past bridges, where there were idlers too, loitering and looking over. Below stone balconies, erected at a giddy height, before the loftiest windows of the loftiest houses. Past plots of garden, theatre, shrines, prodigious piles of architecture—Gothic—Saracenic—fanciful with all the fancies of all times and countries. Past buildings that were high, and low, and black, and white, and straight, and crooked, mean and grand, crazy and strong. Twining among a tangled lot of boats and barges, and shooting out at last into a Grand Canal! There, in the errant fancy of my dream, I saw old Shylock passing to and fro upon a bridge, all built upon with shops and humming with the tongues of men; a form I seemed to know for Desdemona's leaned down through a latticed blind to pluck a flower. And in the dream, I thought that Shakespeare's spirit was abroad upon the water somewhere: stealing through the city.

At night, when two votive lamps burnt before an image of the Virgin, in a gallery outside the great cathedral, near the roof, I fancied that the great piazza of the Winged Lion was a blaze of cheerful light, and that its whole arcade was thronged with people, while crowds were diverting themselves in splendid coffee-houses opening from it—which were never shut, I thought, but open all night long. When the bronze giants struck the hour of midnight on the bell, I thought the life and animation of the city were all centered here; and as I rowed away, abreast the silent quays, I only saw them dotted, here and there, with sleeping boatmen wrapped up in their cloaks, and lying at full length upon the stones.

But close about the quays and churches, palaces and prisons: sucking at their walls, and welling up into the secret places of the town: crept the water always. Noiseless and watchful: coiled round and round it, in its many folds, like an old serpent: waiting for the time, I thought, when people should look down into its depths for any stone of the old city that had claimed to be its mistress.

Thus it floated me away, until I awoke in the old marketplace at Verona. I have, many and many a time, thought since, of this strange dream upon the water: half-wondering if it lie there yet, and if its name be *Venice*.

Euphemia Gray Ruskin

⊰ 1828–1897 ⊱

Euphemia Gray shared John Ruskin's life in Venice while he was writing
The Stones of Venice. *Her exuberant personal correspondence written
from the Hotel Danieli and then from the Casa Wetzlar (now the Gritti
Palace Hotel) describing their daily lives was published more than a
hundred years later, in 1965.* Effie in Venice: Her Picture of Society and
Life with John Ruskin, 1849–1852, *edited by Mary Lutyens, covers two
periods of residence in Austria-occupied Venice, with an interval in
England March, 1850–September, 1851. During their second residence,
the Austrians had resumed the social order that was broken off in 1848 by
the unsuccessful attempt of the Venetians, under Daniele Manin, to
re-establish the Republic overthrown by Napoleon. "Effie's" letters,
composed in the flush of her desire to "shine in society" are now a
valuable document of the lavish revels of the Austrian overlords of the
city. The Ruskin marriage was annulled after six years and Euphemia
Gray married the pre-Raphaelite painter, John Everett Millais.*

EFFIE IN VENICE, 1849–1852

Venice, 13th November, 1849

My dearest Mother

. . . It is the most exquisite place I have ever seen and we shall not quit
it in a hurry if I can help it, and at any rate not till this time next month.

Your letters take exactly 8 days so that you can always count. We are
living in Danieli's Hotel, formerly a splendid Palace with marble staircase and doors and Balconies looking out on the sea covered with ships
and churches and the Doge's Palace, the finest building in the world, with
St. Mark's Place and Church 100 yards off. There, every night the

Austrian Band plays, the finest trained I ever heard, numbering about 60 men. The whole of Venice seems to turn in there at that time. The place is like a vast drawing room lighted enough by the gas from the arcades all round the square under which sit all the Ladies & gentlemen at their coffee, iced water and cigars with a dense crowd in the center of men, women, children, soldiers, Turks, magnificent Greek costumes and sky above studded with innumerable twinkling stars. I was walking there with John last night till past eight without any bonnet but my hair dressed— walking about like all the rest amongst the crowd, taking our coffee under the Arcade and enjoying ourselves extremely. The women here have the most magnificent black hair I ever saw, so beautifully plaited and stand- ing in a complete circle of three to four inches in width all round their heads but I can't draw it to give you the slightest idea, but the conse- quence is that whenever a bonnet is put on over such a mass they look the most extraordinary antics you ever saw & any Ladies that do wear bonnets, they are the shape worn some six years ago and look as if they had been brought out of the ark. I intend getting the black veils of the country and discarding our bonnets till the winter begins as it is far too warm yet for velvet or satin. . . .

I cannot understand why Dr Macfarlane had not enough exercise here. It must have been entirely his own fault because there is no better or more delightful exercise for every muscle than standing and rowing a Gondola and not easy either, and if he did not like that, there are most charming little streets intersecting the whole of Venice like a puzzle, none more than ten feet broad where you could run about and lose yourself in for a whole day as we did yesterday for a couple of hours, and it is so delicious to think that you can never be run over, no carriages, carts, horses, barrows or anything but people and gondolas. This last is the most luxurious conveyance in the world if you can fancy yourself moved through canals of oil. There is no more motion on the green canals and you lie all your length on soft cushions and pass other people in the same happy ease as yourself. I often wish you were all here for nothing could be more enjoyable.

We had a delightful sail across the lagoon from Mestre on Saturday having passed Vicenza and Padua in the railway. Formerly it brought you into Venice across the lagoon but parts of the Bridge were thrown down during the Bombardment and they are now repairing it. If I was Radetzky not one stone of it should be left on another. It completely destroys your first impressions of Venice and it cost the Italians £1,500,000, and no good has come of it so far & the everlasting shame besides of turning half their Churches into Mills because they can't be troubled to keep them in order, covered with invaluable Frescoes of Titian, Giorgione, the Bellinis & others and giving all that money for a Railway bridge, but they have been dreadfully punished already. . . .

Venice, 15th November, 1849

Dearest George [George Gray, Effie's brother],

I have been intending for some days to answer your kind note but I have got an Italian master and what with writing exercises and learning Dialogue I find all my spare time taken up as our afternoons and evenings are spent in the open air. . . . I find myself much better since I came here and the air seems to agree very well with me. John thinks, if his Father will allow him, of buying a little house here and he finds so much work before him, and I think if one lived years in Venice there would still be half of its treasures to explore. . . .

John and the Gondolier rowed me over to Lido, one of the outer Islands between Venice and the Adriatic. I wished to see the open sea and we walked across the Island over the Jews' burying Ground, where they formerly were all obliged to be buried. All the tombstones were well sculptured and with Hebrew writing on them. On the other side we ran down to the sea. The tide was coming in and the green waves crested with white foam were very splendid, and pretty shells striped in many colors were lying on the sand. When we returned the wind rose and it was quite stormy. A fleet of Venetian fishing boats literally flew past us with their beautiful sails spread. They are of a rich orange color with a cross and the world in black painted on them and when the sun shines on them you cannot conceive anything more vivid in color or more elegant in form. John is very busy in the Doge's Palace all day and as yet he has only drawn one capital of one Pillar and there is something like hundreds on each side. He is going to return however for us today at two & take us through the picture Gallery inside. . . .

Many of the Italians here appear to have no homes at all and to be perfectly happy. At eight o'clock in the evening when we return from hearing the Band we see them all lying packed together at the edge of the bridges, wrapped in their immense brown cloaks and large hoods as warm as fires. Then in the morning there are little stands on all parts of the Quay where they can get hot fish, rice soup, hot elder wine, all kinds of fruit, cigars, and this eating al fresco goes on the whole day, with the occasional interruption of Punch or a Juggler or a storyteller when immediately an immense crowd is collected. Here also some of the Austrian Infantry are exercised and sometimes it is very merry and exciting. The other day an immense Fire and a large cauldron was put in the Square where they burned all the paper money issued by the Provisional Government here while it lasted. I saw the ashes of above 2,000,000 of notes. I must stop now. . . .

Venice, 19th November, 1849

My dear Mama,

 . . ."I have so much to do for my Italian Master whom I like very much now that I have little time for writing and sometimes I feel inclined to adopt John's plan of never writing anywhere but home. On Saturday he took us into the Doge's Palace and showed us the suite of rooms. . . . Its chief riches are in several pictures of enormous dimensions of Tintoretto's and Paul Veronese, one of the former, the three circles of Paradise, covering one entire end of a hall and of most wonderful invention and the coloring wonderful. . . .

Several others of his, one I admired exceedingly, are in other rooms, the Marriage of Bacchus & Adriadne, the Bacchus most lovely, crowned & girt with vine leaves & grapes and such a face, and one can imagine exactly where he got his model, for there is a Cigar boy on the Piazza below, the very creature that I see every day I go out, and that is always the case here showing you that the race is the same although much degraded to what it was, for every where you see men, women, children & dogs here that you think have stepped out of the canvasses of Titian, Tintoretto, Veronese, Giorgione, the Bellinis, &c. and so remarkably so, that we are perpetually turning in the street and saying, "Oh, there is the boy in Tintoretto's Mercury & the Graces," or, "There is the Europa of Paul Veronese."

Mark Twain

Mark Twain delighted his guide when he said that at moments Venice "suggested a half-submerged Arkansas town in a spring freshet." The journalist, novelist, lecturer arrived in Venice July 20, 1867, nine months after the annexation of Venice to the Kingdom of Italy, as part of a tour aboard "The Quaker City" making its way to the Holy Land. The articles he wrote on this "pilgrimage" became The Innocents Abroad *(1869). Criticism of the book by Italians, as one that would make their country unsympathetic to foreigners, was so severe that it was not published in Italy until 1960, almost a hundred years after its original publication. Twain returned to Venice again, in 1878 in the company of his wife and their two daughters. Under the guidance of William Dean Howells Twain viewed Venice in an altogether different light, reflected in his opinions of the art and architecture of Venice in* A Tramp Abroad *(1878).*

THE INNOCENTS ABROAD, 1867

We reached Venice at eight in the evening, and entered a hearse belonging to the Grand Hotel d'Europe. At any rate, it was more like a hearse than anything else, though, to speak by the card, it was a gondola. And this was the storied gondola of Venice!—the fairy boat in which the princely cavaliers of the olden time were wont to cleave the waters of the moonlit canals and look the eloquence of love into the soft eyes of patrician beauties, while the gay gondolier in silken doublet touched his guitar and sang as only gondoliers can sing! This the famed gondola and this the gorgeous gondolier!—the one an inky, rusty old canoe with a sable hearse-body clapped on to the middle of it, and the other a mangy, barefooted gutter-snipe with a portion of his raiment on exhibition which should have been sacred from public scrutiny. Presently, as he turned a

155

corner and shot his hearse into a dismal ditch between two long rows of towering, untenanted buildings, the gay gondolier began to sing, true to the traditions of his race. I stood it a little while. Then I said:

"Now, here, Roderigo Gonzales Michael Angelo, I'm a pilgrim, and I'm a stranger, but I am not going to have my feelings lacerated by any such caterwauling as that. If that goes on, one of us has got to take water. It is enough that my cherished dreams of Venice have been blighted forever as to the romantic gondola and the gorgeous gondolier; this system of destruction shall go no farther; I will accept the hearse, under protest, and you may fly your flag of truce in peace, but here I register a dark and bloody oath that you shan't sing. Another yelp, and overboard you go."

I began to feel that the old Venice of song and story had departed forever. But I was too hasty. In a few minutes we swept gracefully out into the Grand Canal, and under the mellow moonlight the Venice of poetry and romance stood revealed. Right from the water's edge rose long lines of stately palaces of marble; gondolas were gliding swiftly hither and thither and disappearing suddenly through unsuspected gates and alleys; ponderous stone bridges threw their shadows athwart the glittering waves. There was life and motion everywhere, and yet everywhere there was a hush, a stealthy sort of stillness, that was suggestive of secret enterprises of bravoes and of lovers; and, clad half in moonbeams and half in mysterious shadows, the grim old mansions of the Republic seemed to have an expression about them of having an eye out for just such enterprises as these at that same moment. Music came floating over the waters—Venice was complete.

It was a beautiful picture—very soft and dreamy and beautiful. But what was this Venice to compare with the Venice of midnight? Nothing. There was a fête—a grand fête in honor of some saint who had been instrumental in checking the cholera three hundred years ago,* and all Venice was abroad on the water. It was no common affair, for the Venetians did not know how soon they might need the saint's services again, now that the cholera was spreading everywhere. So in one vast space—say a third of a mile wide and two miles long—were collected two thousand gondolas, and every one of them had from two to ten, twenty, and even thirty colored lanterns suspended about it, and from four to a dozen occupants. Just as far as the eye could reach, these painted

---

* The Festa of the Redentore is still observed each year on the third weekend of July to commemorate the Church on the Giudecca designed by Andreas Palladio, and completed in 1592, as a token of thanks for the end of a plague.

lights were massed together—like a vast garden of many-colored flowers, except that these blossoms were never still; they were ceaselessly gliding in and out, and mingling together, and seducing you into bewildering attempts to follow their mazy evolutions. Here and there a strong red, green, or blue glare from a rocket that was struggling to get away splendidly illuminated all the boats around it. Every gondola that swam by us, with its crescents and pyramids and circles of colored lamps hung aloft, and lighting up the faces of the young and the sweet-scented and lovely below, was a picture; and the reflections of those lights, so long, so slender, so numberless, so many-colored and so distorted and wrinkled by the waves, was a picture likewise, and one that was enchantingly beautiful. Many and many a party of young ladies and gentlemen had their state gondolas handsomely decorated, and ate supper on board, bringing their swallow-tailed, white-cravated varlets to wait upon them, and having their tables tricked out as if for a bridal supper. They had brought along the costly globe lamps from their drawing-rooms, and the lace and silken curtains from the same places, I suppose. And they had also brought pianos and guitars, and they played and sang operas, while the plebeian paper-lanterned gondolas from the suburbs and the back alleys crowded around to stare and listen.

There was music everywhere—choruses, string bands, brass bands, flutes, everything. I was so surrounded, walled in with music, magnificence, and loveliness, that I became inspired with the spirit of the scene, and sang one tune myself. However, when I observed that the other gondolas had sailed away, and my gondolier was preparing to go overboard, I stopped.

The fête was magnificent. They kept it up the whole night long, and I never enjoyed myself better than I did while it lasted.

* * * *

The Venetian gondola is as free and graceful, in its gliding movement, as a serpent. It is twenty or thirty feet long, and is narrow and deep, like a canoe; its sharp bow and stern sweep upward from the water like the horns of a crescent with the abruptness of the curve slightly modified.

The bow is ornamented with a steel comb with a battle-axe attachment which threatens to cut passing boats in two occasionally, but never does. The gondola is painted black because in the zenith of Venetian magnificence the gondolas became too gorgeous altogether, and the Senate decreed that all such display must cease, and a solemn unembellished black be substituted. If the truth were known, it would doubtless appear that rich plebeians grew too prominent in their affectation of patrician show on the Grand Canal, and required a wholesome snubbing. Reverence for the hallowed Past and its traditions keeps the dismal fashion in force now that the compulsion exists no longer. So let it remain. It is the color of mourning. Venice mourns. The stern of the boat is decked over and the gondolier stands there. He uses a single oar—a long blade, of course, for he stands nearly erect. A wooden peg, a foot and a half high, with two slight crooks or curves in one side of it and one in the other, projects above the starboard gunwale. Against that peg the gondolier takes a purchase with his oar, changing it at intervals to the other side of the peg or dropping it into another of the crooks, as the steering of the craft may demand—and how in the world he can back and fill, shoot straight ahead, or flirt suddenly around a corner, and make the oar stay in those insignificant notches, is a problem to me and a never-diminishing matter of interest. I am afraid I study the gondolier's marvelous skill more than I do the sculptured palaces we glide among. He cuts a corner so closely, now and then, or misses another gondola by such an imperceptible hair-breadth, that I feel myself "scrooching," as the children say, just as one does when a buggy wheel grazes his elbow. But he makes all his calculations with the nicest precision, and goes darting in and out among a Broadway confusion of busy craft with the easy confidence of the educated hackman. He never makes a mistake.

Sometimes we go flying down the great canals at such a gait that we can get only the merest glimpses into front doors, and again, in obscure alleys in the suburbs, we put on a solemnity suited to the silence, the mildew, the stagnant waters, the clinging weeds, the deserted houses, and the general lifelessness of the place, and move to the spirit of grave meditation.

The gondolier *is* a picturesque rascal for all he wears no satin harness, no plumed bonnet, no silken tights. His attitude is stately; he is lithe and supple; all his movements are full of grace. When his long canoe, and his fine figure, towering from its high perch on the stern, are cut against the evening sky, they make a picture that is very novel and striking to a foreign eye.

We sit in the cushioned carriage-body of a cabin, with the curtains drawn, and smoke, or read, or look out upon the passing boats, the houses, the bridges, the people, and enjoy ourselves much more than we could in a buggy jolting over our cobblestone pavements at home. This is the gentlest, pleasantest locomotion we have ever known.

But it seems queer—ever so queer—to see a boat doing duty as a private carriage. We see business men come to the front door, step into a gondola, instead of a street car, and go off down town to the counting-room. . . .

Spectators

We see little girls and boys go out in gondolas with their nurses, for an airing. We see staid families, with prayer book and beads, enter the gondola dressed in their Sunday best, and float away to church. And at midnight we see the theatre break up and discharge its swarm of hilarious youth and beauty; we hear the cries of the hackman-gondoliers, and behold the struggling crowd jump aboard, and the black multitude of boats go skimming down the moonlit avenues; we see them separate here and there, and disappear up divergent streets; we hear the faint sounds of laughter and of shouted farewells floating up out the distance; and then, the strange pageant being gone, we have lonely stretches of glittering water—of stately buildings—of blotting shadows—of weird stone faces creeping into the moonlight—of deserted bridges—of motionless boats at anchor. And over all broods that mysterious stillness that stealthy quiet, that befits so well this old dreaming Venice. . . .

* * * *

Yes, I think we have seen all of Venice. We have seen, in these old churches, a profusion of costly and elaborate sepulchre ornamentation such as we never dreamt of before. We have stood in the dim religious light of these hoary sanctuaries, in the midst of long ranks of dusty monuments and effigies of the great dead of Venice, until we seemed drifting back, back, back, into the solemn past, and looking upon the scenes and mingling with the peoples of a remote antiquity. We have been in a half-waking sort of dream all the time. I do not know how else to describe the feeling. A part of our being has remained still in the nineteenth century, while another part of it has seemed in some unaccountable way walking among the phantoms of the tenth.

We have seen famous pictures until our eyes are weary with looking at them and refuse to find interest in them any longer. And what wonder, when there are twelve hundred pictures by Palma the Younger in Venice and fifteen hundred by Tintoretto? And behold, there are Titians and the works of other artists in proportion. We have seen Titian's celebrated Cain and Abel, his David and Goliah, his Abraham's Sacrifice. We have seen Tintoretto's monster picture, which is seventy-four feet long and I do not know how many feet high, and thought it a very commodious picture. We have seen pictures of martyrs enough, and saints enough, to regenerate the world. I ought not to confess it, but still, since one has no opportunity in America to acquire a critical judgment in art, and since I could not hope to become educated in it in Europe in a few short weeks, I

159

may therefore as well acknowledge with such apologies as may be due, that to me it seemed that when I had seen one of these martyrs I had seen them all. They all have a marked family resemblance to each other, they dress alike, in coarse monkish robes and sandals, they are all bald-headed, they all stand in about the same attitude, and without exception they are gazing heavenward with countenances which the Ainsworths, the Mortons, and the Williamses, *et fils*, inform me are full of "expression." To me there is nothing tangible about these imaginary portraits, nothing that I can grasp and take a living interest in. If great Titian had only been gifted with prophecy, and had skipped a martyr, and gone over to England and painted a portrait of Shakespeare, even as a youth, which we could all have confidence in now, the world down to the latest generations would have forgiven him the lost martyr in the rescued seer. I think posterity could have spared one more martyr for the sake of a great historical picture of Titian's time and painted by his brush— such as Columbus returning in chains from the discovery of a world, for instance. The old masters did paint some Venetian historical pictures, and these we did not tire of looking at, notwithstanding representations of the formal introduction of defunct Doges to the Virgin Mary in regions beyond the clouds clashed rather harshly with the proprieties, it seemed to us.

But, humble as we are, and unpretending, in the matter of art, our researches among the painted monks and martyrs have not been wholly in vain. We have striven hard to learn. We have had some success. We have mastered some things, possibly of trifling import in the eyes of the learned, but to us they give pleasure, and we take as much pride in our little acquirements as do others who have learned far more, and we love to display them full as well. When we see a monk going about with a lion and looking tranquilly up to heaven, we know that that is St. Mark. When we see a monk with a book and a pen, looking tranquilly up to heaven, trying to think of a word, we know that that is St. Matthew. When we see a monk sitting on a rock, looking tranquilly up to heaven, with a human skull beside him, and without other baggage, we know that that is St. Jerome. Because we know that he always went flying light in the matter of baggage. When we see a party looking tranquilly up to heaven, unconscious that his body is shot through and through with arrows, we know that that is St. Sebastian. When we see other monks looking tranquilly up to heaven, but having no trademark, we always ask who those parties are. We do this because we humbly wish to learn. We have seen thirteen thousand St. Jeromes, and twenty-two thousand St. Marks, and sixteen thousand St. Matthews, and sixty thousand St. Sebastians, and four millions of assorted monks, undesignated, and we feel encouraged to believe that when we have seen some more of these various pictures, and had a larger experience, we shall begin to take an absorbing interest in them like our cultivated countrymen from *Amerique*. . . .

If I did not so delight in the grand pictures that are spread before me every day of my life by that monarch of all the old masters, Nature, I should come to believe, sometimes, that I had in me no appreciation of the beautiful, whatsoever.

It seems to me that whenever I glory to think that for once I have discovered an ancient painting that is beautiful and worthy of all praise, the pleasure it gives me is an infallible proof that it is *not* a beautiful picture and not in any wise worthy of commendation. This very thing has occurred more times than I can mention, in Venice. In every single instance the guide has crushed out my swelling enthusiasm with the remark:

"It is nothing—it is of the *Renaissance*."

I did not know what in the mischief the Renaissance was, and so always I had to simply say:

"Ah! so it is—I had not observed it before."

I could not bear to be ignorant before a cultivated Negro, the offspring of a South Carolina slave. But it occurred too often for even my self-complacency, did that exasperating "It is nothing—it is of the *Renaissance*." I said at last:

"*Who* is this Renaissance? Where did he come from? Who gave him permission to cram the Republic with his execrable daubs?"

We learned, then, that Renaissance was not a man; that *renaissance* was a term used to signify what was at best but an imperfect rejuvenation of art. The guide said that after Titian's time and the time of the other great names we had grown so familiar with, high art declined; then it partially rose again—an inferior sort of painters sprang up, and these shabby pictures were the work of their hands. Then I said, in my heat, that I "wished to goodness high art had declined five hundred years sooner." The Renaissance pictures suit me very well, though sooth to say its school were too much given to painting real men and did not indulge enough in martyrs.

The guide I have spoken of is the only one we have had yet who knew anything. He was born in South Carolina, of slave parents. They came to Venice while he was an infant. He has grown up here. He is well educated. He reads, writes, and speaks English, Italian, Spanish, and French, with perfect facility; is a worshiper of art and thoroughly conversant with it; knows the history of Venice by heart and never tires of talking of her illustrious career. He dresses better than any of us, I think, and is daintily polite. Negroes are deemed as good as white people, in Venice, and so this man feels no desire to go back to his native land. His judgment is correct.

PART V

RE-ENACTMENTS:

Venice in Literature

She is the Shakespeare of cities—
unchallenged, incomparable, and beyond envy.

JOHN ADDINGTON SYMONDS

Lord Byron

(George Gordon Noel Byron)

◄ 1788–1824 ►

Lord Byron, Percy Bysshe Shelley (1797–1822), Elizabeth Barrett (1806–1861), Robert Browning (1812–1889) and Walter Savage Landor (1775–1864), compatriots, were the celebrated English poets of their day and shared a voluntary exile in Italy from the social and personal restraints of their native country. Inevitably, they became more closely associated with Italy than with England because their adopted country became the inspiration for a large part of their poetry. Landor— although he resided elsewhere in Italy—thought Venice was "among cities what Shakespeare is among men"; Shelley's visits with Byron in Venice gave us incomparable portraits of the city in several poems; Elizabeth Barrett championed the cause of Italian freedom from Austrian rule; and Robert Browning composed a number of poems about Venice. One of his finest of these is about a Venetian composer of Burano, Baldassare Galuppi. Browning died in the Ca' Rezzonico, a eighteenth-century palazzo on the Grand Canal which bears the plaque:

> Open my heart and you will see
> Graved inside of it "Italy"

Lord Byron's surrender to Venetian life was total. "It is my intention," he wrote in November, 1816, "to remain at Venice during the winter, probably, as it has always been (next to the East) the greenest island of my imagination. It has not disappointed me; though its evident decay would, perhaps, have that effect upon others. But I have been familiar with ruins too long to dislike desolation." By March, 1818: "the city . . . is decaying daily, and does not gain in population. However, I prefer it to any other in Italy; and here have I pitched my staff, and here do I purpose [sic] to reside for the remainder of my life . . ." Byron was assimilated, hung the tricolor from his balcony, spoke and wrote the language ("more fluently than correctly") and finally the famed, handsome and outrageously scandalous poet, freed from all constraints was "to work the *mine of my youth to the last veins of the ore and then—good night. I have lived, and am content."*

In "Childe Harold," Byron's passionate verse diary of his travels, his "own sentiments of Venice were thrown" into the opening stanzas of Canto IV, probably the best known English poetry written about the city. "It was the sight of the numerous English travellers following in the footsteps of 'Childe Harold' . . . that suggested the first Baedeker," said Herr Baedeker. In his opening lines of "Ode on Venice," Byron would sound the knell that galvanized future generations of his English countrymen into a concern for the future of the city that is unrivaled:

> Oh Venice! Venice! when thy marble walls
> Are level with the waters there shall be
> A cry of nations o'er thy sunken halls
> A loud lament along the sweeping sea!

CHILDE HAROLD CANTO IV
(Abridged)

1

I stood in Venice, on the 'Bridge of Sighs';
A palace and a prison on each hand:
I saw from out the wave her structures rise
As from the stroke of the Enchanter's wand:
A thousand Years their cloudy wings expand
Around me, and a dying Glory smiles
O'er the far times, when many a subject land
Looked to the wingèd Lion's marble piles,
Where Venice sate in state, throned on her hundred isles!

2

She looks a sea Cybele, fresh from Ocean,
Rising with her tiara of proud towers
At airy distance, with majestic motion,

A Ruler of the waters and their powers:
And such she was;—her daughters had their dowers
From spoils of nations, and the exhaustless East
Poured in her lap all gems in sparkling showers:
In purple was she robed, and of her feast
Monarchs partook, and deemed their dignity increased.

3

In Venice Tasso's echoes are no more,
And silent rows the songless Gondolier;
Her palaces are crumbling to the shore,
And Music meets not always now the ear:
Those days are gone—but Beauty still is here.
States fall—Arts fade—but Nature doth not die,
Nor yet forget how Venice once was dear,
The pleasant place of all festivity,
The Revel of the earth—the Masque of Italy!

4

But unto us she hath a spell beyond
Her name in story, and her long array
Of mighty shadows, whose dim forms despond
Above the Dogeless city's vanished sway;
Ours is a trophy which will not decay
With the Rialto; Shylock and the Moor,
And Pierre, can not be swept or worn away—
The keystones of the Arch! though all were o'er,
For us repeopled were the solitary shore.

5

The Beings of the Mind are not of clay:
Essentially immortal, they create
And multiply in us a brighter ray
And more beloved existence: that which Fate
Prohibits to dull life in this our state
Of mortal bondage, by these Spirits supplied,
First exiles, then replaces what we hate;
Watering the heart whose early flowers have died,
And with a fresher growth replenishing the void.

6

Such is the refuge of our youth and age—
The first from Hope, the last from Vacancy;
And this wan feeling peoples many a page—
And, may be, that which grows beneath mine eye:
Yet there are things whose strong reality
Outshines our fairy-land; in shape and hues
More beautiful than our fantastic sky,
And the strange constellations which the Muse
O'er her wild universe is skilful to diffuse:

7

I saw or dreamed of such,—but let them go,—
They came like Truth—and disappeared like dreams;
And whatsoe'er they were—are now but so:
I could replace them if I would; still teems
My mind with many a form which aptly seems
Such as I sought for, and at moments found;
Let these too go—for waking Reason deems
Such over-weening phantasies unsound,
And other voices speak, and other sights surround.

8

I've taught me other tongues—and in strange eyes
Have made me not a stranger; to the mind
Which is itself, no changes bring surprise;
Nor is it harsh to make, nor hard to find
A country with—aye, or without mankind;
Yet was I born where men are proud to be,—
Not without cause; and should I leave behind
The inviolate Island of the sage and free,
And seek me out a home by a remoter sea,

9

Perhaps I loved it well; and should I lay
My ashes in a soil which is not mine,
My Spirit shall resume it—if we may

Unbodied choose a sanctuary. I twine
My hopes of being remembered in my line
With my land's language: if too fond and far
These aspirations in their scope incline,—
If my Fame should be, as my fortunes are,
Of hasty growth and blight, and dull Oblivion bar

10

My name from out the temple where the dead
Are honoured by the Nations—let it be—
And light the Laurels on a loftier head!
And be the Spartan's epitaph on me—
'Sparta hath many a worthier son than he.'
Meantime I seek no sympathies, nor need—
The thorns which I have reaped are of the tree
I planted,—they have torn me,—and I bleed:
I should have known what fruit would spring from such a seed.

11

The spouseless Adriatic mourns her Lord,
And annual marriage now no more renewed—
The Bucentaur lies rotting unrestored,
Neglected garment of her widowhood!
St. Mark yet sees his Lion where he stood
Stand, but in mockery of his withered power,
Over the proud Place where an Emperor sued,
And monarchs gazed and envied in the hour
When Venice was a Queen with an unequalled dower.

12

The Suabian sued, and now the Austrian reigns—
An Emperor tramples where an Emperor knelt;
Kingdoms are shrunk to provinces, and chains
Clank over sceptred cities; Nations melt
From Power's high pinnacle, when they have felt
The sunshine for a while, and downward go
Like Lauwine loosened from the mountain's belt;
Oh for one hour of blind old Dandolo!
Th' octogenarian chief, Byzantium's conquering foe.

13

Before St. Mark still glow his Steeds of brass,
Their gilded collars glittering in the sun;
But is not Doria's menace come to pass?
Are they not bridled?—Venice, lost and won,
Her thirteen hundred years of freedom done,
Sinks, like a sea-weed, unto whence she rose!
Better be whelmed beneath the waves, and shun,
Even in Destruction's depth, her foreign foes,
From whom Submission wrings an infamous repose.

14

In youth She was all glory,—a new Tyre,—
Her very by-word sprung from Victory,
The 'Planter of the Lion,' which through fire
And blood she bore o'er subject Earth and Sea;
Though making many slaves, Herself still free,
And Europe's bulwark 'gainst the Ottomite;
Witness Troy's rival, Candia! Vouch it, ye
Immortal waves that saw Lepanto's fight!
For ye are names no Time nor Tyranny can blight.

15

Statues of glass—all shivered—the long file
Of her dead Doges are declined to dust;
But where they dwelt, the vast and sumptuous pile
Bespeaks the pageant of their splendid trust;
Their sceptre broken, and their sword in rust,
Have yielded to the stranger: empty halls,
Thin streets, and foreign aspects, such as must
Too oft remind her who and what enthrals,
Have flung a desolate cloud o'er Venice' lovely walls.

16

When Athens' armies fell at Syracuse,
And fettered thousands bore the yoke of war,
Redemption rose up in the Attic Muse,

Her voice their only ransom from afar:
See! as they chant the tragic hymn, the car
Of the o'ermastered Victor stops—the reins
Fall from his hands—his idle scimitar
Starts from its belt—he rends his captive's chains,
And bids him thank the Bard for Freedom and his strains.

17

Thus, Venice! if no stronger claim were thine,
Were all thy proud historic deeds forgot—
Thy choral memory of the Bard divine,
Thy love of Tasso, should have cut the knot
Which ties thee to thy tyrants; and thy lot
Is shameful to the nations,—most of all,
Albion! to thee: the Ocean queen should not
Abandon Ocean's children; in the fall
Of Venice think of thine, despite thy watery wall.

18

I loved her from my boyhood—she to me
Was as a fairy city of the heart,
Rising like water-columns from the sea—
Of Joy the sojourn, and of Wealth the mart;
And Otway, Radcliffe, Schiller, Shakespeare's art,
Had stamped her image in me, and even so,
Although I found her thus, we did not part;
Perchance even dearer in her day of woe,
Than when she was a boast, a marvel, and a show.

19

I can repeople with the past—and of
The present there is still for eye and thought,
And meditation chastened down, enough;
And more, it may be, than I hoped or sought;
And of the happiest moments which were wrought
Within the web of my existence, some
From thee, fair Venice! have their colours caught:
There are some feelings Time can not benumb,
Nor Torture shake, or mine would now be cold and dumb.

James Fenimore Cooper

·◄ 1789–1851 ►·

Cooper went to Europe in 1826 as American Consul in Lyons, France, and in 1828 he became the third American writer of note—after Washington Irving and Henry Wadsworth Longfellow—to visit Italy. Irving's Tales of a Traveller (1824) *was the first American work of fiction with an Italian setting. Cooper's sojourn in Italy, October 1828–May, 1830, included ten days in Venice, less than in Florence, Naples, Sorrento or Rome. Cooper wrote that "although Venice was attractive at first, in the absence of acquaintances it became monotonous and wearying. A town," he continued, "in which the sound of wheels and hoofs is never known, in which the stillness of the narrow, ravine-like canals is seldom broken, unless by the fall of an oar or the cry of a gondolier, fatigues one by its unceasing calm. . . yet no other place ever struck my imagination so forcibly" and he had to "disburthen" it in the novel* The Bravo. *This selection is a fictional account of one of the gondola regattas that at one time played a much more important role in Venetian life than they do today.*

THE BRAVO

The narrowness of most of the canals of Venice, with the innumerable angles and the constant passing, have given rise to a fashion of construction and of rowing that are so peculiar to that city and its immediate dependencies as to require some explanation. The reader has doubtless already understood that a gondola is a long, narrow, and light boat, adapted to the uses of the place, and distinct from the wherries of all other towns. The distance between the dwellings on most of the canals is so small, that the width of the latter does not admit of the use of oars on both sides at the same time. The necessity of constantly turning aside to give room for others, and the frequency of the bridges and the corners, have

173

suggested the expediency of placing the face of the waterman in the direction in which the boat is steering, and, of course, of keeping him on his feet. As every gondola, when fully equipped, has its pavilion in the center the height of the latter renders it necessary to place him who steers on such an elevation as will enable him to overlook it. From these several causes a one-oared boat in Venice is propelled by a gondolier, who stands on a little angular deck in its stern, formed like the low roof of a house, and the stroke of the oar is given by a push, instead of a pull, as is common elsewhere. This habit of rowing erect, however, which is usually done by a forward, instead of a backward movement of the body, is not unfrequent in all the ports of the Mediterranean, though in no other is there a boat which resembles the gondola in all its properties or uses. The upright position of the gondolier requires that the pivot on which the oar rests should have a corresponding elevation; and there is, consequently, a species of bumkin raised from the side of the boat to the desired height, and which, being formed of a crooked and very irregular knee of wood, has two or three row-locks, one above the other, to suit the stature of different individuals, or to give a broader or a narrower sweep of the blade as the movement shall require. As there is frequent occasion to cast the oar from one of these row-locks to the other, and not unfrequently to change its side, it rests in a very open bed; and the instrument is kept in its place by great dexterity alone, and by a perfect knowledge of the means of accommodating the force and the rapidity of the effort to the forward movement of the boat and the resistance of the water. All these difficulties united render skill in a gondolier one of the most delicate branches of a waterman's art, as it is clear that muscular strength alone, though of great aid, can avail but little in such a practice.

The great canal of Venice, following its windings, being more than a league in length, the distance in the present race was reduced nearly half, by causing the boats to start from the Rialto. At this point, then, the gondolas were all assembled, attended by those who were to place them. As the whole of the population which before had been extended along the entire course of the water, was now crowded between the bridge and the Bucintoro the long and graceful avenue resembled a vista of human heads. It was an imposing sight to look along that bright and living lane, and the hearts of each competitor beat high, as hope, or pride, or apprehension, became the feeling of the moment.

"Gino of Calabria," cried the marshal who placed the gondolas, "thy station is on the right. Take it, and St. Januarius speed thee!"

The servitor of Dom Camillo assumed his oar, and the boat glided gracefully into its berth.

"Thou comest next, Enrico of Fusina. Call stoutly on thy Paduan patron, and husband thy strength; for none of the main have ever yet borne away a prize in Venice."

He then summoned, in succession, those whose names have not been mentioned, and placed them side by side, in the center of the canal.

"Here is place for thee, Signore," continued the officer, inclining his head to the unknown gondolier; for he had imbibed the general impression that the face of some young patrician was concealed beneath the mask, to humor the fancy of some capricious fair. "Chance hath given thee the extreme left."

"Thou hast forgotten to call the fisherman," observed the masker, as he drove his own gondola into its station.

"Does the hoary fool persist in exposing his vanity and his rags to the best of Venice?"

"I can take place in the rear," meekly observed Antonio. "There may be those in the line it doth not become one like me to crowd, and a few strokes of the oar, more or less, can differ but little in so long a strife."

"Thou hadst better push modesty to discretion, and remain."

"If it be your pleasure, Signore, I would rather see what St. Anthony may do for an old fisherman, who has prayed to him, night and morning, these sixty years?"

"It is thy right; and, as thou seemest content with it, keep the place thou hast in the rear. It is only occupying it a little earlier than thou would'st otherwise. Now, recall the rules of the games, hardy gondoliers, and make your last appeal to your patrons. There is to be no crossing, or other foul expedients; naught except ready oars, and nimble wrists. He who varies needlessly from his line until he leadeth, shall be recalled by name; and whoever is guilty of any act to spoil the sports, or otherwise to offend the patricians, shall be both checked and punished. Be ready for the signal."

The assistant, who was in a strongly manned boat, fell back a little, while runners, similarly equipped, went ahead to order the curious from the water. The preparations were scarcely made, when a signal blasted on the nearest dome. It was repeated on the campanile, and a gun was fired at the arsenal. A deep but suppressed murmur arose in the throng, which was as quickly succeeded by suspense.

Each gondolier had suffered the bows of his boat to incline slightly towards the left shore of the canal, as the jockey is seen, at the starting-post, to turn his courser aside, in order to repress its ardor, or divert its attention. But the first long and broad sweep of the oar brought them all in a line again, and away they glided in a body.

For the first few minutes there was no difference in speed, nor any sign by which the instructed might detect the probable evidence of defeat or success. The whole ten, which formed the front line, skimmed the water with an equal velocity, beak to beak, as if some secret attraction held each in its place, while the humble, though equally light bark of the fisherman steadily kept its position in the rear.

The boats were soon held in command. The oars got their justest poise and widest sweep, and the wrists of the men accustomed to their play. The line began to waver. It undulated, the glittering prow of one protruding beyond the others; and then it changed its form. Enrico of Fusina shot ahead, and, privileged by success, he insensibly sheered more into the center of the canal, avoiding by the change the eddies, and the other obstructions of the shore. This maneuver which, in the language of the course, would have been called "taking the track," had the additional advantage of throwing upon those who followed some trifling impediment from the backwater. The sturdy and practiced Bartolomeo of the Lido, as his companions usually called him, came next, occupying the space on his leader's quarter, where he suffered least from the reaction caused by the stroke of his oar. The gondolier of Dom Camillo, also, soon shot out of the crowd, and was seen plying his arms vigorously still farther to the right, and a little in the rear of Bartolomeo. Then came in the center of the canal, and near as might be in the rear of the triumphant waterman of the main, a dense body, with little order and varying positions, compelling each other to give way, and otherwise increasing the difficulties of their struggle. More to the left, and so near to the palaces as barely to allow room for the sweep of his oar, was the masked competitor, whose progress seemed retarded by some unseen cause, for he gradually fell behind all the others, until several boats' lengths of open water lay between him and even the group of his nameless opponents. Still he plied his arms steadily, and with sufficient skill. As the interest of mystery had been excited in his favor, a rumor passed up the canal, that the young cavalier had been little favored by fortune in the choice of a boat. Others, who reflected more deeply on causes, whispered of the folly of one of his habits taking the risk of mortification by a competition with men whose daily labor had hardened their sinews and whose practice enabled them to judge closely of every chance of the race. But when the eyes of the multitude turned from the cluster of passing boats to the solitary barge of the fisherman, who came singly on in the rear, admiration was again turned to derision.

Antonio had cast aside the cap he wore of wont, and the few straggling hairs that were left streamed about his hollow temples, leaving the whole of his swarthy features exposed to view. More than once, as the gondola came on, his eyes turned aside reproachfully, as if he keenly felt the stings of so many unlicensed tongues applied to feelings which, though blunted by his habits and condition, were far from extinguished. Laugh arose above laugh, however, and taunt succeeded taunt more bitterly, as the boats came among the gorgeous palaces which lined the canal nearer to the goal. It was not that the owners of these lordly piles indulged in the unfeeling triumph, but their dependents, constantly subject themselves to the degrading influence of a superior presence, let loose the long-pent torrents of their arrogance on the head of the first unresisting subject which offered.

Antonio bore all these jibes manfully, if not in tranquillity, and always without retort, until he again approached the spot occupied by his companions of the Lagoon. Here his eye sank under the reproaches, and his oar faltered. The taunts and denunciations increased as he lost ground, and there was a moment when the rebuked and humbled spirit of the old man seemed about to relinquish the contest. But dashing a hand across his brow, as if to clear a sight which had become dimmed and confused, he continued to ply the oar, and, happily he was soon past the point most trying to his resolution. From this moment the cries against the fisherman diminished, and as the Bucintoro, though still distant, was now in sight, interest in the issue of the race absorbed all other feelings.

Enrico still kept the lead; but the judges of the gondolier's skill began to detect signs of exhaustion in his faltering stroke. The waterman of the Lido pressed him hard, and the Calabrian was drawing more into a line with them both. At this moment, too, the masked competitor exhibited a force and skill that none had expected to see in one of his supposed rank. His body was thrown more upon the effort of the oar, and as his leg was stretched behind to aid the stroke, it discovered a volume of muscle and an excellence of proportion that excited murmurs of applause. The consequence was soon apparent. His gondola glided past the crowd in the center of the canal, and by a change that was nearly insensible, he became the fourth in the race. The shouts which rewarded his success had scarcely parted from the multitude, ere their admiration was called to a new and an entirely unexpected aspect in the struggle.

Left to his own exertions, and less annoyed by that derision and contempt which often defeat even more generous efforts, Antonio had drawn nearer to the crowd of nameless competitors. Though undistinguished in this narrative, there were seen, in that group of gondoliers, faces well known on the canals of Venice, as belonging to watermen in whose dexterity and force the city took pride. Either favored by his isolated position, or availing himself of the embarrassment these men gave to each other, the despised fisherman was seen a little on their left coming up abreast with a stroke and velocity that promised further success. The expectation was quickly realized. He passed them all, amid a dead and wondering silence, and took his station as fifth in the struggle.

From this moment all interest in those who formed the vulgar mass was lost. Every eye was turned towards the front, where the strife increased at each stroke of the oar, and where the issue began to assume a new and doubtful character. The exertions of the waterman of Fusina were seemingly redoubled, though his boat went no faster. The gondola of Bartolomeo shot past him; it was followed by those of Gino and the masked gondolier, while not a cry betrayed the breathless interest of the multitude. But when the boat of Antonio also swept ahead, there arose such a hum of voices as escapes a throng when a sudden and violent change of feeling is produced in their wayward sentiments. Enrico was frantic with the disgrace. He urged every power of his frame to avert the dishonor, with the desperate energy of an Italian, and then he cast himself into the bottom of the gondola, tearing his hair and weeping in agony. His example was followed by those in the rear, though with more governed feelings, for they shot aside among the boats which lined the canal and were lost to view.

From this open and unexpected abandonment of the struggle, the spectators got the surest evidence of its desperate character. But as a man has little sympathy for the unfortunate when his feelings are excited by competition, the defeated were quickly forgotten. The name of Bartolomeo was borne high upon the winds by a thousand voices, and his fellows of the Piazzetta and the Lido called upon him, aloud, to die for the honor of their craft. Well did the sturdy gondolier answer to their wishes, for palace after palace was left behind, and no further change was made in the relative positions of the boats. But, like his predecessor, the leader redoubled his efforts with a diminished effect, and Venice had the mortification of seeing a stranger leading one of the most brilliant of her regattas. Bartolomeo no sooner lost place, than Gino, the masker, and the despised Antonio, in turn, shot by, leaving him who had so lately been first in the race, the last. He did not, however, relinquish the strife, but continued to struggle with the energy of one who merited a better fortune.

When this unexpected and entirely new character was given to the contest, there still remained a broad sheet of water between the advancing gondolas and the goal. Gino led, and with many favorable symptoms of his being able to maintain his advantage. He was encouraged by the shouts of the multitude, who now forgot his Calabrian origin in his success, while many of the servingmen of his master cheered him on by name. All would not do. The masked waterman, for the first time, threw the grandeur of his skill and force into the oar. The ashen instrument bent to the power of an arm whose strength appeared to increase at will, and the movements of his body became rapid as the leaps of the greyhound. The pliant gondola obeyed, and amid a shout which passed from the Piazzetta to the Rialto, it glided ahead.

If success gives force and increases the physical and moral energies, there is a fearful and certain reaction in defeat. The follower of Don Camillo was no exception to the general law, and when the masked competitor passed him the boat of Antonio followed as if it were impelled by the same strokes. The distance between the two leading gondolas even now seemed to lessen, and there was a moment of breathless interest when all there expected to see the fisherman, in despite of his years and boat, shooting past his rival.

But expectation was deceived. He of the mask, notwithstanding his previous efforts, seemed to sport with the toil, so ready was the sweep of his oar, so sure its stroke, and so vigorous the arm by which it was impelled. Nor was Antonio an antagonist to despise. If there was less of the grace of a practiced gondolier of the canals in his attitudes than in those of his companion, there was no relaxation in the force of his sinews. They sustained him to the last with that enduring power which had been begotten by threescore years of unremitting labor, and while his still athletic form was exerted to the utmost there appeared no failing of its energies.

A few moments sent the leading gondolas several lengths ahead of their nearest followers. The dark beak of the fisherman's boat hung upon the quarter of the more showy bark of his antagonist, but it could do no more. The port was open before them, and they glanced by church, palace, barge, and felucca, without the slightest inequality in their relative speed. The masked waterman glanced a look behind as if to calculate his advantage, and then bending again to his pliant oar he spoke, loud enough to be heard only by him who pressed so hard upon his track.

"Thou hast deceived me, fisherman!" he said. "There is more of manhood in thee yet than I had thought."

"If there is manhood in my arms, there is childlessness and sorrow at the heart," was the reply.

"Dost thou so prize a golden bauble? Thou art second; be content with thy lot."

"It will not do; I must be foremost or I have wearied my old limbs in vain!"

This brief dialogue was uttered with an ease that showed how far use had accustomed both to powerful bodily efforts, and with a firmness of tones that few could have equalled in a moment of so great physical effort. The masker was silent, but his purpose seemed to waver. Twenty strokes of his powerful oarblade and the goal was attained, but his sinews were not so much extended, and that limb which had shown so fine a development of muscle, was less swollen and rigid. The gondola of old Antonio glided abeam.

"Push thy soul into the blade," muttered he of the mask, "or thou wilt yet be beaten!"

The fisherman threw every effort of his body on the coming effort, and he gained a fathom. Another stroke caused the boat to quiver to its center and the water curled from its bows like the ripple of a rapid. Then the gondola darted between the two goal-barges and the little flags that marked the point of victory fell into the water. The action was scarce noted ere the glittering beak of the masquer shot past the eyes of the judges, who doubted for an instant on whom success had fallen. Gino was not long behind, and after him came Bartolomeo, fourth and last in the best contested race which had ever been seen on the waters of Venice.

When the flags fell, men held their breaths in suspense. Few knew the victor, so close had been the struggle. But a flourish of the trumpets soon commanded attention, and then a herald proclaimed, "Antonio, a fisherman of the Lagoon, favored by his holy patron of the Miraculous Draught, has borne away the prize of gold—while a waterman who wore his face concealed, but who hath trusted to the care of the blessed San Giovanni of the Wilderness, is worthy of the silver prize and the third had fallen to the fortunes of Gino of Calabria, a servitor of the illustrious Don Camillo Monforte, Duca di Sant' Agata, and lord of many Neapolitan Seignories."

When this formal announcement was made, there succeeded a silence like that of the tomb. Then there arose a general shout among the living mass, which bore on high the name of Antonio as if they celebrated the success of some conqueror. All feeling of contempt was lost in the influence of his triumph. The fishermen of the Lagoon who so lately had loaded their aged companion with contumely, shouted for his glory with a zeal that manifested the violence of the transition from mortification to pride; and, as has ever been and ever will be the meed of success, he who was thought least likely to obtain it was most greeted with praise and adulation when it was found that the end had disappointed expectation. Ten thousand voices were lifted in proclaiming his skill and victory, and young and old, the fair, the gay, the noble, the winner of sequins and he who lost, struggled alike to catch a glimpse of the humble old man, who had so unexpectedly wrought this change of sentiment in the feelings of a multitude.

Antonio bore his triumph meekly. When his gondola had reached the goal, he checked its course and without discovering any of the usual signs of exhaustion he remained standing, though the deep heaving of his broad and tawny chest proved that his powers had been taxed to their utmost. He smiled as the shouts arose on his ear, for praise is grateful even to the meek; still he seemed oppressed with an emotion of a character deeper than pride. Age had somewhat dimmed his eye, but it was now full of hope. His features worked, and a single burning drop fell on each rugged cheek. The fisherman then breathed more freely.

Like his successful antagonist, the waterman of the mask betrayed none of the debility which usually succeeds great bodily exertion. His knees were motionless, his hands still grasped the oar firmly, and he too kept his feet with a steadiness that showed the physical perfection of his frame. On the other hand, both Gino and Bartolomeo sank in their respective boats as they gained the goal in succession; so exhausted was each of these renowned gondoliers, that several moments elapsed before either had breath for speech. It was during this momentary pause that the multitude proclaimed its sympathy with the victor by their longest and loudest shouts. The noise had scarcely died away, however, before a herald summoned Antonio of the Lagoon, masked waterman and Gino the Calabrian, to the presence of the Doge, whose princely hand was to bestow the promised prizes of the regatta.

Marcel Proust

·◄ 1871–1922 ►·

Marcel Proust got his formative impression of Venice as a boy from a drawing of Titian, as he relates in Remembrance of Things Past. *At twenty-five he discovered and was strongly influenced by the theories of John Ruskin from reading Robert de la Sizaranne's book* Ruskin and the Religion of Beauty (1896). *Under the powerful spell of Ruskin Proust saw Venice for the first time, in 1900. In 1904 Proust translated two volumes by Ruskin. Ruskin's* The Stones of Venice *would surely have enhanced the hypnotic spell the city played in the fantasies, dreams and creative imagination of Proust. Proust's first encounter with the reality of Venice is "recalled" in* Albertine Disparue—*called in English* The Sweet Cheat Gone—*one of the sixteen volumes in the famous semi-autobiographical series* Remembrance of Things Past.

REMEMBRANCE OF THINGS PAST

My mother had brought me for a few weeks to Venice and—as there may be beauty in the most precious as well as in the humblest things—I was receiving there impressions analogous to those which I had felt so often in the past at Combray, but transposed into a wholly different and far richer key. When at ten o'clock in the morning my shutters were thrown open, I saw ablaze in the sunlight, instead of the black marble into which the slates of Saint-Hilaire used to turn, the Golden Angel on the Campanile of San Marco. In its dazzling glitter, which made it almost impossible to fix it in space, it promised me with its outstretched arms, for the moment, half an hour later, when I was to appear on the Piazzetta, a joy more certain than any that it could ever in the past have been bidden to announce to men of good will. I could see nothing but itself, so long as I remained in bed, but as the whole world is merely a vast sundial, a single lighted segment of which enables us to tell what o'clock it is, on the very first morning I was reminded of the shops in the Place de l'Eglise at Combray, which, on Sunday mornings, were always on the point of shutting when I arrived for mass, while the straw in the market place smelt strongly in the already hot sunlight. But on the second morning, what I saw, when I awoke, what made me get out of bed (because they had taken the place in my consciousness and in my desire of my memories of Combray), were the impressions of my first morning stroll in Venice, Venice whose daily life was no less real than that of Combray, where as at Combray on Sunday mornings one had the delight of emerging upon a festive street, but where that street was paved with water of a sapphire blue, refreshed by little ripples of cooler air, and of so solid a color that my tired eyes might, in quest of relaxation and without fear of its giving way, rest their gaze upon it. Like, at Combray, the worthy folk of the Rue de l'Oiseau, so in this strange town also, the inhabitants did indeed emerge from houses drawn up in line, side by side, along the principal street, but the part played there by houses that cast a patch of shade before them was in Venice entrusted to palaces of porphyry and jasper, over the arched door of which the head of a bearded god (projecting from its alignment, like the knocker on a door at Combray) had the effect of darkening with its shadow, not the brownness of the soil but the splendid blue of the water. On the piazza, the shadow that would have been cast at Combray by the linen-draper's awning and the barber's pole, turned into the tiny blue flowers scattered at its feet upon the desert of sun-scorched tiles by the silhouette of a Renaissance façade, which is not to say that, when the sun was hot, we were not obliged, in Venice as at Combray, to pull down the blinds between ourselves and the Canal, but they hung behind the quatre-foils and foliage of gothic windows. . . .

And as I went indoors to join my mother . . . I did indeed recapture, coming from the warm air outside, that feeling of coolness that I had known long ago at Combray when I went upstairs to my room, but at Venice it was a breeze from the sea that kept the air cool, and no longer upon a little wooden staircase with narrow steps, but upon the noble surfaces of blocks of marble, splashed at every moment by a shaft of greenish sunlight, which to the valuable instruction in the art of Chardin, acquired long ago, added a lesson in that of Veronese. And since at Venice it is to works of art, to things of priceless beauty, that the task is entrusted of giving us our impressions of everyday life, we may sketch the character of this city, using the pretext that the Venice of certain painters is coldly aesthetic in its most celebrated parts, by representing only (let us make an exception of the superb studies of Maxime De-thomas) its poverty-stricken aspects, in the quarters where everything that creates its splendor is concealed, and to make Venice more intimate and more genuine give it a resemblance to Aubervilliers. It has been the mistake of some very great artists, that, by a quite natural reaction from the artificial Venice of bad painters, they have attached themselves exclusively to the Venice which they have found more realistic, to some humble *campo,* some tiny deserted *rio*. It was this Venice that I used often to explore in the afternoon, when I did not go out with my mother. The fact was that it was easier to find there women of the industrial class, match-makers, pearl-stringers, workers in glass or lace, working women in black shawls with long fringes. My gondola followed the course of the small canals; like the mysterious hand of a Genie leading me through the maze of this oriental city, they seemed, as I advanced, to be carving a road for me through the heart of a crowded quarter which they clove asunder, barely dividing with a slender fissure, arbitrarily carved, the tall houses with their tiny Moorish windows; and, as though the magic guide had been holding a candle in his hand and were lighting the way for me, they kept casting ahead of them a ray of sunlight for which they cleared a path.

One felt that between the mean dwellings which the canal had just parted and which otherwise would have formed a compact whole, no open space had been reserved. With the result that the belfry of the church, or the garden-trellis rose sheer above the *rio* as in a flooded city. But with churches as with gardens, thanks to the same transposition as in the Grand Canal, the sea formed so effective a way of communication, a substitute for street or alley, that on either side of the *canaletto* the churches rose from the water in this ancient, plebeian quarter, degraded into humble, more frequented mission chapels, bearing upon their surface the stamp of their necessity, of their use by crowds of simple folk, that the gardens crossed by the line of the canal allowed their astonished leaves or fruit to trail in the water and that on the doorstep of the house whose roughly hewn stone was still wrinkled as though it had only just been sawn, little boys surprised by the gondola and keeping their balance allowed their legs to dangle vertically, like sailors seated upon a swing-bridge the two halves of which have been swung apart, allowing the sea to pass between them.

Now and again there appeared a handsomer building that happened to be there, like a surprise in a box which we have just opened, a little ivory temple with its Corinthian columns and its allegorical statue on the pediment, somewhat out of place among the ordinary buildings in the midst of which it had survived, and the peristyle with which the canal provided it resembled a landing-stage for market gardeners.

The sun had barely begun to set when I went to fetch my mother from the Piazzetta. We returned up the Grand Canal in our gondola. We watched the double line of palaces between which we passed reflect the light and angle of the sun upon their rosy surfaces, and alter with them, seeming not so much private habitations and historic buildings as a chain of marble cliffs at the foot of which people go out in the evening in a boat to watch the sunset. In this way, the mansions arranged along either bank of the canal made one think of objects of nature, but of a nature which seemed to have created its works with a human imagination. But at the same time (because of the character of the impressions, always urban, which Venice gives us almost in the open sea, upon those waves whose flow and ebb make themselves felt twice daily, and which alternately cover at high tide and uncover at low tide the splendid outside stairs of the palaces), as we should have done in Paris upon the boulevards, in the Champs-Elysées, in the Bois, in any wide thoroughfare that was a fashionable resort, in the powdery evening light, we passed the most beautifully dressed women, almost all foreigners, who, propped luxuriously upon the cushions of their floating vehicle, took their place in the procession, stopped before a palace in which there was a friend whom they wished to see, sent to inquire whether she was at home; and while, as they waited for the answer, they prepared to leave a card, as they would have done at the door of the Hôtel de Guermantes, they turned to their guidebook to find out the period, the style of the palace, not without being shaken, as though upon the crest of a blue wave, by the thrust of the flashing, prancing water, which took alarm on finding itself pent between the dancing gondola and the slapping marble. And thus any excursion, even when it was only to pay calls or to go shopping, was threefold and unique in this Venice where the simplest social coming and going assumed at the same time the form and the charm of a visit to a museum and a trip on the sea. . . .

*   *   *   *

After dinner, I went out by myself, into the heart of the enchanted city where I found myself wandering in strange regions like a character in the Arabian Nights. It was very seldom that I did not, in the course of my wanderings, hit upon some strange and spacious piazza of which no guidebook, no tourist had ever told me.

I had plunged into a network of little alleys, *calli* dissecting in all directions by their ramifications the quarter of Venice isolated between a canal and the lagoon, as if it had crystallized along these innumerable, slender, capillary lines. All of a sudden, at the end of one of those little streets, it seemed as though a bubble had occurred in the crystallized matter. A vast and splendid *campo* of which I could certainly never, in this network of little streets, have guessed the importance, or even found room for it, spread out before me flanked with charming palaces silvery in the moonlight. It was one of those architectural wholes towards which, in any other town, the streets converge, lead you and point the way. Here it seemed to be deliberately concealed in a labyrinth of alleys, like those palaces in oriental tales to which mysterious agents convey by night a person who, taken home again before daybreak, can never again find his way back to the magic dwelling which he ends by supposing that he visited only in a dream.

On the following day I set out in quest of my beautiful nocturnal piazza, I followed *calli* which were exactly like one another and refused to give me any information, except such as would lead me farther astray. Sometimes a vague landmark which I seemed to recognize led me to suppose that I was about to see appear, in its seclusion, solitude and silence, the beautiful exiled piazza. At that moment, some evil genie which had assumed the form of a fresh *calle* made me turn unconsciously from my course, and I found myself suddenly brought back to the Grand Canal. And as there is no great difference between the memory of a dream and the memory of a reality, I ended by asking myself whether it was not during my sleep that there had occurred in a dark patch of Venetian crystallization that strange interruption which offered a vast piazza flanked by romantic palaces, to the meditative eye of the moon.

Frederick Rolfe

(Baron Corvo)

◄ 1860–1913 ►

Frederick William Rolfe, better known as the self-titled Baron Corvo, was born in London and died in abject poverty in Venice as his fictionalized autobiography The Desire and the Pursuit of the Whole: A Romance of Modern Venice *prophesies. The outrageously eccentric and gifted author of* Hadrian the Seventh, *called by A. J. A. Symonds "one of the most remarkable books in the English language," spent the last five years of his life 1908–1913, in Venice. The Desire and the Pursuit of the Whole, written in 1909, was only brought to light by Symonds twelve years later and finally published in 1934. In his Foreword, W.H. Auden wrote: "If there was nothing but Rolfe's nightmare and his day dream it might be too depressing to read except as a clinical study; luckily there is a third story behind both which is a real love story, the story of Rolfe's love for Venice . . . for him The Great Good Place, a city built by strong and passionate men in the image of their mother, the perfect embodiment of everything he most craved and admired, beauty, tradition, grace and ease."*

THE DESIRE AND THE PURSUIT OF THE WHOLE

Nicholas [Crabbe] wondered when the gods would have done with sending him such detestable samples, mocking his desire and impeding his pursuit of alliance. He didn't go one centimeter out of his way to seek them. They flopped to him, or barged up against him; and he was afraid to refuse the job of testing them. Cowardice of that refusing kind he abominated. No one knew how he outraged his tastes and senses and ambitions over these testings: but they seemed to be his duty, and he did it. This last experiment, however, brimmed his chalice of endurance. He never would touch any of his past subjects any more, unless they voluntarily came and began at once with a full and spontaneous apology for their stupidity. That was all he wanted: but he insisted on it. And he would contract no new relations, unless one came and began with a business-like propostion for putting him in working order. He believed these conditions to be sufficiently prohibitive. "So much the better," he told God: "I'm sick of this life, which is just one damned thing after another."

There was a week of his tenure of the garret in the Calle del Anzolo yet to run. He spent most of it in bed, storing up a good provision of sleep against the time when he might want it. As for food—*qui dort dine*—he kept the forty *centesimi*, which remained in his pocket, for some desperate emergency. But, of course, on the sixth day, a matter of four guineas came from his secret sowing: so that he was able to leave the Alley of the Angel, fed, and with a bold carriage deceptive to all observers. This money—his last—he set out to economize. Life in the pupparin was clearly indicated for the two remaining summer months. Only alone, on the lagoon, could he avoid fighting with beasts. Only on the lagoon could sun and sea keep him in life: little there was really needed for eating and drinking when one took one's time about it; and cash could be spun out; and there would be peace for really poetic work.

Life on the lagoon was good for his soul as well. It crystallized determination: it sifted out the urgencies of desires. Little by little his system of meditation by incantation renewed its efficacy, carrying him once more to the heights where the spirit breathes in Conspectu. The festival of Marymas in August filled him with joy. There was an Armenian Mass in Saint Mark's. The byzantine Madonna of Nikopoieia was exposed at the high altar, on an antependium and dossal of gold brocade veiling the Pala d'Oro. The extreme dignity of the bearded celebrant in a high-collared cope of filmy tissue, and of the two Armenian children who served him, made a deep impression upon Crabbe: here was catholocity untainted by influences of the nonsensical modern fetish of uniformity. He treated himself to a regular debauch of religious observances that day, going from church to church between dawn and noon. At Sansalvador, high over the great silver altar, he found the very latest modern ideal of Mary Virgin, a glorified handmaiden, humbly and pathetically and triumphantly emerging from a background all of shadowy gold with distance in it, coming from a distant world of gold, crowned with a most marvellous nimbus of electricity, through an archway of ivory, down into this world of a myriad stars on a forest of tapers. . .

About the middle of the last month of summer, he found to his horror that his physical fitness was diminishing. He had been into the city to buy his weekly provision of seven rolls, costing twenty-three *centesimi*: for he had got himself down to the dull and strait diet of one hard roll a day. And, just out of the defiant devilry which invariably stiffened him when his back was against the wall, he must needs row up and down Canalazzo, with the aspect of one merely taking pleasure of his leisure. At the great curve of the canal by the Rio di Ca' Foscari, he was caught between two steamboats: there is always a disconcerting wash set up by these nuisances, specially at that point where the swirlings of cross-currents also have to be considered. He was sufficiently master of his mystery to preserve his poise on the lofty poop, easing the long light bark with dexterous oar as it jumped with sounding slaps from billow to billow; and passengers on the steamers looked with amusement at the Englishman's grim insuperability amid perturbations which made Venetians bellow for *Mariavergine*. All was happening as usual, and Crabbe was holding his own, when (from behind him) came swooping two motor-launches—the heavy omnibus of a Lido hotel, and the vicious cigar-shaped racer of Palazzo Contarini, adding their waves to the wash of the Vaporetti. An instant of vertigo took him; and, to save himself from cascading into the canal, he stepped down. It was the kind of thing which every gondolier has to do occasionally: but that was the very reason why the action of leaving the poop for the floor of the bark upset Crabbe's equanimity. He had lost confidence in his physique; and, for the sake of appearances, he ceased to risk himself publicly where difficulties were likely to occur. In fact, he confined his rowing hereafter to the daily journey between the club (where he showed himself, while Zildo polished the pupparin) and the canals of Fasiol and Scoazze on the lagoon south of Spinalonga.

By the first week of October, not only his nerve but his strength had waned to such an extent that he gave up life on the water. The pupparin was not actually his own; and he no longer felt secure about returning it in decent condition to the club. Its bottom was weed-clogged after the summer's warmth of water; and it was very much heavier to row, as Zildo repeatedly warned him. He had no objection to being found dead in a club bark: but no one should find his gift to the club damaged, or oar-robbed, with him moribund on the floor of it.

He made out a duplicate list of the four hundred and sixty-one bridges of the city; and instructed his servant. "Listen, Zildo," he said. 'You are to understand, *o toso mio,* that I now know all the waterways of Venice. And it becomes necessay for my writing that I should affright myself to study the streets. *Sa?*"

"*Mi lo so ben.*"

Nicholas looked sharply at him. Was there a second intention in that lovely unruffleable voice? How much knowledge was there, actually, in the brain behind those translucent innocent ignorant wistful eyes? "What do you know so well?" he demanded.

"That my *Paròn* knows the *rii*, and wants to study the alleys."

"*Va benòn*. Take, then, this list of bridges. See, I have its companion. Tomorrow, at 8 o'clock, you will bring the pupparin to the first bridge. Wait there five minutes. If you see me, I shall give you certain commandments. If not, take the pupparin to your house. At 4 o'clock, bring the pupparin to the second bridge. Wait there five minutes. If you see me, I shall give you certain commandments. If not, take the pupparin to the *Bucintoro;* and chain it for the night. You have your key: I have mine. I can take the bark if I want it: you can take it at the hours appointed. Have you understood?"

"*Go ben capiò, Sior.*"

"And, on the next day, you will go to the next two bridges at the same hours, observing the same rules. And, on the day after, the two next two. And so on, till the list is exhausted. And, remember, when I desire service I shall speak: but, when I am silent, favor me with a touch of tranquillity for my studies."

"*Sissior—con permesso,* one little word of my own. *Sior*, be pleased to consider certain things. I am a faithful servant, and I speak only of the well-being of the pupparin—though I could, and I would, speak of other—"

"And what about the pupparin?"

"This, *Sior.* The *Bucintoro* moorings are at the entrance of *Rio Palazzo Reale*. Within one stroke of an oar is the open Basin of Saint Mark. Within two—three—strokes is the steamboat pontoon of Calle Vallareso. Autumn is here. There will occur winds, storms, and always the wash of those quintuply accursed and ill-created steamboats. *Va ben*. Also, the *pali* of the Bucintoro are rotten, badly fixed with rusty wire to broken nails in a rotting wall. Wherefore I demand whether my *Paròn* would not rather command his pupparin to be chained, at night, under his faithful servant's eye, at my house in Santrovaso?"

"*Benissimo*. Moor at your *pali* at night. In the morning, after you have visited the bridge, moor at the Bucintoro for the day. But tell the barcariol of the club that I still reserve the bark: otherwise members may seize it for their diversions—"

"*Nòssior*. They shall not. That is my affair. And, regarding other matters—"

"*Basta, basta: go caplo.*"

"*Sissior.*"

It remained to maneuver a private life on land. He spent much time on the islet of Santelena—or rather on the new islet, the grassclad Field of Mars used for football and military drill, which has been built on the lagoon mud between the islet of Santelena and the Public Gardens. The adding of fresh islets to the hundred and eighteen which compose Venice goes on slowly though surely. Recent mud-banks are staked off with double rows of massive wooden piles well rammed down: the space between is filled with concrete, and a stone wall built on the sea-face: the enclosed mud-bank is then pumped dry, and filled with rubbish stamped to a certain degree of solidity. In course of time houses spring up for the increasing population, which necessitates fresh pile-driving as foundations for the walls. But the Campo di Marte has not yet reached this stage: it is only a huge uneven plot of rough grass raised about a meter and a half above high-water mark so far. Crabbe very much wanted to get on the actual island of Santelena. The modern iron-foundry there, which was made of the old church and monastery, seems to have failed financially; and the place is deserted, but for a caretaker. But the bridge, which connects it with the new Campo di Marte, is gated; and attempts to pass, with or without permission, might have aroused undesirable curiosity. The life of the homeless half-starving man, whose one aim is to evade attention, is a very singular one in Venice. Venice, serenely walled-in by her lagoon, is not a city where Lazarus can hide his sores without the exercise of masterly and continuous ingenuity. Refuges there are, such as the *Asili dei Senza Tetto:* but he had no use for them. To apply for shelter at any of the Asylums for the Without-Roofs would be to accept charity, which was out of the question; and, further, it would have proclaimed his nationality and procured his instant deportation beyond the frontier under military escort, foreigners not being permitted to be homeless and starving in Italy. It pleased him to remember that he was not the first, however.

Crabbe began his last wanderings by walking and walking (with one of his leathern satchels slung on his shoulder and a sketch-book in his hand) about the new Campo di Marte, till there was no nook or recess or inequality of its sea-wall unknown to him: he tested them all by daylight, day after day, apparently jotting down sketches of skies and clouds above the wide lagoon for the benefit of chance observers, but really sampling their qualities of wind- or rain-shelter for use as a coach at night. This was his main retreat. It was the loneliest place accessible to him. And, because of its value, he used it only in cases of necessity when rain made the quays a sodden horror, or when he felt that he must either sleep or rave. Most of the time he spent in the streets. From the moment when the

churches opened at dawn, he heard Mass after Mass, the roof of God's
House being his for three—five—hours each day. Often he strolled about
the harbor of Marittima, watching loading and unloading, and the long
line of lusty grain-sack-laden dancers daintily dancing lithely barefoot
down long planks from ship to shore. This excited him: he knew himself
capable of carrying those sacks on his shoulders, but doubted the steadiness of his head for the passage along swaying planks slight as slack-
wire—a slip, a failure, would have attracted notice to an English curiously circumstanced, which was above all to be meticulously avoided.
The last stretch of the Fondamente Nuove also was a favourite haunt of
his. The wide quay ends abruptly on the Sacca della Misericordia, that
great square bay of the northern lagoon where the floats of timber are
stored. There is no cross-alley within thirty meters of the quay-end.
Those thirty meters are almost empty: no one howls the horrible ditty here
about "Adelaide": the view of the cemetery-island, and the Island-City
of Murano, and all the lagoon to the mainland twenty miles away and to
the ridge of the Alps seventy miles away, is broken only by the outjutting
ghost-haunted Casa dei Spiriti which an American artist uses for a studio
and occasional lugubrious carnivals. Here, and in similar seclusions, he
dawdled by day, waiting for fruits of his sure but secret sowing, or (of
course) for that which he never ceased to hope for in the depth of his
heart—the repentance of those who had wronged and robbed him. Work
for a living? Try to get a job? No. He could not dig: he would not beg: six
months' exposure and starvation had brought him low: and was it likely
that for a mere matter of keeping himself in life he should consult the
convenience of Erastians? He mocked the bare idea. "Where is the
injustice if I, or anyone who feels himself superior to another, refuse to be
on a level with him?" he said, in the words of splendid Alcibiades.
Beside, he had worked, he had done far more than his share of work, and
he confidently left the fruition of it to The Authorities. . . .

After two nights on the open shore of the Lido, where a mere hour's
rest on the sand soaked him with frost—thick white frost—and so
stiffened him that he could have cried like a baby with the fearful aching,
he noticed that his shabby clothes were notably conspicuous from exposure to rain and sun: specially his cap had changed color from indigo to
the odious violet worn by knights of the Order of Sanctissima Sophia. His
visits to the club had been fewer and shorter: but now he knew that he
must relinquish them altogether. Shabbiness might pass: but clothes
obviously rotting might not be exhibited by England to young Venice. He
went to the Bucintoro at mid-morning, when no one was there, and
substituted the greenish-grey boat-cloak of Harris Mixture for the

blue one which he had been carrying; it would not show stains so easily. He put his Wilkinson razors and some washing-gear with a towel into his largest pigskin satchel; and filled it up with manuscripts. Then he put all his other belongings into his locker and snapped the padlock for good and all. If fortune turned, he could come back for them. He promised himself employment for the next fine day, sitting on the grass of the sea-wall of the Campo di Marte, sorting his papers—the incomplete manuscript of *Toward Aristocracy,* his draft-letter book, diary, and all the letters received since his return from Calabria. . . .

No fruit came from his sowing. Nothing was left in him, or of him, but an unconquerable capacity of endurance till sweet white Death should have leave to touch him, with an insuperable determination to keep his crisis from the hideous eyes of all men. Terrible as was his bodily emaciation, languid as was his mind, aching and stiff and feeble as were his weary weary limbs, he contrived to preserve his leisured imperscrutable carriage, and to present to the world a face offensive, disdainful, slightly sardonic, utterly unapproachable. The short pipe, which he always sported, was long empty but not (as he believed) noticeably empty; and it added that tinge of casual insolence which freed him from suspicion of dying fast of privation and exposure.

He went, every evening, to the sermon and benediction at the church of the Gesuati on the Zattere: first, to pay the prodigious debt of the present to the past—the duty of love and piety to the dead; and, second, for the sake of an hour in quiet sheltered obscurity. The grand temple, prepared for the Month of the Dead, draped in silver and black, with its forest of slim soaring tapers crowned with primrose stars in mid-air half-way up the vault, and the huge glittering constellation aloft in the apse where God in His Sacrament was enthroned, replenished his beauty-worshipping soul with peace and bliss. The patter of the preacher passed him unheard. His wordless prayer, for eternal rest in the meanest crevice of purgatory, poured forth unceasingly with the prayers of the dark crowd kneeling with him in the dimness below.

On the Day of All Saints he strolled carelessly (one would have said)—he successfully accomplished the giddy feat of not staggering (if one must speak accurately)—across the long wooden bridge of barks to the cemetery on the islet of Sanmichele. It was a last pious pilgrimage, with the holy and wholesome thought of praying for the dead, that they (in turn) might pray for him who had none living to spit him a suffrage. The place was a garden. On all sides thronged the quick, to deck the graves of their dead with tapers and lamps and flowers. The place was a garden, hallowed by prayer, hallowed by human love. In the place where God deigned to mount upon The Cross, and to be crucified for love, also, there was a garden.

He slowly paced along cypress-avenues, between the graves of little children with blue or white standards and the graves of adults marked by more somber memorials. All around him were patricians bringing sheaves of painted candles and gorgeous garlands of orchids and everlastings, or plebeians on their knees grubbing up weeds and tracing pathetic designs with cheap chrysanthemums and farthing night-lights. Here, were a baker's boy and a telegraph-messenger, repainting their father's grave-post with a tin of black and a bottle of gold. There, were half a dozen ribald venal dishonest licentious young *gondolieri,* quiet and alone on their wicked knees round the grave of a comrade. And there went Zildo, creeping swiftly somewhere, with an armful of dark red roses hiding his face. Nicholas turned away to the open gates of private chapels, revealing byzantine interiors, with gold-winged suns in turquoise vaults, over altars of porphyry and violet marble and alabaster inlaid with mother-o'-pearl in dull silver, and triptychs of hammered silver set with lapis lazuli and ivory, blazing with slender tapers, starred with lanthorns of beaten bronze, carpeted with dewy-fresh flowers. Even the *loculi,* the tombs in the cemetery-walls, each had its bordure of brilliant bloom with tapers to burn on the pavement before it. All the morning, masses were offered in the church of Saint Michael and in the chapel of Saint Christopher. From time to time a minor friar, in surplice and stole, went, with some black-robed family, to bless the new memorial on a recent grave.

He found himself in the field where Venice buries strangers, and looked for the grave of the engineer who died at the Universal Infirmary nine months before. He remembered its site, but it was unmarked, totally neglected, unrecognizable. Evidently the grave had not been bought in perpetuity; and the bones had gone (or would go) to the common ossuary, with none to care or make memorial. He went on, praying, and entered the columbarium. Here was the plain marble urn of an English baby, Lawrence, burned and forgotten. Here was the plain marble urn of that other Englishman who died at the Universal Infirmary in March: one had remembered him, then, with red roses and a card of love: but flowers fade, and love—Love can move the sun and the other stars. O loyal love! Zildo had not forgotten his father.

It was the eighth day since Nicholas had tasted any food at all. He had a bit of bread in his pocket—a half of one of those biscuit-like rings of the poor, hard as stone, which are so satiating. He had two *lire* and sixty *centesimi* also. But he could not eat. The last morsel had nauseated him so cataclysmically. He had tried milk, but it had made him reel. Water, a handful of it, surreptitiously taken, at night, from the fountain in some campo, satisfied him now.

It was the eleventh day since he had caught a glimpse of Zildo's face, at the Ponte dei Pugni in Sanbarnaba. He dared not submit to the scrutiny of those lovely wistful pellucid eyes, which, somehow, seemed to be beginning to know all things hidden since the world began. Of course he avoided Santrovaso by daylight; and, at night, when he walked swiftly by, closed window-shutters veiled the gleam of candles. He would have liked to have seen that wonderful exquisite dear child again. He would have liked many other indecorous things: but nothing could justify invasion or confusion of a young life like Zildo's. Never—never. Alone he had lived: he would at least pluck up enough sense of propriety to do his dying by himself. He sauntered on.

Late at night he came to the gated bridge of the islet of Sanelena. The torrential rain of Sunday had not made his favorite nook impracticable; and, though his long-soaked clothes clung heavily and stickily to him, he rather glowed than felt their chill. But Sleep had deserted him; for five days and nights he had been wide-awake. Oh that the suave twin-brothers might come very soon—first, kind Sleep—then, gentle Death.

But, "Not my will—"

And, "Though He slay me, yet I will trust in Him: but I will maintain mine own ways before Him."

Stars spangled the blackness of heaven. Over the distant lagoon the Bear prowled away from the Lido, and Orion the Huntsman rushed across the sky between the islands of Burano and Santerasmo. Later, the waning moon made shift to rise. The deadly cold and damp struck and unnerved him. "God, do give me a home," he sighed, shivering, too stiff to move without crying, all night long.

At 5½ o'clock the black horizon beyond the Lido channel seemed to develop a monstrous interminable blacker wall, with a paler black light behind it, which showed above it. At 6½ o'clock an orange-colored stripe unrolled itself along the base of the wall which shimmered in deepest greys; and a pink sun peered out of the sea with a certain air of urgency. Another day in this world! Surely he had untied all the strings which bound him here? Had he? Had He? No: not quite all.

He rose, moving delicately to ease his stiffness, till he felt fit and able to ramble, in freedom from remark, on an errand which his angel-guardian indicated for him. Something more seemed to be expected from him. "Nothing in my hand I bring," but his hand was not yet empty.

Once more he went toward the cemetery. In Campo Sanzancristomo he bought an armful of white crysanthemums and a handful of white rose-buds with his last coins. Let the forgotten Dead remember him, as he remembered them. Let them.

There were many people, also bearing flowers: but not the close-packed mob of yesterday. This was the Day of the Dead. Later, all Venice would throng the bridge of barks. He must do his errand swiftly.

In the columbarium he placed rose-buds at the urn containing the ashes of the unremembered baby, and a nosegay in place of the faded roses at the urn of the Englishman. No one was about, yet. He went to the forgotten grave of the engineer, and marked out a great white cross of chrysanthemums on the level grass. And he prayed long for the repose of their Protestant souls, that they also might pray for him in his great loneliness. Even now he was alone, faint, yet pursuing.

From those secluded enclosures he went into the crowded church of Saint Michael Archangel and Soul-Weigher, to hear a mass and commemorate his own dear dead whose remains lay far away. In those ancestral memories, fragrant, most beloved, he offered what merit there was in his remembrance of forgotten dead whom (in life) he had never even seen. Thence he travelled to the chapel of Saint Christopher Giant and God-bearer. The Cardinal Patriarch was saying mass, a gentle courtly white-haired elder, with the delicate hands and ordered manner of reticent but pregnant gesture and utterance of the hierarchy. Nicholas prayed near the door till the prelate emerged to the open to bless and absolve all those whose remains awaited resurrection in the earth around him. The grey and orange of dawn had lightened, and a clear sky of pink and silver and pale violet with paler gold hung like a canopy above.

To escape the observation (and exhalation) of the mob he returned to the city, now nearly deserted, and wandered all day through quieter alleys between the Ghetto and Santalvise in the *sexter* of Cannarezo. A brace of sandy-haired black-shawled wenches gave him a scratch of annoyance by glancing from his boots to his face and back to his boots, as he paced the long quay of La Senza near the Abbey of Pity. They grinned. He wondered how haggard he really was. His boots, he knew, were purely frightful. But how ghastly was unintelligent note and criticism. He thanked God for that crowning mercy which is called blind night.

By dusk he strayed southward over the station-bridge into Santacroxe and Sanpolo. The magnificent bells, and the splendid sweetly-rolling diapason of the organ, in the huge dim church of the Frari, enormously revived him at an early Benediction. He rested there awhile, after, between the shades of Titian and Canova, till intonation of the Vespers of

The Dead began. Then, on again—he must not fail to finish his sequence of nine-days' prayer at the church of the Gesuati. . .

Eternal rest. . . . Everlasting light. . . . It was dark. Where should he find rest? He could not get to Santelena now. There was no way but through the most flaring and crowded parts of the city, and the glances of a mob would send him raving mad. He ought to have economized his forces, to get there before he became so dead-tired—tired, but not yet dead. The time was here when he would cry God mercy—man, never—Kyrie eleèson.

When they closed the church he went up the Zattere, as far as the gated bridge of the Doganale over Rio della Salute. He rested here by the wood-store, pretending to admire the view across the Canal of Zuecca. But no one apprached. Venice itself was tired, and refrained from dissipation on the night of the Day of The Dead. He crept down the dark little alley by Ca' Struan, and crossed the bridge to the great quay and stairs of the Salute. Just by the bridge, the empty bark of old Bastian Vianello was moored to its *pali,* littered and dirty with the fragments of faggots. He wondered whether the firewood merchant would let him sleep there. No. There were darker nooks high up on the steps of the church.

After an hour or so he moved back, through the Rio Terrà dei Catecumeni, where Ottoman infidels used to be confined till they knew their catechism. One of his old *gondolieri* kennelled here, a bluff plausible faithless little dog. The wide long stretch of the Zattere invited him. He hesitated; and presently went toward Marittima, very slowly, and with frequent pauses, for he seemed to have lost all sense of his limbs, and walked but automatically. Kyrie eleèson. At every post he stopped, to lean against it with the cultivated air of leisured pensive meditation which cost no effort, having been made habitual. Time tore on. Passers-by became fewer and very far between. He had whole sections of the quay entirely to himself. The last lights went out in the wine-shop by the ferry-pontoons. Sometimes he lost consciousness for several minutes. Kyrie eleèson, he murmured all the while.

He turned, apathetically, under the arcade at the corner of Rio di Santrovaso to take one more look at Zildo's window. All was dark.

And instantaneous coruscation burst in his brain, and something broke—breast—heart—Kyrie eleèson.

He found himself on his hands and knees on the pavement, with a sound of rushing water surging. He must move. He must move very far away from there, at once. It could not be a flood, for he remembered no sirocco. No: it was only a sudden squall—but how sudden, how violent! Kyrie eleèson. He picked himself up and tottered to the parapet of the quay of support, just while he satisfied himself as to the state of the tide in the canal.

Right beneath him was the pupparin, chained to its *pali*. The pupparin! The very thing! And his own key of its padlock was in his trousers-pocket. What luck! He would paddle it, with a floor-board, out on the great canal of Zuecca, and let the flood—for undoubtedly there was a terrible sudden flood—carry him where it would. If he could but get as far as the friendly solitary sea! Kyrie eleèson.

At least he was in the bark again. How the water roared in his ears! He must be very calm. Kyrie eleèson. Perhaps it would be as well to lie down, satchel for pillow, and rest—only for a few minutes. How very dark the night was! Or, had the wind blown out the lamps? Yes: he would lie down, and recollect a little strength before doing anything. Then he would fumble for the padlock; set the bark free. Kyrie eleèson.

This was not suicide. On the contrary, it was a precaution of safety. Moored barks were often swamped, or hung up on their own moorings and battered to bits, in storms like this. Whereas, if he let her go, nothing could upset her: she would ride bravely on any swell: and one could rest more securely in her than on inundated quays—and in perfect privacy too. Kyrie eleèson. Yes: he would count up to a hundred. Then he would take the key from his pocket, and count fifty. Then he would find the padlock, in this dense rocking din, and count another fifty—fifty Kyries, a hundred Kyries, counted on his fingers, understood. Then he would paddle under the bridge to the open. Kyrie eleèson.

He was lying on his back in the bark. Why? Where was she now?—The rushing and the rocking of the water in the dark. No one could see.—He had unlocked the chain? Had he? He couldn't remember. Kyrie eleèson.—The long strong booming of the wind in the dark. What did that matter? He was all alone.—Now it was imperatively necessary to be extremely artful. He must make quite sure about the dark. Kyrie eleèson.—Key—pocket . . . Hand . . . Where? . . . The crashing of great stormy streams in the dark. . . . *Deus, in adiutorium meum intende* . . . .

Thomas Mann

·⊲ 1875–1955 ⊳·

Thomas Mann was the pre-eminent German writer of the first half of the twentieth century. Born in Lübeck, Mann first attracted attention with a story written during a year spent in Italy in 1898, but it was the publication in 1901 of Buddenbrooks, *a novel dealing with the rise and fall of a German merchant family, that made him famous. His subsequent work added to his reputation world-wide and earned him the 1929 Nobel Prize in Literature. An outspoken opponent of anti-intellectualism, and so of Fascism and Nazism, Mann left Germany voluntarily in 1933, going first to Switzerland, and then, after the Nazis had deprived him of his German citizenship, to the United States. There he lived until 1953, when he returned to Switzerland.*

Death in Venice, *published in 1912, contains representative themes from Mann's fiction: the interaction of psychological and cultural values and problems, the interconnection of neurosis and art, genius and disease.*

DEATH IN VENICE

In the afternoon Aschenbach spent two hours in his room, then took the *vaporetto* to Venice, across the foul-smelling lagoon. He got out at San Marco, had his tea in the Piazza, and then, as his custom was, took a walk through the streets. But this walk of his brought about nothing less than a revolution in his mood and an entire change in all his plans.

There was a hateful sultriness in the narrow streets. The air was so heavy that all the manifold smells wafted out of houses, shops, and cookshops—smells of oil, perfumery, and so forth—hung low, like exhalations, not dissipating. Cigarette smoke seemed to stand in the air, it drifted so slowly away. Today the crowd in these narrow lanes oppressed the stroller instead of diverting him. The longer he walked, the more was

201

he in tortures under that state, which is the product of the sea air and the sirocco and which excites and enervates at once. He perspired painfully. His eyes rebelled, his chest was heavy, he felt feverish, the blood throbbed in his temples. He fled from the huddled, narrow streets of the commercial city, crossed many bridges, and came into the poor quarter of Venice. Beggars waylaid him; the canals sickened him with their evil exhalations. He reached a quiet square, one of those that exist at the city's heart, forsaken of God and man; there he rested awhile on the margin of a fountain, wiped his brow, and admitted to himself that he must be gone.

For the second time, and now quite definitely, the city proved that in certain weathers it could be directly inimical to his health. Nothing but sheer unreasoning obstinacy would linger on, hoping for an unprophesiable change in the wind. A quick decision was in place. He could not go home at this stage, neither summer nor winter quarters would be ready. But Venice had not a monopoly of sea and shore: there were other spots where these were to be had without the evil concomitants of lagoon and fever-breeding vapors. He remembered a little bathing place not far from Trieste of which he had had a good report. Why not go there? At once, of course, in order that this second change might be worth the making. He resolved, he rose to his feet and sought the nearest gondola-landing, where he took a boat and was conveyed to San Marco through the gloomy windings of many canals, beneath balconies of delicate marble traceries flanked by carven lions; round slippery corners of wall, past melancholy façades with ancient business shields reflected in the rocking water. It was not too easy to arrive at his destination, for his gondolier, being in league with various lace-makers and glass-blowers, did his best to persuade his fare to pause, look, and be tempted to buy. Thus the charm of this bizarre passage through the heart of Venice, even while it played upon his spirit, yet was sensibly cooled by the predatory commercial spirit of the fallen queen of the seas.

Once back in his hotel, he announced at the office, even before dinner, that circumstances unforeseen obliged him to leave early next morning. The management expressed its regret, it changed his money and receipted his bill. He dined, and spent the lukewarm evening in a rockingchair on the rear terrace, reading the newspapers. Before he went to bed, he made his luggage ready against the morning.

His sleep was not of the best, for the prospect of another journey made him restless. When he opened his window next morning, the sky was still overcast, but the air seemed fresher—and there and then his rue began. Had he not given notice too soon? Had he not let himself be swayed by a slight and momentary indisposition? If he had only been patient, not lost heart so quickly, tried to adapt himself to the climate, or even waited for a change in the weather before deciding! Then, instead of the hurry and flurry of departure, he would have before him now a morning like yesterday's on the beach. Too late! He must go on wanting what he had wanted yesterday. He dressed and at eight o'clock went down to breakfast.

When he entered the breakfast-room it was empty. Guests came in while he sat waiting for his order to be filled. As he sipped his tea, he saw the Polish girls enter with their governess, chaste and morning-fresh, with sleep-reddened eyelids. They crossed the room and sat down at their table in the window. Behind them came the porter, cap in hand, to announce that it was time for him to go. The car was waiting to convey him and other travellers to the Hôtel Excelsior, whence they would go by motorboat through the company's private canal to the station. Time pressed. But Aschenbach found it did nothing of the sort. There still lacked more than an hour of train time. He felt irritated at the hotel habit of getting the guests out of the house earlier than necessary; and requested the porter to let him breakfast in peace. The man hesitated and withdrew, only to come back again five minutes later. The car could wait no longer. Good, then it might go, and take his trunk with it, Aschenbach answered with some heat. He would use the public conveyance, in his own time; he begged them to leave the choice of it to him. The functionary bowed. Aschenbach, pleased to be rid of him, made a leisurely meal, and even had a newspaper of the waiter. When at length he rose, the time was grown very short. And it so happened that at that moment Tadzio came through the glass doors into the room.

To reach his own table he crossed the traveller's path, and modestly cast down his eyes before the gray-haired man of the lofty brows—only to lift them again in that sweet way he had and direct his full soft gaze upon Aschenbach's face. Then he was past. "For the last time, Tadzio," thought the elder man. "It was all too brief!" Quite unusually for him, he shaped a farewell with his lips, he actually uttered it, and added: "May God bless you!" Then he went out, distributed tips, exchanged farewells with the mild little manager in the frockcoat, and, followed by the porter with his hand luggage, left the hotel. On foot as he had come, he passed through the white-blossoming avenue, diagonally across the island to the boat landing. He went on board at once—but the tale of his journey across the lagoon was a tale of woe, a passage through the very valley of regrets.

It was the well-known route: through the lagoon, past San Marco, up the Grand Canal. Aschenbach sat on the circular bench in the bows, with his elbow on the railing, one hand shading his eyes. They passed the

Public Gardens, once more the princely charm of the Piazzetta rose up before him and then dropped behind, the next came the great row of palaces, the canal curved, and the splendid marble arches of the Rialto came in sight. The traveller gazed—and his bosom was torn. The atmosphere of the city, the faintly rotten scent of swamp and sea, which had driven him to leave—in what deep, tender, almost painful draughts he breathed it in! How was it he had not known, had not thought, how much his heart was set upon it all! What this morning had been slight regret, some little doubt of his own wisdom, turned now to grief, to actual wretchedness, a mental agony so sharp that it repeatedly brought tears to his eyes, while he questioned himself how he could have foreseen it. The hardest part, the part that more than once it seemed he could not bear, was the thought that he should never more see Venice again. Since now for the second time the place had made him ill, since for the second time he had had to flee for his life, he must henceforth regard it as a forbidden spot, to be forever shunned; senseless to try it again, after he had proved himself unfit. Yes, if he fled it now, he felt that wounded pride must prevent his return to this spot where twice he had made actual bodily surrender. And this conflict between inclination and capacity all at once assumed, in this middle-aged man's mind, immense weight and importance; the physical defeat seemed a shameful thing, to be avoided at whatever cost; and he stood amazed at the ease with which on the day before he had yielded to it.

Meanwhile the steamer neared the station landing; his anguish of irresolution amounted almost to panic. To leave seemed to the sufferer impossible, to remain not less so. Torn thus between two alternatives, he entered the station. It was very late, he had not a moment to lose. Time pressed, it scourged him onward. He hastened to buy his ticket and looked round in the crowd to find the hotel porter. The man appeared and said that the trunk had already gone off. "Gone already?" "Yes, it has gone to Como." "To Como?" A hasty exchange of words—angry questions from Aschenbach, and puzzled replies from the porter—at length made it clear that the trunk had been put with the wrong luggage even before leaving the hotel, and in company with other trunks was now well on its way in precisely the wrong direction.

Aschenbach found it hard to wear the right expression as he heard this news. A reckless joy, a deep incredible mirthfulness shook him almost as with a spasm. The porter dashed off after the lost trunk, returning very soon, of course, to announce that his efforts were unavailing. Aschenbach said he would not travel without his luggage; that he would go back and wait at the Hôtel des Bains until it turned up. Was the company's motorboat still outside? The man said yes, it was at the door. With his native eloquence he prevailed upon the ticket agent to take back the ticket already purchased; he swore that he would wire, that no pains should be spared, that the trunk would be restored in the twinkling of an eye. And the unbelievable thing came to pass; the traveller, twenty minutes after he had reached the station, found himself once more on the Grand Canal on his way back to the Lido.

What a strange adventure indeed, this about face of destiny— incredible, humiliating, whimsical as any dream! To be passing again, within the hour, these scenes from which in profoundest grief he had but now taken leave forever! The little swift-moving vessel, a furrow of foam at its prow, tacking with droll agility between steamboats and gondolas, went like a shot to its goal; and he, its sole passenger, sat hiding the panic and thrills of a truant schoolboy beneath a mask of forced resignation. His breast still heaved from time to time with a burst of laughter over the contretemps. Things could not, he told himself, have fallen out more luckily. There would be the necessary explanations, a few astonished faces—then all would be well once more, a mischance prevented, a grievous error set right; and all he had thought to have left forever was his own once more, his for as long as he liked. . . . And did the boat's swift motion deceive him, or was the wind now coming from the sea?

The waves struck against the tiled sides of the narrow canal. At Hôtel Excelsior the automobile omnibus awaited the returned traveller and bore him along by the crisping waves back to the Hôtel des Bains. The little mustachioed manager in the frockcoat came down the steps to greet him.

In dulcet tones he deplored the mistake, said how painful it was to the management and himself; applauded Aschenbach's resolve to stop on until the errant trunk came back; his former room, alas, was already taken, but another as good awaited his approval. *"Pas de chance, monsieur,"* said the Swiss lift porter, with a smile, as he conveyed him upstairs. And the fugitive was soon quartered in another room which in situation and furnishings almost precisely resembled the first.

He laid out the contents of his handbag in their wonted places; then, tired out, dazed by the whirl of the extraordinary forenoon, subsided into the armchair by the open window. The sea wore a pale-green cast, the air felt thinner and purer, the beach with its cabins and boats had more color, notwithstanding the sky was still gray. Aschenbach, his hands folded in his lap, looked out. He felt rejoiced to be back, yet displeased with his vacillating moods, his ignorance of his own real desires. Thus for nearly an hour he sat, dreaming, resting, barely thinking. At midday he saw Tadzio, in his striped sailor suit with red breastknot, coming up from the sea, across the barrier and along the boardwalk to the hotel. Aschenbach recognized him, even at this height, knew it was he before he actually saw him, had it in mind to say to himself: "Well, Tadzio, so here you are again too!" But the casual greeting died away before it reached his lips, slain by the truth in his heart. He felt the rapture of his blood, the poignant pleasure, and realized that it was for Tadzio's sake the leavetaking had been so hard.

He sat quite still, unseen at his high post, and looked within himself. His features were lively, he lifted his brows; a smile, alert, inquiring, vivid, widened the mouth. Then he raised his head, and with both hands, hanging limp over the chairarms, he described a slow motion, palms outward, a lifting and turning movement, as thought to indicate a wide embrace. It was a gesture of welcome, a calm and deliberate acceptance of what might come.

Ernest Hemingway

Ernest Hemingway, one of the great American writers of the twentieth century and winner of the 1954 Nobel Prize in Literature, joined the American Red Cross as a volunteer during the First World War, not long after graduating from Oak Park (Illinois) High School and after working briefly as a reporter for the Kansas City Star. *Assigned to the Italian Army, he was stationed at first near Schio and later along the front between Mount Grappa and the Piave River, at a time when the Austrian Army was threatening the Veneto and Venice. There, in mid-summer, Hemingway was wounded, the first American casualty in Italy. He was not quite nineteen years old.*

The experience of war and of the Veneto left a lasting mark on the young man. As he once said, "I am a man that has five home towns, Oak Park (where I was born), Paris, Key West, Havana . . . and Venice." Across the River and into the Trees *was his lovesong to Venice. In 1948 he returned to the city for the first time after the Second World War, and his first extended visit to Italy since 1918. There, on Torcello, the original island settlement of the Venetians, he began the story that became the novel. When it was published in 1950, an elaborate disclaimer stated that "there are no real people in this volume." But Hemingway knew better, intending to delay publication in Italian until two years after English publication. In fact, the novel was not published in Italy until 1965, four years after Hemingway's death.*

ACROSS THE RIVER AND INTO THE TREES

He was looking ahead now to see where the canal road joined the main highway again. There he knew that he would see it on a clear day such as this was. Across the marshes, brown as those at the mouths of the Mississippi around Pilot Town are in winter, and with their reeds bent by the heavy north wind, he saw the squared tower of the church at Torcello and the high campanile of Burano beyond it. The sea was a slate blue and he could see the sails of twelve sailing barges running with the wind for Venice.

I'll have to wait until we cross the Dese River above Noghera to see it perfectly, he thought. It is strange to remember how we fought back there along the canal that winter to defend it and we never saw it. Then one time, I was back as far as Noghera and it was clear and cold like today, and I saw it across the water. But I never got into it. It is my city, though, because I fought for it when I was a boy, and now that I am half a hundred years old, they know I fought for it and am a part owner and they treat me well.

Do you think that's why they treat you well, he asked himself.

Maybe, he thought. Maybe they treat me well because I'm a chicken colonel on the winning side. I don't believe it, though. I hope not, anyway. It is not France, he thought. . . .

"Jackson," he said, "are you happy?"

"Yes, sir."

"Good. Shortly, we are coming to a view that I want you to see. You only have to take one look at it. The entire operation will be practically painless."

I wonder what he's riding me for now, the driver thought. Just because he was a BG once he knows everything. If he was any good as a BG why didn't he hold it? He's been beat up so much he's slug-nutty.

"There's the view, Jackson," the Colonel said. "Stop her by the side of the road and we'll take a look."

The Colonel and the driver walked over to the Venice side of the road and looked across the lagoon that was whipped by the strong, cold wind from the mountains that sharpened all the outlines of buildings so that they were geometrically clear.

"That's Torcello directly opposite us," the Colonel pointed. "That's where the people lived that were driven off the mainland by the Visigoths. They built that church you see there with the square tower. There were thirty thousand people lived there once and they built that church to honor their Lord and to worship him. Then, after they built it, the mouth of the Sile River silted up or a big flood changed it, and all that land we came through just now got flooded and started to breed mosquitoes and malaria hit them. They all started to die, so the elders got together and decided they should pull out to a healthy place that would be defensible with boats, and where the Visigoths and the Lombards and the other bandits couldn't get at them, because these bandits had no sea power. The

Torcello boys were all great boatmen. So they took the stones of all their houses in barges, like that one we just saw, and they built Venice."

He stopped. "Am I boring you, Jackson?"

"No, sir. I had no idea who pioneered Venice."

"It was the boys from Torcello. They were very tough and they had very good taste in building. They came from a little place up the coast called Caorle. But they drew on all the people from the towns and the farms behind when the Visigoths overran them. It was a Torcello boy who was running arms into Alexandria, who located the body of St. Mark and smuggled it out under a load of fresh pork so the infidel customs guards wouldn't check him. This boy brought the remains of St. Mark to Venice, and he's their patron saint and they have a cathedral there to him. But by that time, they were trading so far to the east that the architecture is pretty Byzantine for my taste. They never built any better than at the start there in Torcello. That's Torcello there."

It was, indeed.

"St. Mark's Square is where the pigeons are and where they have that big cathedral that looks sort of like a moving-picture palace, isn't it?"

"Right, Jackson. You're on the ball. If that's the way you look at it. Now you look beyond Torcello you will see the lovely campanile on Burano that has damn near as much list on it as the leaning tower of Pisa. That Burano is a very over-populated little island where the women make wonderful lace, and the men make *bambinis* and work daytimes in the glass factories in that next island you see on beyond with the other campanile, which is Murano. They make wonderful glass daytimes for the rich of all the world, and then they come home on the little vaporetto and make *bambinis*. Not everyone passes every night with his wife though. They hunt ducks nights too, and with punt guns, out along the edge of the marshes on this lagoon you're looking across now. All night long on a moonlight night you hear the shots." He paused.

"Now when you look past Murano you see Venice. That's my town. There's plenty more I could show you, but I think we probably ought to roll now. But take one good look at it. This is where you can see how it all happened. But nobody ever looks at it from here."

"It's a beautiful view. Thank you, sir."

"Okay," the Colonel said. "Let's roll." . . .

*   *   *   *

This country meant very much to him, more than he could, or would ever tell anyone and now he sat in the car happy that in another half hour they would be in Venice. He took two mannitol hexanitrate tablets; since

209

he had always been able to spit since 1918, he could take them dry, and asked, "How are you doing, Jackson?"

"Fine, sir."

"Take the left outside road when we hit the fork for Mestre and we'll be able to see the boats along the canal and miss that main traffic."

"Yes, sir," the driver said. "Will you check me on the fork?"

"Of course," the Colonel said.

They were coming up on Mestre fast, and already it was like going to New York the first time you were ever there in the old days when it was shining, white and beautiful. I stole that, he thought. But that was before the smoke. We are coming into my town, he thought, Christ, what a lovely town.

They made the left turn and came along the canal where the fishing boats tied up, and the Colonel looked at them and his heart was happy because of the brown nets and the wicker fish traps and the clean, beautiful lines of the boats. It's not that they are picturesque. The hell with picturesque. They are just damned beautiful. . . .

They were up on the causeway from Mestre to Venice now with the ugly Breda works that might have been Hammond, Indiana.

"What do they make there, sir?" Jackson asked.

"The company makes locomotives in Milan," the Colonel said. "Here they make a little of everything in the metallurgic line."

It was a miserable view of Venice now and he always disliked this causeway except that you made such good time and you could see the buoys and the channels.

"This town makes a living on its own," he said to Jackson. "She used to be the queen of the seas and the people are very tough and they give less of a good goddamn about things than almost anybody you'll ever meet. It's a tougher town than Cheyenne when you really know it, and everybody is very polite." . . .

"Well, there's the Fiat garage where we leave the car," the Colonel said. "You can leave the key at the office. They don't steal. I'll go in the bar while you park upstairs. They have people that will bring the bags."

"Is it okay to leave your gun and shooting gear in the trunk, sir?"

"Sure. They don't steal here. I told you that once."

"I wanted to take the necessary precautions, sir, on your valuable property."

"You're so damned noble that sometimes you stink," the Colonel said. "Get the wax out of your ears and hear what I say the first time."

"I heard you, sir," Jackson said. The Colonel looked at him contemplatively and with the old deadliness.

He sure is a mean son of a bitch, Jackson thought, and he can be so goddamn nice.

"Get my and your bag out and park her up there and check your oil, your water and your tires." the Colonel said, and walked across the oil and rubber stained cement of the entry of the bar. . . .

*   *   *   *

At the *imbarcadero,* the Colonel tipped the man who had carried their two bags and then looked around for a boatman he knew.

He did not recognize the man in the launch that was first on call, but the boatman said, "Good day, my Colonel. I'm the first."

"How much is it to the Gritti?"

"You know as well as I, my Colonel. We do not bargain. We have a fixed tariff."

"What's the tariff?"

"Three thousand five hundred."

"We could go on the vaporetto for sixty."

"And nothing prevents you going," the boatman, who was an elderly man with a red but uncholeric face, said. "They won't take you to the Gritti but they will stop at the *imbarcadero* past Harry's, and you can telephone for someone from the Gritti to get your bags."

And what would I buy with the goddamn three thousand five hundred lire; and this is a good old man.

"Do you want me to send that man there?" he pointed to a destroyed old man who did odd jobs and ran errands around the docks, always ready with the unneeded aid to the elbow of the ascending or descending passenger, always ready to help when no help was needed, his old felt hat held out as he bowed after the unneeded act. "He'll take you to the vaporetto. There's one in twenty minutes."

"The hell with it," the Colonel said. "Take us to the Gritti."

"*Con piacere*," the boatman said.

The Colonel and Jackson lowered themselves into the launch which looked like a speed boat. It was radiantly varnished and lovingly kept and was powered with a marine conversion of a tiny Fiat engine that had served its allotted time in the car of a provincial doctor and had been purchased out of one of the graveyards of automobiles; those mechanical elephant cemeteries that are the one certain thing you may find in our world near any populated center; and been reconditioned and reconverted to start this new life on the canals of this city.

"How is the motor doing?" the Colonel asked. He could hear her sounding like a stricken tank or T.D., except the noises were in miniature from the lack of power.

"So-so," the boatman said. He moved his free hand in a parallel motion.

"You ought to get the smallest model Universal puts out. That's the best and lightest small marine engine I know."

"Yes," the boatman said. "There are quite a few things I should get."

"Maybe you'll have a good year."

"It's always possible. Lots of *pescecani* come down from Milano to gamble at the Lido. But nobody would ride twice in this thing on purpose. As a boat, it is fine, too. It is a well built, pleasant boat. Not beautiful as a gondola is, of course. But it needs an engine."

"I might get you a jeep engine. One that was condemned and you could work it over."

"Don't talk about such things," the boatman said. "Things like that don't happen. I don't want to think about it."

"You can think about it," the Colonel said. "I'm talking true."

"You mean it."

"Sure. I don't guarantee anything. I'll see what I can do. How many children have you got?"

"Six. Two male and four female."

"Hell, you mustn't have believed in the Régime. Only six."

"I *didn't* believe in the Régime."

"You don't have to give me that stuff," the Colonel said. "It would have been quite natural for you to *have* believed in it. Do you think I hold that against a man after we've won?"

They were through the dull part of the canal that runs from Piazzale Roma to Ca'Foscari, though none of it is dull, the Colonel thought.

It doesn't all have to be palaces nor churches. Certainly that isn't dull. He looked to the right, the starboard, he thought. I'm on the water. It was a long low pleasant building and there was a *trattoria* next to it.

I ought to live here. On retirement pay I could make it all right. No Gritti Palace. A room in a house like that and the tides and the boats going by. I could read in the mornings and walk around town before lunch and go every day to see the Tintorettos at the Accademia and to the Scuola San Rocco and eat in good cheap joints behind the market or, maybe, the woman that ran the house would cook in the evenings.

I think it would be better to have lunch out and get some exercise walking. It's a good town to walk in. I guess the best, probably. I never walked in it that it wasn't fun. I could learn it really well, he thought, and then I'd have that.

It's a strange, tricky town and to walk from any part to any other given part of it is better than working crossword puzzles. It's one of the few things to our credit that we never smacked it, and to *their* credit that they respected it.

Christ, I love it, he said, and I'm so happy I helped defend it when I was a punk kid, and with an insufficient command of the language and I never even saw her until that clear day in the winter when I went back to have that small wound dressed, and saw her rising from the sea. *Merde,* he thought, we did very well that winter up at the junction.

I wish I could fight it again, he thought. Knowing what I know now and having what we have now. But they'd have it too and the essential problem is just the same, except who holds the air.

And all this time he had been watching the bow of the beat-up beautifully varnished, delicately brass-striped boat, with the brass all beautifully polished, cut the brown water and seen the small traffic problems.

They went under the white bridge and under the unfinished wood bridge. Then they left the red bridge on the right and passed under the first high-flying white bridge. Then there was the black iron fret-work bridge on the canal leading into the Rio Nuovo and they passed the two stakes chained together but not touching: like us the Colonel thought. He watched the tide pull at them and he saw how the chains had worn the wood since he first had seen them. That's us, he thought. That's our monument. And how many monuments are there to us in the canals of this town?

Then they still went slowly until the great lantern that was on the right of the entrance to the Grand Canal where the engine commenced its metallic agony that produced a slight increase in speed.

Now they came down and under the Accademia between the pilings where they passed, at touching distance, a heavily loaded black diesel boat full of cut timber, cut in chunks, to burn for firewood in the damp houses of the Sea City. . . .

They were moving up the Grand Canal now and it was easy to see where your friends lived.

"That's the house of the Contessa Dandolo," the Colonel said.

He did not say, but thought, she is over eighty, and she is as gay as a girl and does not have any fear of dying. She dyes her hair red and it looks very well. She is a good companion and an admirable woman.

Her palazzo was pleasant looking, set well back from the Canal with a garden in front and a landing place of its own where many gondolas had come, in their various times, bringing hearty, cheerful, sad and disil-

213

lusioned people. But most of them had been cheerful because they were going to see the Contessa Dandolo.

Now, beating up the Canal, against the cold wind off the mountains, and with the houses as clear and sharp as on a winter day, which, of course, it was, they saw the old magic of the city and its beauty. But it was conditioned, for the Colonel, by his knowing many of the people who lived in the palazzos; or if no one lived there now, knowing to what use the different places had been put.

There's Alvarito's mother's house, he thought, and did not say.

She never lives there much and stays out at the country house near Treviso where they have trees. She's tired of there not being trees in Venice. She lost a fine man and nothing really interests her now except efficiency.

But the family at one time lent the house to George Gordon, Lord Byron, and nobody sleeps now in Byron's bed nor in the other bed, two flights below, where he used to sleep with the gondolier's wife. They are not sacred, nor relics. They are just extra beds that were not used afterwards for various reasons, or possibly to respect Lord Byron who was well loved in this town, in spite of all the errors he committed. You have to be a tough boy in this town to be loved, the Colonel thought. They never cared anything for Robert Browning, nor Mrs. Robert Browning, nor for their dog. They weren't Venetians no matter how well he wrote of it. And what is a tough boy, he asked himself. You use it so loosely you should be able to define it. I suppose it is a man who will make his play and then backs it up. Or just a man who backs his play. And I'm not thinking of the theatre, he thought. Lovely as the theatre can be. . . .

But now he was passing the house where the poor beat-up old boy had lived with his great, sad and never properly loved actress and he thought of her wonderful hands and her so transformable face, that was not beautiful, but that gave you all love, glory and delight and sadness; and of the way the curve of her forearm could break your heart, and he thought, Christ they are dead and I do not know where either one is buried even. But I certainly hope they had fun in that house.

"Jackson," he said, "that small villa on the left belonged to Gabriele d'Annunzio, who was a great writer."

"Yes, sir," said Jackson, "I'm glad to know about him. I never heard of him."

"I'll check you out on what he wrote if you ever want to read him," the Colonel said. "There are some fair English translations."

"Thank you, sir," said Jackson. "I'd like to read him any time I have time. He has a nice practical looking place. What did you say the name was?"

"D'Annunzio," the Colonel said. "Writer."

He added to himself, not wishing to confuse Jackson, nor be difficult, as he had been with the man several times that day, writer, poet, national hero, phraser of the dialectic of Fascism, macabre egotist, aviator, commander, or rider, in the first of the fast torpedo attack boats, Lieutenant-Colonel of Infantry without knowing how to command a company, nor a platoon properly, the great, lovely writer of *Notturno* whom we respect, and jerk.

Up ahead now there was a crossing place of gondolas at the Santa Maria del Giglio and, beyond, was the wooden dock of the Gritti.

"That's the hotel where we are stopping at, Jackson."

The Colonel indicated the three-story, rose-colored, small, pleasant palace abutting on the Canal. It had been a dependence of the Grand Hotel—but now it was its own hotel and a very good one. It was probably the best hotel, if you did not wish to be fawned on, or fussed over, or over-flunkied, in a city of great hotels and the Colonel loved it.

"It looks okay to me, sir," Jackson said.

"It is okay," the Colonel said.

EPILOGUE

. . . if Enrico Dandolo or Francesco Foscari could be summoned from their tombs, and stood each on the deck of his galley at the entrance of the Grand Canal . . . the mighty Doges would not know in what part of the world they stood, would literally not recognize one stone of the great city, for whose sake, and by whose ingratitude, their grey hairs had been brought down with bitterness to the grave. The remains of *their* Venice—more gorgeous a thousandfold than that which now exists—lie hidden . . . in many a grass-grown court, and silent pathway, and lightless canal, where the slow waves have sapped their foundations . . . and must soon prevail over them for ever.

JOHN RUSKIN

Maladies of Venice

BY DORA JANE HAMBLIN

Reports of her death have been exaggerated, but there is no doubt that regal Venice, the dowager empress of the Adriatic, is desperately ill.

Her lovers, and the merely curious, call upon her assiduously: five million or so a year. They admire the Titians and Tintorettos, misquote Shakespeare at the Rialto Bridge, feed the messy pigeons in front of that ultimate Byzantine monument, St. Mark's Basilica. Most go home happy, all unaware that Venice still has no viable sewer system, that almost 58 percent of the dwellings have no central heat, that more than one-third of the population has fled across the famous lagoon in less than 25 years to the relative comfort of dry apartments on the mainland.

Yet even the most art-drenched tourist must see the deterioration. Blocks of weathered Istrian stone slip periodically from their moorings beside the stations of the vaporetti, or water buses, and subside into the canals. Church facades crack down the middle. Eroded marble reliefs lack noses and fingers, and pigeons nest quietly behind the ears of sculptured saints. Plaster falls from exterior walls of once-glorious palaces on the Grand Canal, exposing the damp brick beneath. First floors, too wet for habitation, are closed off and their windows boarded up.

All this despite the fact that, for more than a decade, millions of dollars have been borrowed, begged, donated or appropriated to save the city. The big trouble is that the dowager's doctors have been paralyzed by the complexity of the illness. A strangling bureaucracy at all levels (the national government, the regional government, the city administration), convoluted politics and stridently competing aims and claims have induced Italian administrators to behave like lifeguards arguing over who should throw out the cork ring—and who will have to pay for it if it doesn't work. Meanwhile, would-be rescuers from UNESCO, the United States, half of Europe, even Japan, Iran and Brazil, not to mention thousands of concerned Italian citizens, are constrained to dance around the perimeter alternately urging haste and crying "shame" at too hastily conceived cures.

The shocking state of Venice might have remained only a local sorrow had it not been for the big flood of 1966. Eleven years ago this month, heavy storms spread havoc across much of northern Italy, drove the Arno

River out of its banks to devastate Florence, and sent more than six feet of high water rampaging through the homes, shops and piazzas of Venice.

At first, both Italian and world attention focused on Florence, but within weeks a cry for aid came from the lagoon city. Led by UNESCO, dozens of private organizations rushed to help: from the United States the Committee to Rescue Italian Art (CRIA) and Colonel James A. Gray's International Fund for Monuments (IFM); Great Britain's Venice in Peril Fund and Italian Art and Archives Rescue Unit; hastily formed committees in West Germany, France, Yugoslavia, Australia and other countries; plus a host of Italian public and private institutions. In the years since the flood, this cadre of international volunteers has done wonders and spent from 3.5 to 4 million dollars in the process. This year, 33 groups from 13 nations are funneling funds and experts into the rescue. The Italian financial contribution (from ten distinct groups) ranks second only to that of the United States.

Thousands of square yards of frescoes and paintings have been restored. Churches have been renovated and structurally repaired, palaces put in order, bridges and facades cleaned. All this is wonderful, but it is in a sense only cosmetic. What good to save the treasures, if the whole city is doomed to wash away or perish in its own pollution, erosion and neglect?

The basic cure for Venice is a job only Italians can do, and it has become a classic case of the collision of warring interests: ecologists versus industrialists, city planners versus regional planners, developers versus preservationists. It is, to be fair, a staggering problem; "Everything that must be done in Venice must be done at the same time," complains the hard-working Communist assistant mayor, Gianni Pellicani.

Venice has been in peril, no doubt, since the first settlers sank wooden piles into the ooze of the lagoon in the fifth century A.D. and decided, against all odds, to build a city there. They had astonishing luck for centuries, grew rich and powerful, famous and decadent. Venice was the longest-lived republic the world had ever known, until it fell in 1797 to Napoleon, who then handed it over to Austria. In 1866 it was incorporated into the brand-new Italian unified state, and lurched uncertainly into the more complex perils of the 20th century.

In the middle of World War I the renowned Venetian Arsenal, which since the 12th century had massproduced men-of-war and armaments, closed down and turned 8, ooo men out of work. A group of local patriots, led by Count Giuseppe Volpi and including members of the Cini and Gaggia families, rushed to the rescue with a plan: Venice could once again become an important port, an industrial center, if it would build modern facilities. The men placed their dream on the mainland, on the other side of the causeway which Austria had built in 1846 to connect the island city for the first time with terra firma.

The new industrial zone, called Porto Marghera, was created by filling in about 500 hectares (1,235 acres) of mud flats. It thrived and attracted the beneficent attention of Mussolini. As Marghera grew, an adjoining tiny community called Mestre became its bedroom. By 1927 these satellite areas had grown important enough to be incorporated into "Greater Venice," which included the historic center and the islands of the lagoon.

Venice survived World War II relatively unscathed, though Marghera was bombed, and shortly after the war a second industrial zone grew up nearby. This one took another 500 hectares of what Venetians call the *barene,* or mud flats, and gobbled up twice that amount of adjacent farmland. Petrochemical, aluminum and other heavy industries, ship-yards and oil refineries went up. The three ancient channels of Chioggia, Malamocco and Lido, which link the lagoon with the Adriatic Sea, were deepened to facilitate access to the factory areas. Tourists suddenly were treated to the sight of 60,000-ton tankers cruising through the Giudecca Canal less than a hundred yards from the Doge's Palace.

For a while in the 1950s it seemed that happy days were here again. Employment on the mainland rose steadily; a third and even more gigantic industrial zone was projected. Yet in the rush of postwar build-ing, some of it illegal and some just ineptly designed, the face of Venice began to change. The clashingly modern railway station in the center and a towering, ugly parking garage across from it were joined by several architecturally unsuitable hotels and innumerable "elevations," *i.e.,* extra floors perched atop older existing buildings. Rich foreigners rushed to acquire palaces or a piece of a palace, as did rich Italians for whom "a second home in Venice" seemed desirable.

There were a few danger signals. Some days the sun was obscured by pollutants either from within the city or from across the lagoon. Fish began to vanish from the canals. Pieces of stone—small, at first—began to fall from buildings. Most ominous of all was the increasing incidence of *acque alte,* or high waters. Venice has always been subject to ex-ceptionally high tides, caused by meteorological events such as low-pressure systems or sirocco winds from the southeast which fill the Adriatic gulf to overflowing. These are dramatic but less dangerous in the long run than smaller, but more frequent, inundations. *Acque alte* are described specifically as tides of 1.1 meters, or about 43 inches higher than a so-called "normal" tide reference-level established in 1897. In the 20th century their occurrence increased, and waters of three and a half feet or higher have come with monotonous regularity. Even more alarming was the increasing difference between high and low water. The highs were higher and the lows were lower.

Although not immediately apparent to tourists, these fluctuations create near-intolerable problems for Venetians. In high water the boats have trouble getting beneath small bridges, and in low water even emergency craft—fire and ambulance boats—cannot navigate the smaller canals. Furthermore, the exaggerated changes between high and low cause structural damage. Stone, wood, even brick, will survive for a long time if they are either totally wet or totally dry. But the alternation of wet-and-dry, dry-and-wet, sharply increases the disintegration of the basic fabric.

Complicating the phenomenon was the now-celebrated "subsidence" of the city. Greater Venice was plagued by the existence of about 20,000 deep artesian wells dug to suck up water for public use and for the needs of the increasingly greedy industries on the mainland. As this sustaining underground water table fell, so did the lagoon bed above it.

Oceanographers, marine biologists, even ordinary Venice-lovers with boats knew what was wrong: Man had tampered too long and too drastically with the delicate balance of the lagoon and its underpinnings. When the Venetian Republic was at its height, the most powerful citizen in it, after the Doge himself, was the Superintendent of the Waters. His authority was awesome: he could forbid fishermen to dam the lagoon to make hatcheries; he could keep people from building on or filling up the vast mud flats into which the incoming tides rushed twice a day, and from which they retreated, slowly, when high tide was over; he oversaw the cleaning and dredging of the 160-plus large and small canals of the city.

The happy Venetians of that era had no need for man-made sewers because the unimpeded tides came rushing, sucking, evacuating, twice a day. They tended their seawalls carefully, and were so jealous of their limpid waters that they forbade housewives and their slaveys even to beat rugs on balconies, for fear dust would fall into the canals where gondolas plied.

Beginning in the 19th century, after the Austrian occupation, it all changed. For whatever reason, Venice began neglecting its seawalls, left its small canals undredged. Then the industrial zones filled in 2,500 acres of mud flats, the escape valve of other days, and a projected third zone was planned to take away far more. Other acres were filled in to let the town of Mestre grow and to build the airport. By one expert evaluation, an incredible one-fourth of the total area of the lagoon has now been closed to the tides. At the same time, all the channels have been deepened, and a new tanker canal dredged from the Porto di Malamocco to the industrial zone is 40 feet deep. Water rushing through such deep channels has an erosive effect on everything from seawalls to basements, and with the escape hatch of the *barene* so restricted, it has trouble getting out before the next high tide.

When the flood came in 1966, many conservationists and ecologists, both Italian and foreign, were secretly relieved. Now, they thought, at last Rome and the rest of the world would pay attention. The late René Maheu, director-general of UNESCO in Paris, instantly offered his own services, and the concern of the organization, to the stricken city. Within months that body had set up an office in Rome to coordinate international aid to both Florence and Venice. The mere existence of the office, plus some exuberant journalism, convinced most Italians and a great part of the Western world that UNESCO was at the ready with "an international loan" of millions, just as it rushed to the rescue of Egyptian treasures when the Aswan Dam was built.

UNESCO officials today deny that there ever was such a loan, or even the offer of one. The organization did help raise money to enable Venice's Superintendent of Galleries and Monuments to catalog and restore the most gravely endangered major works of art. Money came to help set up a restoration laboratory in the monastery of San Gregorio, and to support an international advisory committee to direct the salvation work. Maheu devoted a great part of the last ten years of his life to lobbying and working for an effective campaign to save the city.

Five years after the flood, the Italian Senate finally passed a special statute to safeguard Venice. That was in December 1971, but the statute had not yet passed the lower house when the government fell and the Venice law was lost among 3,773 others under consideration at the time. Not until April 1973, almost seven years after the flood, did a national law finally pass both houses. It was a painfully obvious compromise between the interests of industry and the preservation of the historic center. It postponed development of the "third zone," but it approved completion of the hotly opposed (by ecologists and hydrologists) deep tanker canal. It threw a bone to labor by guaranteeing that the 40,000 to 50,000 jobs in the Marghera-Mestre area would be maintained. It directed that sewers be built, polluters controlled, artesian wells capped and replaced by aqueducts, home heating switched from oil-based fuels to non-polluting methane gas or electricity.

The law was specific about expenditures. Half a billion dollars would be raised and divided roughly into thirds: one-third for the national government, to repair seawalls and bridges, to combat damage done by high water and to construct barriers in the channels as a defense against high tides; one-third to the regional government, charged with devising antipollution measures and building aqueducts and a sewage-treatment system; one-third to the city of Venice for restoration of decayed housing, palaces, bridges and monuments in the historic center and on the islands of the lagoon.

The latter job turned out to be far more complex than it seemed because of the shift in population from "old Venice" to the mainland. In 1945 the historic center boasted 180,000 residents and the mainland 83,000. But today the balance has shifted, aided by the departure of well over 80,000 Venetians to the mainland, so that almost two out of three citizens of Greater Venice live within the industrialized zones.

Six months after passage of the law, Italy issued a loan contract described as a "prefinancing loan . . . in connection with the preservation project of the city of Venice." Banks all over the world rushed to take up the issue, at favorable terms to Italy, and very quickly one of the biggest loans ever arranged on the Eurodollar market was accomplished.

Then, to the consternation of many, the money didn't go to Venice. For one reason: no official governmental body, on any level, was ready with precise plans for how to spend it. No serious organization will leave such sums lying about, so the Eurodollar loan—it was generally suspected —was used to help prop up the staggering *lira*.

At the risk of boring everybody, it must be explained that passage of a special law in Italy commits the state, but also indicates primarily *intent*. To implement the Special Law on Venice required supplementary issuance of guidelines called *indirizzi*. A government led by Mariano Rumor had some *indirizzi* ready in October 1974, but the government fell four days before the crucial vote. Twenty-three months had dragged by between passage of the Special Law and the final appearance of *indirizzi* in the spring of 1975, endless months during which endless committees had endless meetings.

After the *indirizzi* must come detailed plans and projects for each particular segment of the total problem. And at every turn the warring elements, both political and economic (leaving out for the moment the artistic and historical), collide.

Item: Industrialists insist that Venice needs more and more jobs on the mainland.

Supporters of the historic center counter that most of the present industrial workers come from surrounding mainland areas rather than from Venice itself, and statistics confirm their view: every day about 24,000 residents of Mestre and its surroundings commute back to the historic center to work, while only 1,700 go the other way to mainland jobs.

Item: What to do about deteriorating housing in the center, substandard conditions which forced Venetians to go to the mainland in the first place?

Everyone agrees that the commuting workers should be brought home again and the exodus halted. But no one agrees on how to do it.

The ruling Communist-Socialist city administration is determined to renovate housing for workers and prevent speculators from buying up and restoring property which then might become too expensive for the working class. To this end they have set up rigid rules which make it almost impossible for even an owner to fix up his own property. The result has been a private paralysis which compounds the official one, and an explosion of illegal alterations on the part of those rich or influential enough to risk a fine.

Item: Control of high water. In the wake of the flood, in 1969, the Italian government set up a laboratory with the high-flown title of Institute for the Study of the Dynamics of Large Masses. Its chief was a U.S. trained oceanographer, Roberto Frassetto, who for six years labored mightily with the help of nearly 200 scientific and technical volunteers from all over the world, an IBM computer, and an offshore research platform from which they made field measurements of water levels, currents, waves and tides.

The Institute tested and evaluated a dozen systems for preventing *acque alte*, everything from placing maneuverable barriers in the Adriatic channels to actually raising the land mass. The latter involved a technique called mud jacking, in which a resilient substance is pumped deep into the subsoil to support and raise land levels and the buildings on their backs.

Much more public attention has been devoted to the series of proposals to close the three seaward channels in case of high tide by man-made barriers. One, developed by the Pirelli/Furlanis Consortium, would anchor giant hot-water-bottlelike structures to the bottom and inflate them when necessary. Another would install pivotal metal discs which would be raised or lowered. An international tender was extended for proposals, and by the end of 1976, six firms had submitted plans which are currently under study.

Many oceanologists, hydrologists and Venetian citizens hope the decision will never be made. Further tampering with the natural passages, they argue, would only increase the erosive action of incoming tides: besides, it would impede the outrush of the tides, upset the flushing action and set up stagnation which would become a breeder of disease.

What should be done, ecologists say, is clear and simple: restore the old channels to their previously much shallower depths, abolish the tanker canal and serve the industries with overland oil pipelines, liberate the thousands of acres of *barene* now enclosed for fish hatcheries or the proposed development of the "third zone" (now temporarily halted), dredge the silt-and-garbage-filled secondary canals. Also, restrict the size, speed and traffic patterns of the public and private motorboats which churn through the main thoroughfares, throwing up lashings of waves and the pollution of their motors.

Item: Pollution of air and water. Conservationists blame the industrial zones, industrialists blame Venice itself. Some restorers agree with the industrialists. Even so august a witness as Sir Ashley Clarke, former British ambassador to Italy and now a vice chairman of Britain's Venice in Peril Fund, holds that "Prevailing winds carry industrial pollution inland, not across the lagoon to the historic center."

Yet on any day when the wind blows from the wrong direction, or when there is no wind at all, towering columns of yellow and red and black effluent from the mainland are visible in the historic center, and spread over the city "like an airborne mattress,'" in the words of a stern *Italia Nostra* conservationist.

Air pollution levels, now measured and infrequently reported by city authorities, instead of by the ecologists who set up the system, seldom reach the dangerpoint for long periods of time. But, say conservationists, if the official level (a very permissive .30 parts of sulfur dioxide for every million volumes of air) is exceeded for only one half hour every week, it attacks the stone, marble, brick and bronze of which Venice is made.

Lagoon Venetians have done their part. In response to provisions of the Special Law, they dutifully converted home heating from oil-based to methane fuels. They were supposed to get 40 percent of the cost back from the state, and about one-third of them have been reimbursed, but the other two-thirds are still waiting.

On the mainland, however, the local health officer in 1973 ordered workers in Porto Marghera to wear gas masks to protect them from clouds of nitrogen oxide, sulfur dioxide, phenols, cyanide, formaldehyde, ammonia, methacrylic acid, vitriol and phosgene—the latter a gas used to poison people on purpose during World War I. The workmen largely ignored the order ("gas masks are uncomfortable") and the state failed to enforce it. Even now, ominous little news items buried at the bottom of newspaper columns report that 10 or 15 or 20 workers were carted off to the hospital for treatment after they had inhaled too many fumes of one kind or another.

Throughout the dragging months and years, international crusaders and UNESCO have maintained a stiff upper lip, and in their annual reports have dwelt upon whatever accomplishments they could claim. They have been unfailingly polite to the Italian bureaucracy, although noting from year to year that "We regret this new delay," "What is needed is no possibility of further delay. . . ." and so on.

Their faith may be rewarded. Inner-city pollution has definitely been reduced by the switch to methane. Many artesians wells have been capped, and one new acqueduct has been completed to bring water from the Sile River to the gulping mainland factories. A second aqueduct is on the drawing board, and four pilot sewage plants are in various stages of development. The first doesn't work very well, but maybe the builders will learn by doing.

Italian authorities claim proudly that almost one-third of the total allocation of money has been made (although one-third of that is being held in reserve to cover tenders for the ill-conceived effort to close the channels). Much of the money is being consumed in studies and drawing-board work.

But an international training course for the care and cure of ailing stone, organized and sponsored by UNESCO, is now being held annually in Venice. Then there is the new restoration laboratory in San Gregorio. Eventually the world's aspiring restorers may learn there how to save everything from canvas to marble to wood to glass.

And there has been no disastrous flood in more than a decade. The *acque alte* have receded in intensity if not in frequency, and new scientific measurements indicate that the subsidence of the city has stopped. It might even be rising almost imperceptibly, as underground waters begin to fill the gaps made earlier by the gulping artesian wells.

Finally, no mere foreigner should ever discount the Italians' genius for the last-minute save. If they didn't invent *The Perils of Pauline,* they should have: nobody else is so expert at cutting the bonds of the lady just before the train thunders through, or in leaping from the top of a burning building into a fortuitously passing hay wagon.

Sometimes the save is done thoughtfully instead of instinctively. An organization called the Friends of Museums and Monuments of Venice currently transports children from the industrial zone to the historic center to see the glories of St. Mark's, San Rocco, the Doge's Palace, the Rialto Bridge. The volunteers who run the tours report that 85 percent of these children, Venetians by definition and separated by only 15 minutes of public transport from the historic center, had never seen it before. If these children learn to love old Venice, and if politicians and technicians of all orders can solve one of the knottiest problems of the 20th century, then *La Serenissima* will, truly, rise again.

Chronology of Major Events
in the History of Venice

337
Earliest record of a lagoon settlement. Cassiodorus writes: "They live like marsh birds, in nests of reeds raised on piles, to protect themselves against the waters."

421–452
Successive waves of barbaric invasions of north Italy force the *Veneti* to flee to the safety of the lagoon marshlands.

421
Legendary foundation of Venice.

589
First floods recorded: "The waters changed their usual course and the whole land took on the appearance of a marsh. The inundation lasted an extremely long time and the people said 'we are living neither on land nor on the water.'" Flooding again 875, 1240.

639
Torcello colonized; Bishop Magnus transfers from mainland Altino; Church of Santa Maria Assunta built.

727
Election of First Doge; independence from Byzantine rule.

814
Government and population move to the *Rivo Alto* (Rialto).

FL.1000
Venice, now important maritime power, controls entire Adriatic coast.

1003
The Church of St. Mark's is begun to house remains of Saint Mark stolen from Alexandria.

Chronology

1095–1191

During the early Crusades Doge Domenico Selvo participates in the capture of Tyre.

1177

Venetians effect an accord between Pope Alexander III and Emperor Frederick Barbarossa.

1202–1204

The Fourth Crusade, Sack of Constantinople, creation of a Latin Empire in the Levant with Venice as co-ruler, immense artistic plunder, the famous four bronze horses brought to Venice from Constantinople's Hippodrome.

14TH CENTURY

First walls of clay and wickerwork built as defense against the sea.

1453

Constantinople is re-captured by the Turks; Venetian supremacy ends in the Levant.

1454

The Peace of Lodi. Venetian Republic's triumph over Milanese and French extending her land empire to Bergamo; Venice becomes continental power.

1498

Vasca da Gama, Portugese navigator, journeys to India by rounding the Cape of Good Hope. The loss of the Venetian Republic's monopoly on trade with the Orient begins three centuries of gradual decline of power.

1508

The League of Cambrai unites half of Europe and Italian states against Venetian expansion.

1516

The *Maggior Consiglio* of Venice decrees the creation of a ghetto for the city's Jewish population, the world's first ghetto.

1686, 1691

The first sea walls are swept away by heavy seas.

1744–1751

First section of Istrian stone sea wall completed. Venetian Senate decrees construction of an entire sea wall which is completed in the next thirty nine years. On the section at Pellestrina a tablet reads: "The Guardians of the Water have set this colossal mole of solid marble against the sea so that the sacred estuaries of the city and the Seat of Liberty may be eternally preserved."

1797
Fall of the 1,000 year old Venetian Republic to the French forces of Napoleon.

1805–1814
Venice under Napoleonic rule.

1815–1866
Venice ceded to Austria by Napoleon; Austrian occupation.

1841–1846
Venice joined to mainland by railway.

1848
Unsuccessful uprising of the Venetians under Daniele Manin to expel the Austrians.

1866
The *Risorgimento,* unification of Venice with the Kingdom of Italy under King Victor Emmanuel.

1926
Porto Marghera, developed as an industrial center to provide employment, aluminum, oil refining, steel works, electrometallurgical works, absorbed into Venice proper; peril to land table and art works of the city. The first and second "industrial zones" now re-claim 3,830 acres from the lagoon.

1945
Liberation of Venice from the Nazi occupation by British forces.

1960
Construction of Marco Polo airport. Almost one-fourth of land area of Venice re-claimed from lagoon upsets ecological balance between the city and the sea.

1966
Greatest flood in Venetian history: city is submerged by the Adriatic 6½ feet above normal high level; waves break against the Ducal Palace, with forty billion lire damage. At UNESCO's initiative thirty-four organizations are formed in fourteen countries, among them Italy's own *Italia Nostra,* dedicated to preserving the city.

Chronology

Special Law (Fifth) passed by the government in Rome: Saving Venice and its lagoon is declared a question of essential national interest; three hundred billion lire allotted, Commission to Safeguard Venice established.

Venetian Nomenclature

Calle,	street, usually narrow
Calle larga,	wide street
Campanile,	bell tower
Campo,	square (was once a meadow)
Campiello,	square, smaller
Canale,	canal
Canale Grande,	the Grand Canal
Casa or *Ca',*	house
Corte or *Cortile,*	courtyard
Fondamenta,	broad paved bank along the water; quay
Isola,	island; (Venice is made up of almost one hundred small *isole*)
Motoscafo,	water bus (an express boat on the Grand Canal and the *Circolare* which circles the perimeter of the city)
Palazzo,	palace or mansion
Piazza,	large square (In Venice there is only one *piazza*, the Piazza San Marco)
Piazzetta,	small square
Ponte,	bridge (There are about four hundred in Venice)
Piscina,	a street once filled with rain water and now paved
Ramo,	small narrow street branching out of a larger one
Rio,	small canal
Rio terra,	a street which is a filled-in canal

Riva,	narrow street along the water
Ruga,	street
Rughetta,	little street
Salizzada,	the first paved street
Sestiere,	districts (There are six *sestiere* in Venice: Cannaregio, Castello, Dorsoduro, Santa Croce, San Marco, and San Polo.)
Sottoportico (Italian) or *Sottoportego* (Venetian),	section of a street under a building
Strada,	large street (The Strada Nuova was created by Napoleon for the use of his cavalry.)
Terra ferma,	the mainland
Traghetto,	shuttle, either by vaporetto or gondola between two landings
Vaporetto,	large water bus—local on the Grand Canal and express on the Giudecca Canal

Bibliography of Sources

Berenson, Bernard, *The Italian Painters of the Renaissance*. Oxford University Press, 1930.

Berenson, Bernard. *The Passionate Sightseer, from the Diaries 1947–1956*. London: Thames & Hudson, 1960.

Byron, George Gordon (Lord). "Childe Harold, Canto IV" in *Byron: Selected Verse and Prose Works,* edited by Peter Quennell. London & Glasgow: Collins, 1969.

Casanova de Seingalt, Giacomo. *My Life and Adventures*. London: Julien & Steele, 1932.

Casanova de Seingalt, Giacomo. *Casanova in Rome, in Venice, in Paris: An Appreciation by Havelock Ellis*. Boston: John W. Luce, 1924.

Cooper, James Fenimore. *The Bravo*. New York: Townsend & Co., 1859.

Coryat, Thomas. *Coryat's Crudities*. Reprinted from the edition of 1611 . . . 3 Vols. 1776.

Dickens, Charles. *Hard Times and Pictures from Italy*. London: Chapman & Hall, 1865.

Evelyn, John. *The Life and Writings of J. Evelyn comprising his Diary*. London: Alex Murray, 1870.

Gautier, Theophile. *The Complete Works,* Vol. IV. Translated and edited by F.C. De Sumichrost. London: Postlethwaite, Taylor & Knowles, Ltd., 1901.

Gibbon, Edward. *The History of the Decline and Fall of the Roman Empire*. New York: Harper & Bros., 1884.

Goethe, Johann Wolfgang von. Autobiography, Vol. II. London, 1864–1866.

Hamblin, Dora Jane. "Maladies of Venice: Decay, Delay and That Old Sinking Feeling." *Smithsonian,* November, 1977.

Hemingway, Ernest. *Across the River and into the Trees*. New York: Charles Scribner's Sons, 1950.

Howells, William Dean. *Venetian Life*. Leipzig: B. Tauchnitz, 1866.

Bibliography

James, Henry. *Portraits of Places*. New York: Lear Publishers, 1948.

James, Henry. *Italian Hours*. Boston: Houghton Mifflin, 1909.

McCarthy, Mary. *Venice Observed*. New York: Reynal, 1956.

Machiavelli, Niccolo. *History of Florence, and of the Affairs of Italy from the Earliest Time to the Death of Lorenzo the Magnificent*. New York, London: M. Walter, Dunne, 1901.

Mann, Thomas. *Death in Venice*. Translated from the German by H. T. Lowe–Porter. New York: Knopf, 1925.

Morris, James. *Venice*. London: Faber & Faber, 1974.

Norton, Charles Eliot. *Historical Studies of Church-Building in the Middle Ages, Venice, Siena, Florence*. New York: Harper, 1880, 1902, 1969.

Proust, Marcel. *Remembrance of Things Past*, 4 Vols., Translated by C.K. Scott Moncrieff and Frederick A. Blossom. New York: Random House, 1934.

Rolfe, Frederick. *The Desire and the Pursuit of the Whole: A Romance of Modern Venice*. New York: New Directions, 1953.

Ruskin, Euphemia Gray. Effie in Venice: Her Picture of Society and Life with John Ruskin, 1849–1852, edited by Mary Lutyens. London: John Murray, 1965.

Ruskin, John. *St. Mark's Rest: The History of Venice*. London: George Allen, 1884.

Ruskin, John. *The Stones of Venice*, 3 Vols. London: Smith & Elder, 1873.

Sand, George. *Lettres d' un Voyageur*. Paris Frère Levy.

Twain, Mark. *The Innocents Abroad, or the New Pilgrim's Progress*, 2 Vols. Hartford: The New American Publishing Co., 1901.

A

Accademia Bridge, 61
Accademia Gallery, 63–64, 73 f., 90, 100
Acqua alta (flooding), 221, 225, 227
Acre, 22
Adriatic Sea, 4, 5, 6, 9, 13, 33, 37, 92, 95,
    106, 113, 114, 123, 124, 128, 133,
    135, 141, 147, 153, 219, 221, 225
Adige River, 5, 123
Aegean Sea, 85
Africa, 85
Alexandria, 126, 209
All Saint's Day, 47, 52, 195
All Soul's Day, 52
Alps, 4, 5, 33, 37, 117, 194
Altinum, 33, 34, 91, 92
Amsterdam, 115
Apennines, 4, 117
Apulia, 25
Aquileia, 9, 33, 85
Arabia, 37, 101
Archeological Museum, 104
Aretino, Pietro, 41, 77
Aristo, Ludovico, 44, 47
Armenians in Venice, 127
Arno River, 219
Arsenal, 36, 107, 108, 121, 124, 127–128,
    149, 175, 220
Ascension Week, 124, 126
Asia, 10, 25, 35, 37, 85
Athenaeus, 117
Athens, 85, 86, 101
Attila, 9, 13, 34
Auden, W. H., 189
Australia, 220
Austria, 5, 27–31, 38, 151, 153, 220, 221,
    222
Avars, 33

B

Baedeker, Karl, 34, 65, 166
Barbarossa, Emperor Frederick, 73
Bassano del Grappa, 105
Bellini, Gentile, 59, 72, 73, 74, 75, 90,
    107, 108, 152, 154
Bellini, Giovanni, 72, 104, 107, 152, 154
Bellini, Jacopo, 107, 152, 154
Berenson, Bernard, 69, 89
Bergamasco, Guglielmo, 101
Bergamo, 10
Bocca del Leone, 108, 148
Bon, Bartolomeo, 88 f.
Bosporus, 16, 17, 20
Brazil, 219
Brenta River, 4, 6, 131
Brera Museum (Milan), 80
Brescia, 10
Bridge of Sighs, 43, 148
Brondolo, 114
Browning, Elizabeth Barrett, 165, 214
Browning, Robert, 62, 103, 165, 214
Bucintoro (Official State Barge), 103, 124,
    127, 174, 177, 192
Burano, 91, 103, 165, 208, 209
Byron, Lord, 65, 103, 165–166, 214
Byzantine Architecture, 22, 23, 24, 60, 83,
    84, 88, 89–90, 98, 100, 209, 219
Byzantine Empire, 16, 19, 25, 35, 37

C

Ca d'Oro, 67
Ca' Foscari, 61, 63, 212
Ca' Pesaro, 65, 68
Ca' Rezzonico, 59, 62, 108, 165
Ca' Struan, 199
Calabria, 174, 177, 178, 180, 181

Index

Index

Index

Siena, 73, 83, 86
Sile River, 208, 227
Simeon Stylites (Syria), 39
Smith, Joseph, 134
Sorrento, 173
Spain, 37, 76, 77, 79, 81, 82
Spalato, 85
Specchi Cafe, 30
Spencer, Herbert, 23
Stockholm, 115
Strasburg, 125
Symonds, A. J. A., 189
Symonds, John Addington, 163
Syria, 10, 22, 39

T

Temple of Solomon (Jerusalem), 23
Tiberias, Lake, 95
Tiepolo, Giovanni Battista, 82, 104, 107
Tiepolo, Giovanni Domenico, 107
Tintoretto, 59, 78–80, 81, 104, 107, 108, 154, 159, 212, 219
Titian, 76–78, 79, 81, 107, 125, 152, 154, 159, 160, 161, 183, 198, 219
Torcello, 91–96, 100, 103, 207, 208, 209
Traghetti, 140
Treaty of Villafranca (1859), 30
Tremignon, Alessandro, 101
Treviso, 10, 25, 55, 56
Turandot (Gozzi), 99
Turkey, 22, 36, 39, 105, 108, 127, 128, 151
Tuscany, 14
Twain, Mark, 155
Tyre, 23

U

Ultramontane, 10
U.N.E.S.C.O., 219, 220, 223, 227
United States, 219, 220

V

Vandals, 114
Vaporetti, 66, 67, 103
Veneto, 9, 31, 34, 91
Venice in Peril Fund (English), 220, 226
Vermeer von Delft, 74
Verona, 5, 9, 10, 23, 70, 80, 81, 150
Veronese, 80–81, 82, 108, 154, 184
Vicentine Mountains, 141
Vicenza, 9, 10, 152
Virgil, 44
Visconti, 10
Visigoths, 208, 209
Vittoria, Alessandro, 107
Vivarini, Alvise, 74
Vivarini, Antonio, 100
Voltaire, 39, 98

W

Wordswoth, William, 1

Y

Yugoslavia, 220

Z

Zara, 15
Zattere, 195, 199